# START DRAWING STILL LIFES

Techniques, Composition and Exercises

*by Markus S. Agerer*

# Imprint

Markus S. Agerer

START DRAWING STILL LIFES
Techniques, Composition and Exercises

ISBN: 9798679648319

Original Texts: Markus S. Agerer
Illustrations: Markus S. Agerer
Cover Design: Markus S. Agerer
Translation: Paul Ronning

Copyright: © 2020 Markus S. Agerer

Bürgermeister-Haidacher-Straße 1
82140 Olching
Deutschland

email: markus-agerer@web.de
web: www.markus-agerer.de

This book, sections thereof as well as the pictorial material – if not otherwise noted – are protected by copyright. It may not be used or exploited in any manner divergent from the law without authorization from the creator.

The author/illustrator has produced all contents with the utmost care; nevertheless, liability of any kind can not be assumed for errors and the direct or indirect consequences thereof.

This book contains links (also via QR code) to external third-party websites, on whose content the author of this book has no influence. Therefore, no liability can be assumed for this external content. The linked pages were checked for possible legal violations at the time the link was created. A permanent control of the content of the linked pages is not reasonable without concrete evidence of an infringement.

QR codes: The QR codes in this book contain links to various websites. This expands the content of the book. No guarantee can be given for the continued existence of this online content. It should also be noted that the websites linked in this way may contain advertising, affiliate links etc. The terms of use and the data protection declaration of the respective website must be observed.

# Table of Contents

| | |
|---|---:|
| **INTRODUCTION – STILL LIFES** | **6** |
| **BASIC PRINCIPLES OF DRAWING** | **14** |
| **SIMPLE ARRANGEMENTS** | **60** |
| **DRAWING SIMPLE STILL LIFES** | **66** |
| **REPRESENTATION OF SPACE AND PERSPECTIVE** | **80** |
| **PICTURE DESIGN AND COMPOSITION** | **110** |
| **EXERCISES – COMPLEX STILL LIFES** | **132** |
| **CLOSING REMARKS** | **156** |

# Introduction – Still Lifes

*» All beginnings are light-hearted; the threshold is the place of anticipation. «*

- Johann Wolfgang von Goethe -

# Introduction – Still Lifes

## Preface

This book is my fourth book in the field of drawing. The books I have published in recent years have dealt with the topics of perspective drawing, the basics principles of drawing and image composition. A book about drawing still lifes is the next logical step for me, as the three themes of my other books meet here. After all, in order to depict still lifes, one must first master the basic drawing techniques. Furthermore, the composition of the image is one of the most important components for creating appealing arrangements. But perspective drawing along with the techniques of vanishing points and the creation of an illusion of space and depth are also aspects that come into play when drawing still lifes.

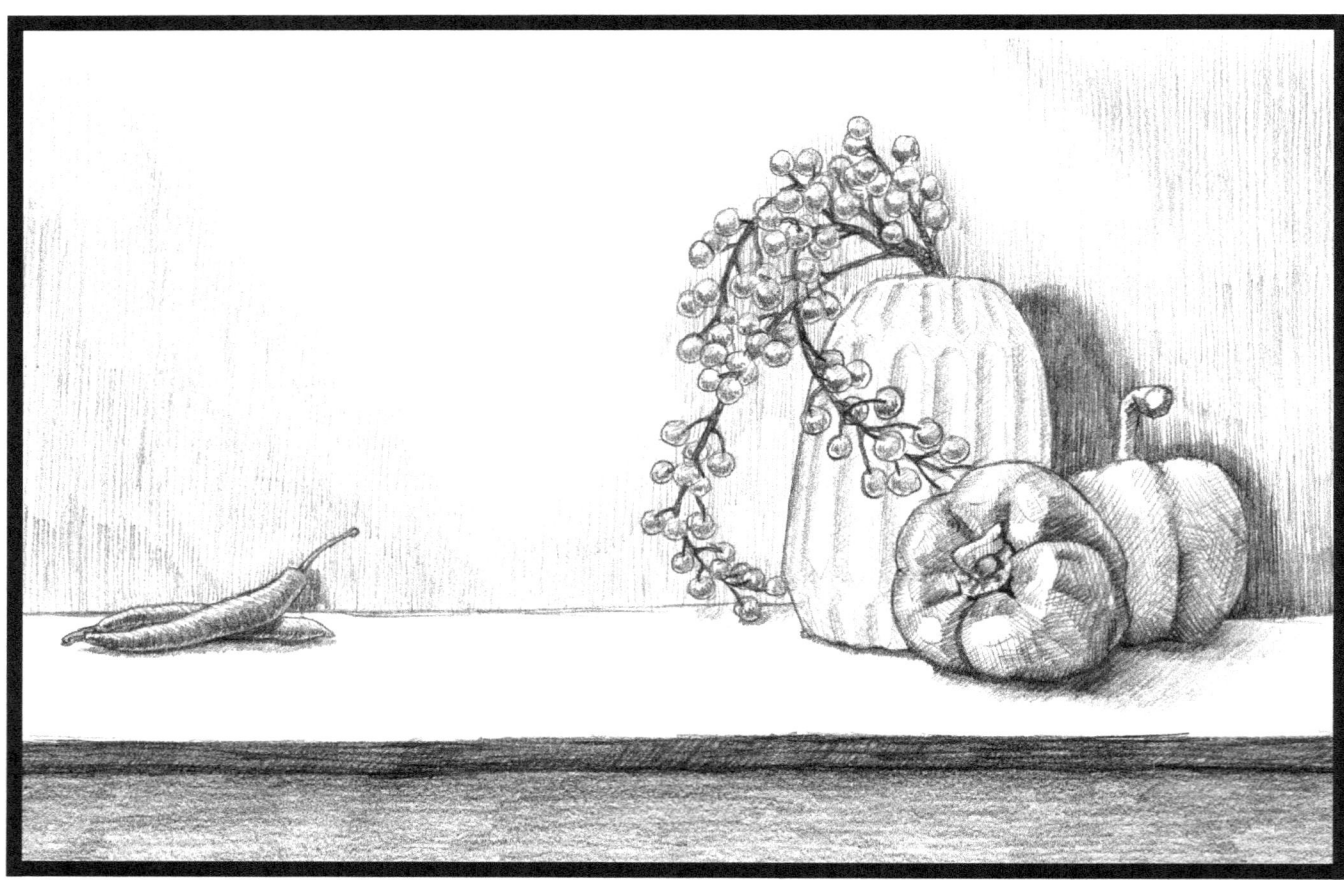

In this book you will find information on all these topics which will teach you the basics of drawing technique, perspective and image composition. This book is therefore an ideal basis for improving your own drawing skills and developing yourself further. Since still lifes depict relatively simple objects that can also be found in one's own four walls, this subject of visual art is also ideal for beginners.

# Introduction

## What is a Still Life?

A still life is a representation of inanimate objects, whether it is a drawing, a photograph or a painting. When drawing a still life, it is important to make the right choice and properly group the objects you want to depict. One should pay attention to an aesthetic arrangement of the objects, on the one hand, and to content aspects on the other hand.

This means, for example, that objects that fit together in terms of content are grouped together in such a way that the overall picture is both coherent and interesting. For example, you can draw various types of fruit in a basket.

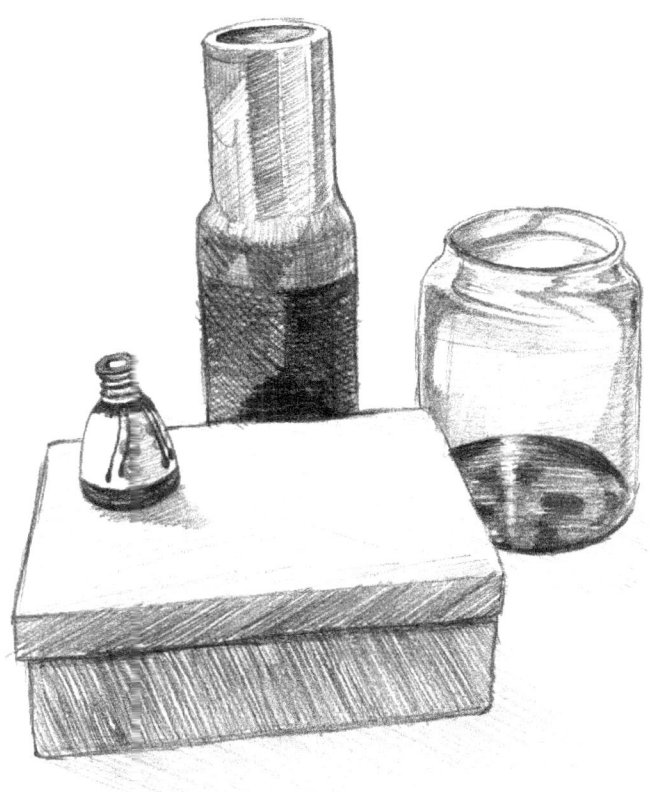

## Term and History of the Term

If the concept of still life is to be defined more precisely, a distinction must be made between a broader and a narrower generic term. In a broader sense, representations of still and inanimate scenes are called still lifes. From this point of view, one can assume that still lifes already existed in antiquity and even before that.

The narrower genre term for still lifes originated in the Netherlands, where they were so named in a list of pictures around 1650. Here the term stil leven (Dutch: stil = unmoved and leven = existence) was first used. Characteristic is also the designation of the paintings, which was determined by the essential pictorial objects.
In further development, different types of still lifes were created such as hunting pieces, kitchen utensils or flower still lifes.

### Still lifes over the course of history

Comparable paintings on walls were known as early as the late antiquity, for example in Pompeii. Silk and porcelain painting in China and Japan developed in medieval times, and can be classified similarly. In the Middle Ages paintings with a statement dominated. Objects as motifs, without intention or statement, had no place there. Between the 14th and 15th centuries, paintings contained objects and plants that are quite well arranged. But these were often, as with Robert Campin or Jan van Eyck, intended as allegory.
Later, still lifes on wall coverings and altar wings can be admired.

This indicates a change: The scene of Christian content recedes behind a magnificently painted still life, for example in Pieter Arten's painting "Christ with Mary and Martha" from 1553. What followed until the 17th century are the vanitas paintings (vanitas meaning emptiness). In this process, the robustness of life is confronted with transience: Skulls, hourglasses, insects and withered flowers appear. The same theme is used in penitent and hermit scenes.

## Still Lifes from the 17th Century

Now the heyday of this style emerged, especially in the Netherlands, but also in Spain and Italy. Some painters were named after their favorite motifs, for example Jan Bruegel, the older one as "Blumenbruegel".

In the academic art of France the still life did not find any recognition. Nevertheless, even famous artists such as Francois Desportes or Jean-Simeon Chardin tried still lifes.

In the second half of the 19th century, Impressionists and Realists took up stylistic means of the still life. To this day, still life continues to express new content.

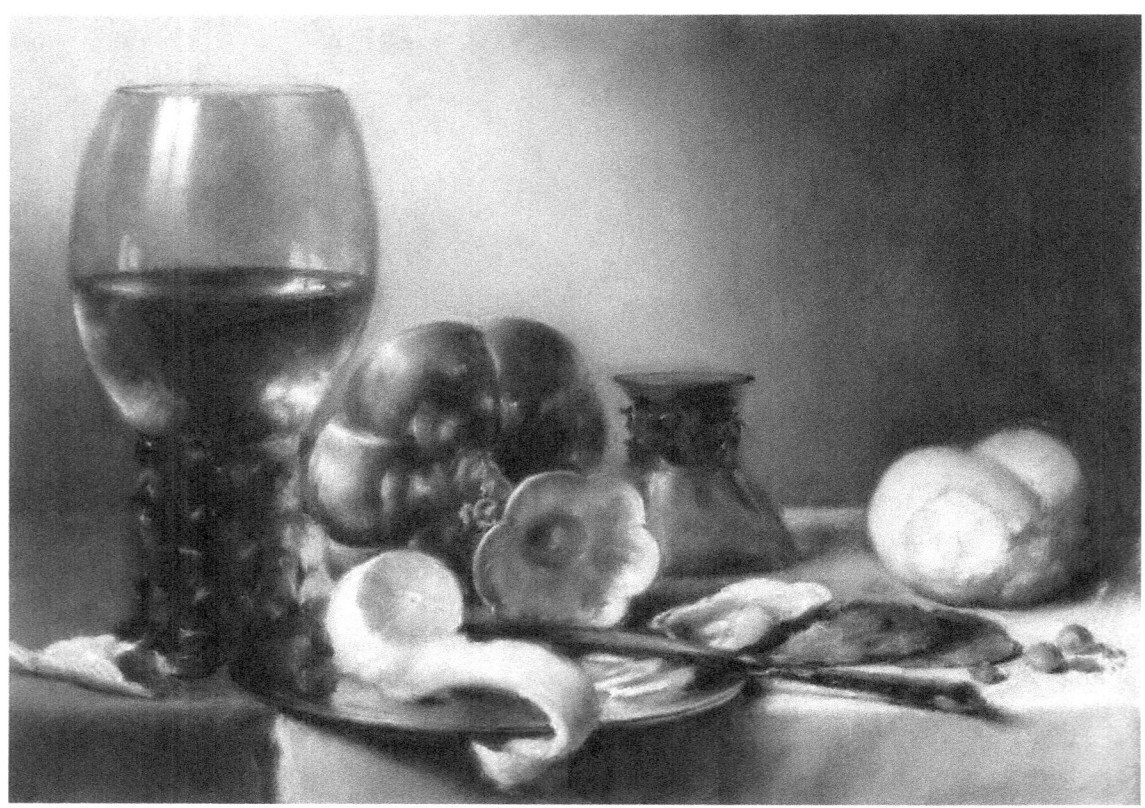

*Still life "Oyster Breakfast" – replica of a painting by Pieter Claesz 1633*

# Types of Still Lifes

Still lifes are differentiated primarily on the basis of their content. Especially in the 18th century still lifes representing fruit and meals were very popular. But also paintings that remind us of the transience of life - so-called vanitas still lifes. Since the 17th century, a distinction has been made between the following

- Vanitas still lifes,
- Mealtime still lifes,
- Flower still lifes,
- Smoker's still lifes,
- Fruit still lifes,
- Hunting still lifes,
- Kitchen still lifes,
- Trophy still lifes,
- Book still lifes,
- Treasure still lifes

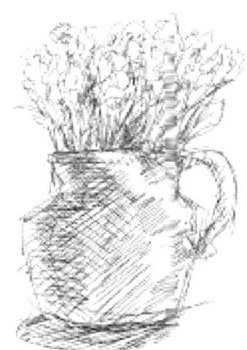

Various types of still lifes are introduced in detail in the following section.

# Vanitas Still Lifes

The word vanitas comes from Latin and means "empty appearance, nothingness, vanity" or "futility". In Jewish and Christian religion the word corresponds to the idea of the transitoriness of all earthly things. Accordingly, vanitas still lifes depict inanimate objects, which are supplemented by symbols of transience. Particularly typical is the depiction of skulls.

Another characteristic is the combination of objects that come from three symbolic groups. Valuable objects that embody an apparent permanence, objects that provide clues to the transience of earthly existence and objects that symbolise rebirth and eternal life are depicted.

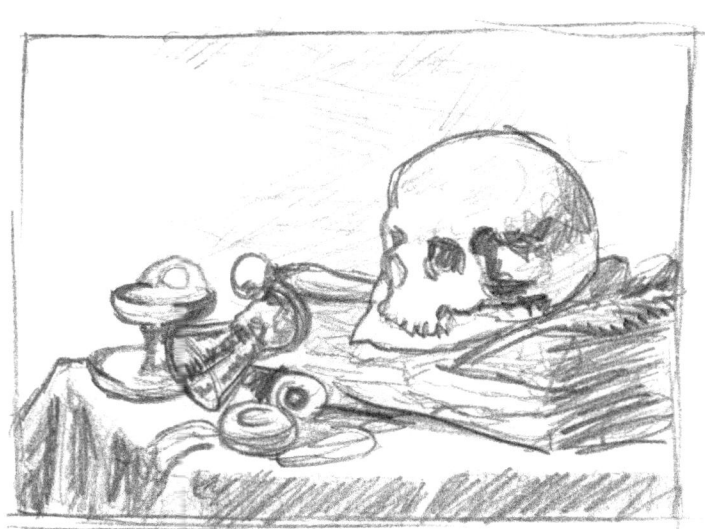

*Sketch of a vanitas still life after an oil painting by Pieter Claesz*

Among the most enduring objects are books, musical instruments, money and precious objects, insignia of power and greatness, and works of fine art. Symbols of transience represent all objects that are subject to decay or remind us of it. Examples are the skull, the hourglass, the fading candle, wilting flowers and fallen or broken glasses. Objects such as ears of corn, laurel and ivy stand for rebirth and eternal life.

# Mealtime Still Lifes

What mealtime still lifes are about is self-explanatory. They are still lifes in which various food, dishes and other objects are depicted that fit the theme of food. The mealtime still life has been known as a separate genre since the 17th century, in the first half of which it had its heyday.

Forerunners of the mealtime still life were market and kitchen pieces. These paintings depicted market or kitchen scenes in which people were also shown. Well-known representatives of this art form were for example the Dutchmen Pieter Aertsen and Frans Snyders and the Frenchman Jean-Baptiste Siméon Chardin

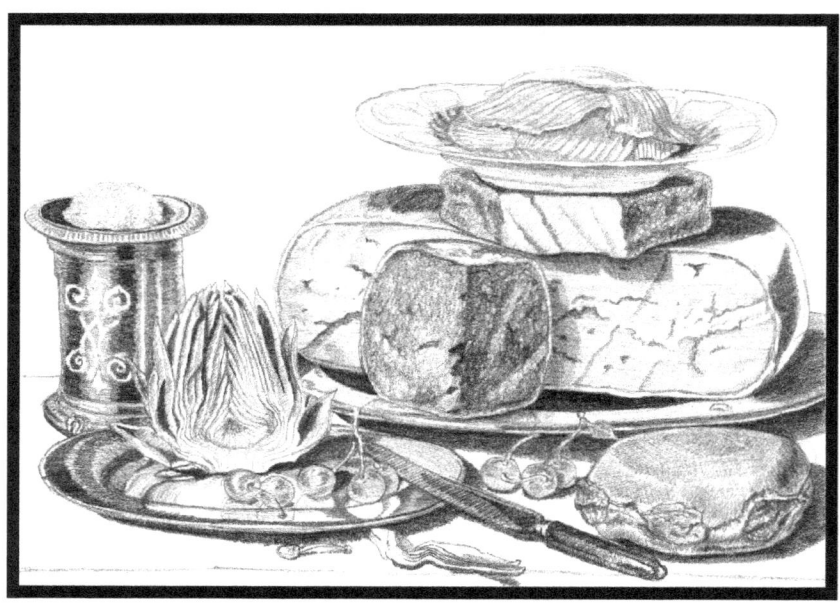

*Drawing after the painting "Still Life with Cheese, Artichokes and Cherries" by Clara Peeters, 1625*

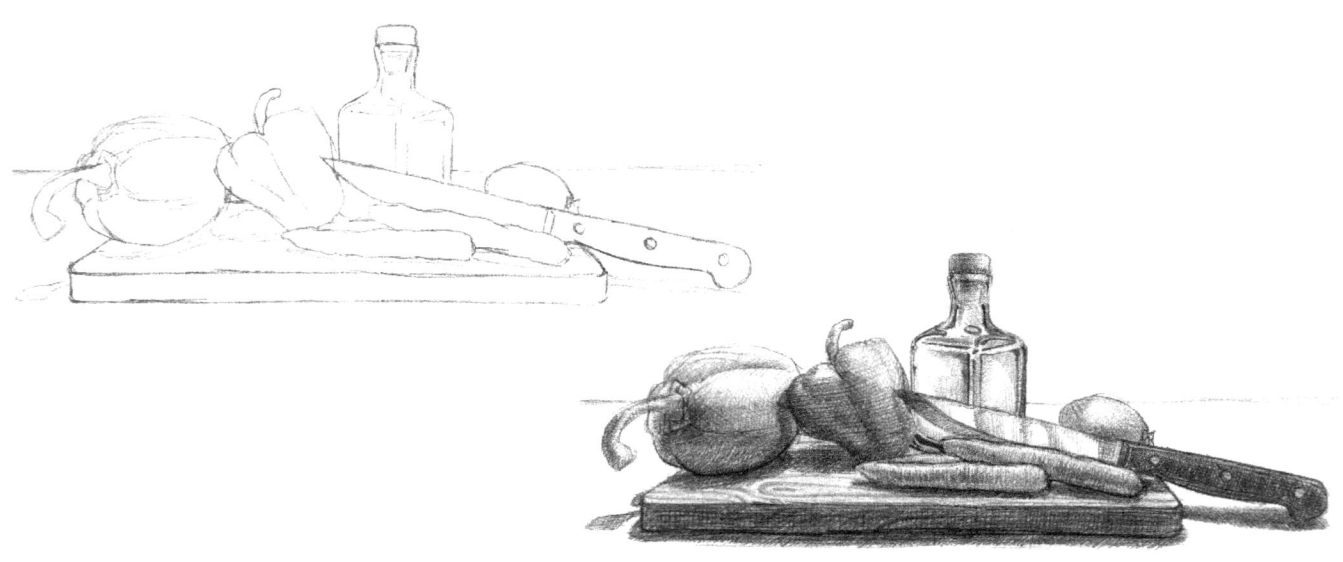

# Flower Still Lifes

Flower still lifes are pictures in which a bouquet of flowers is the main motif. As with most other types of still lifes, flower still lifes experienced their heyday in the 17th century, especially in the Netherlands. The artists mostly painted cut flowers, which were arranged in a vase to form a bouquet that would fill a canvas.

At that time, flower still lifes were the most frequently depicted motif in the field of still lifes. The prices that were achieved were high - some artists sold their paintings at higher prices than, for example, Rembrandt's Night Watch. Yet despite these facts, flower still lifes have received comparatively little explicit attention to this day.

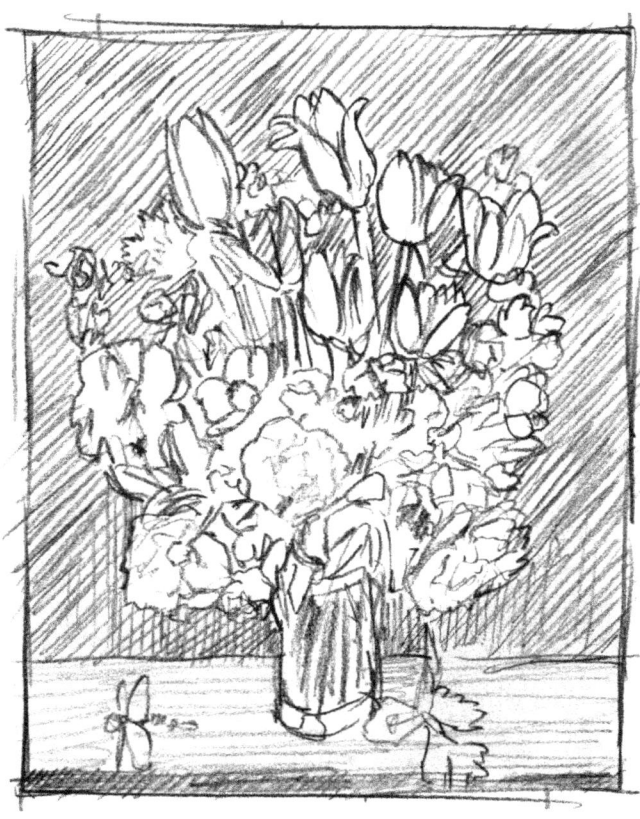

*Sketch of a flower bouquet after a painting by Jacob van Hulsdonck*

What one can interpret from flower still lifes from the 17th century is multifaceted. On the one hand, they were intended to pay homage to the beauty of nature and God's creation - it was not a matter of scientific reproduction. Flowers that actually blossom in different seasons were shown in full bloom at the same time in a bouquet. On the other hand, the transience of all existence should probably also be pointed out, so that flower still lifes also represent a kind of vanitas still life. This is illustrated in paintings in which different flowers are shown in different stages of their life cycle - from bud to wilt

In addition the flower still lifes should also present the wealth of their owner. Central pictorial elements are often tulips, which at that time were extremely sought-after but also expensive. One should also think of the so-called tulip mania, which was an investment phenomenon in the Netherlands at exactly that time - the very country in which the still lifes also experienced their richest expression. Other flowers depicted in the paintings sometimes come from faraway countries and give an indication that the Netherlands was one of the leading sea trading powers of the time.

# Smoker's Still Lifes

Smoker's still lifes are also called toebakje or rookertje and represent a special form of Dutch still life painting. This type of still life was particularly widespread in the 17th century - tobacco had been introduced to Holland by sailors at the end of the previous century.

Smoking was already considered a vice at that time, but was nevertheless very popular. Subjects of this kind were also meant to remind the owner of the painting that one should not completely fall for his vices. Moreover, the depiction of smoking paraphenalia already embodies a clear reference to vanitas. Smoking was regarded as a meaningless and vain activity. Accordingly, objects such as tobacco, pipe and fuse often appear in vanitas still lifes.

Examples of smoker's still lifes are the "Five Senses" (1623) by Pieter Claesz, the "Still Life with Oysters, Wine and Smoking Tools" (1651) by Jan Jansz van de Velde or the "Smoker Still Life in a Niche" (ca. 1630) by Georg Flegel.

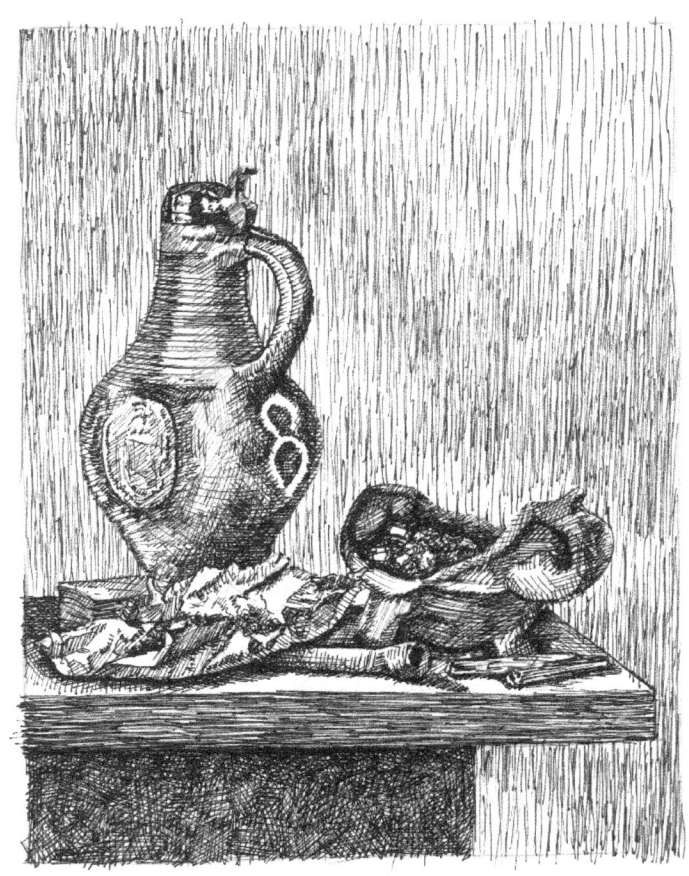

*Still life with clay jug and smoker's paraphernalia after the oil painting by Jan Fris (Amsterdam 1627 – 1672)*

# Basic Principles of Drawing

*» Drawing is the art of taking lines for a walk. «*

- Paul Klee -

# Basic Principles of Drawing

Simple drawing exercises form the basis for the first steps. Get to know your drawing tool and develop an initial understanding of drawing techniques and the illustration of forms.

The basics of drawing also include knowledge of the artist's design tools.

## Drawing Design Tools

The term drawing design tools can be understood primarily as the point and the line, while structure, surface, and light-dark differentiation must also be included here. At least one of these means of design can be found in every drawing - but in most cases there are several.

The point is the smallest and most inconspicuous element in a drawing. The line starts at the point and can be used in different ways: as the outline of a body, as traces of movement, to describe forms and much more.

By drawing points or lines on the paper you can create surfaces, light-dark differentiations, hatching and structures. You can control this through the flow, distribution and density of points or lines.

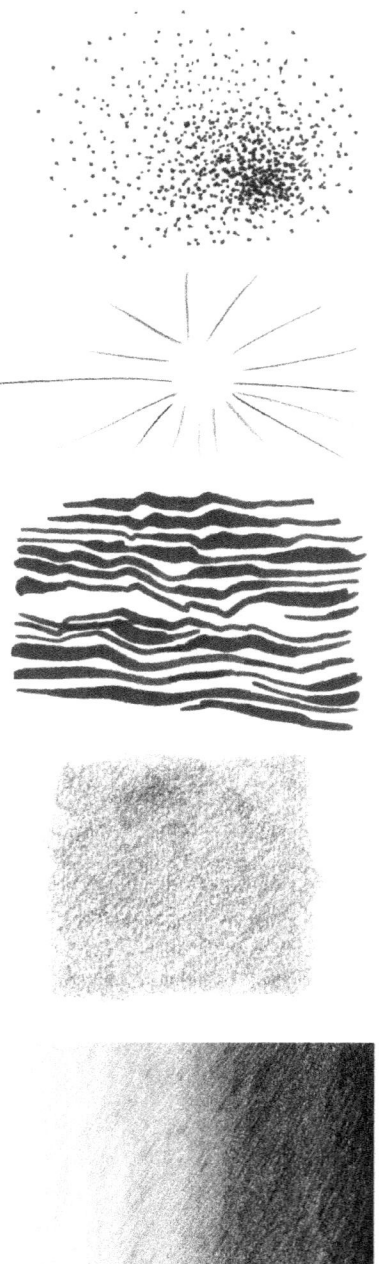

*Drawing design tools: point, line, structure, surface and light-dark differentiation*

# Exercise for Drawing Design Tools

## Line

In a few simple exercises, try to use the design tools of the illustrator (artist). We start with the line. So draw lines in different shapes and different dynamics: straight lines, curved lines, lines carefully drawn or with temperament - anything is allowed.

These simple exercises are especially interesting for beginners and will loosen you up a bit. But the lesson also makes sense for more experienced illustrators, because it is about basic skills.

Lines drawn in a radiant pattern

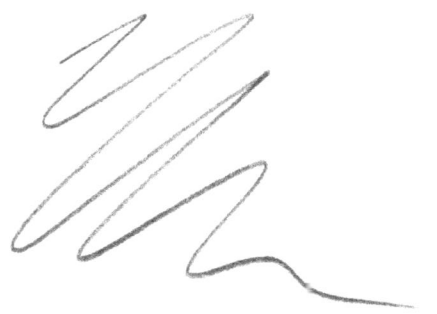
Swiftly drawn scribble line

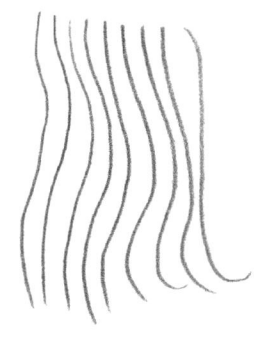
Wavy lines next to one another

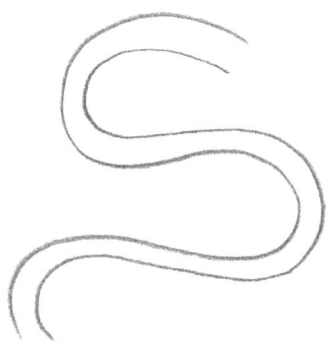
Parallel serpentine lines

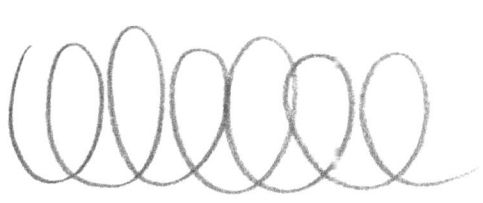
Spring-shaped line

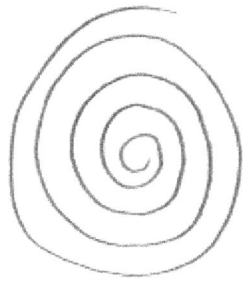
Spiral line

## Structure

Structures can also be represented with lines. Structures must be differentiated from hatchings, since structures are usually not uniform. Each line of a structure can differ in shape, direction, line width and length. Even within a single line, these properties can change. The lines in a structure do not have to have the same distance from one another. Structures are therefore a creative means with which one can also represent a certain rhythm. This allows you to create tension in an image and add effects that are particularly interesting.

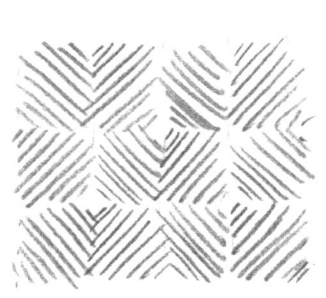

Chessboard structure with lines at a 45°-angle

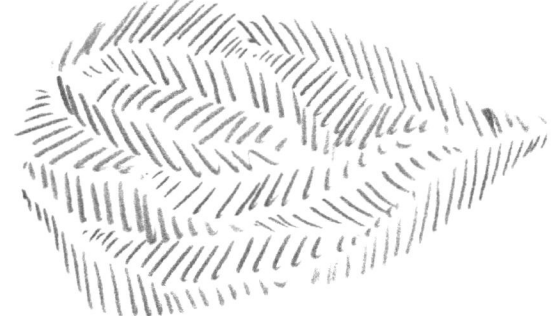

Structure with a series of irregular lines

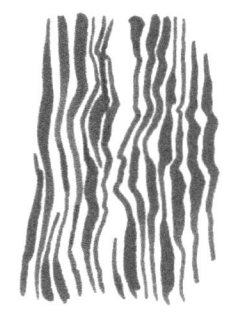

Tree bark-like structure

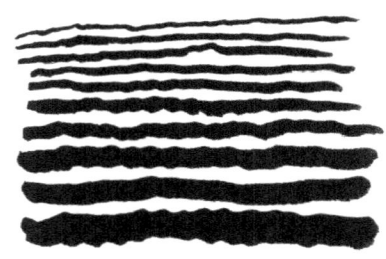

Structure with increasingly thinner lines

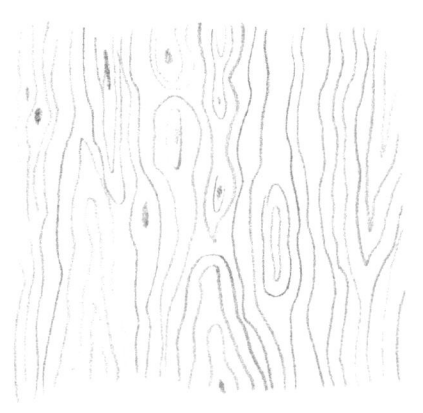

Wood-like structure

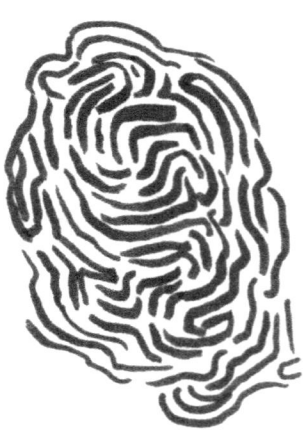

Natural-looking structure

# Basic Principles of Drawing

## Surfaces

Surfaces are a medium for graphic (drawing) design in which a certain drawing technique must inevitably be selected. Drawing techniques for flat-surface working are hatching, shading, wiping and washing. When hatching, the surface is sometimes prepared with a level structure. Additionally, the representation of several surfaces automatically results in the use of the "light-dark" design medium, since several surfaces are formed by different tonal values.

 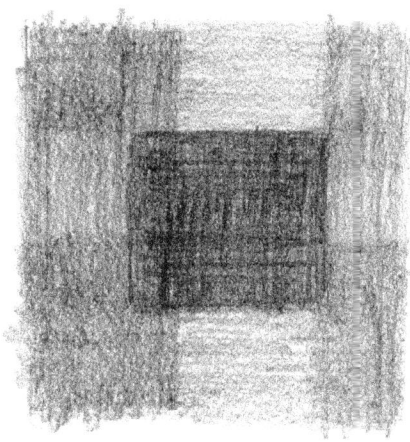 

Level surface · Contrasted surface · Distributed surfaces

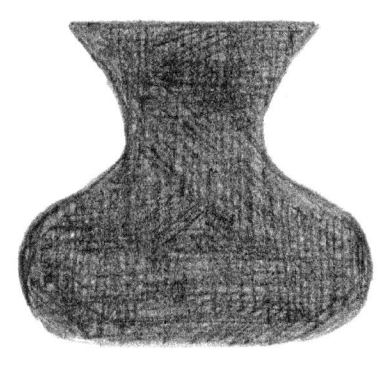 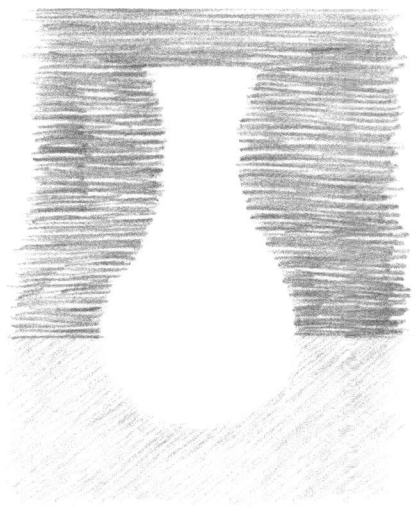 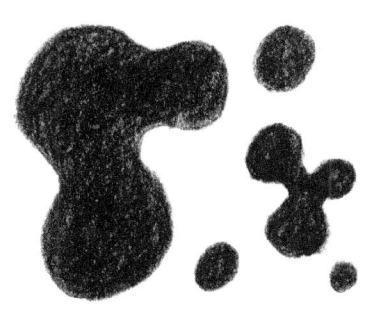

Shaped surface · Negative drawing of a surface · Drop-like surfaces

## Examples in Images

The following image examples illustrate the possibilities which one has with the use of simple graphic design means. Without using more elaborate techniques, such as light-dark gradients using hatching, it is possible to create quite expressive drawings.

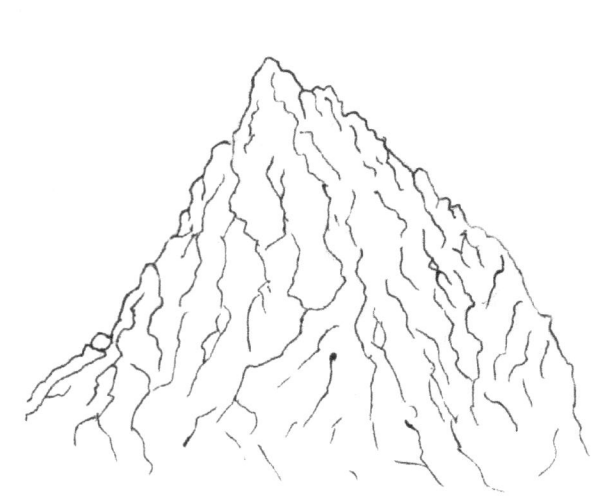

*Line drawing of a mountain*

*Elephant drawn with lines, surfaces and structure*

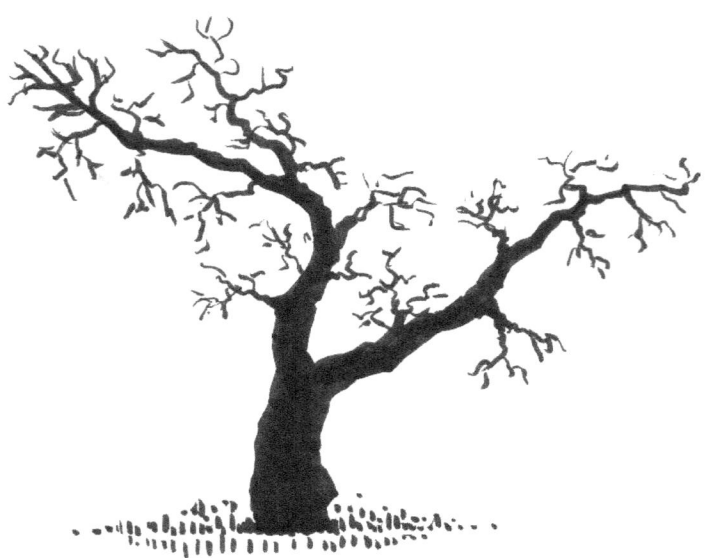

*Leafless tree drawn by deploying surface and line*

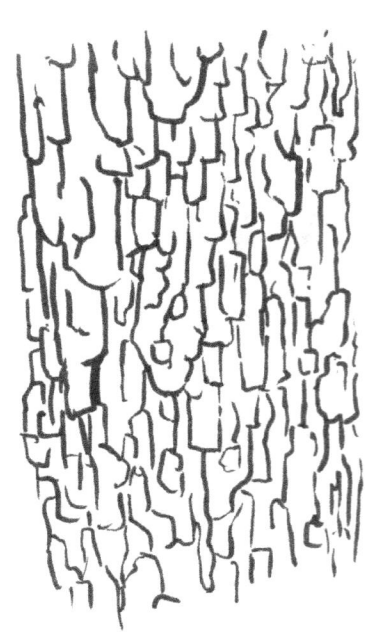

*Structure-drawing used to represent tree bark*

# Drawing Simple Forms

Another good exercise is to sketch basic shapes. This refers to simple geometric figures that are only two-dimensional. In the pictures below you will find examples to trace or reproduce. You can also create your own shapes and sketch them. It makes sense to practice these basic forms, because you will encounter them again and again while drawing different motifs.

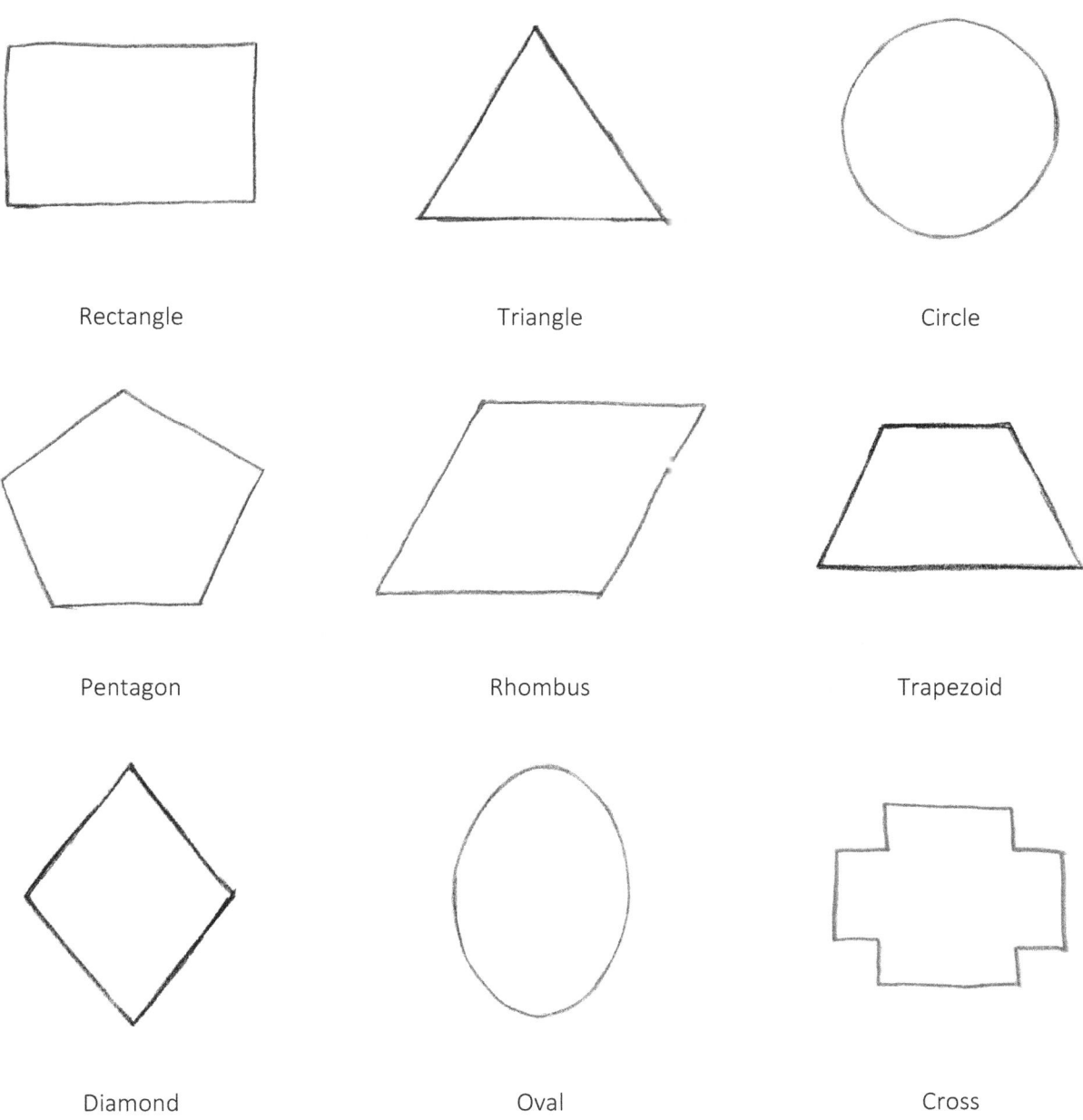

# Representing Three-Dimensional Bodies

In the previous examples and exercises we have limited ourselves to the representation of lines, surfaces and mostly two-dimensional motifs. Space and depth have so far only been represented by surfaces. Now we go one step further and try to depict real bodies.

The term "*body*" refers to a geometric figure that occupies a certain space and is therefore three-dimensional. Drawing a body is much more demanding than sketching two-dimensional forms. For this reason we will start with the simplest objects and slowly improve.

## Simple Geometric Bodies

In the following sketches important and simple bodies are depicted, which you can trace or reproduce for practice:

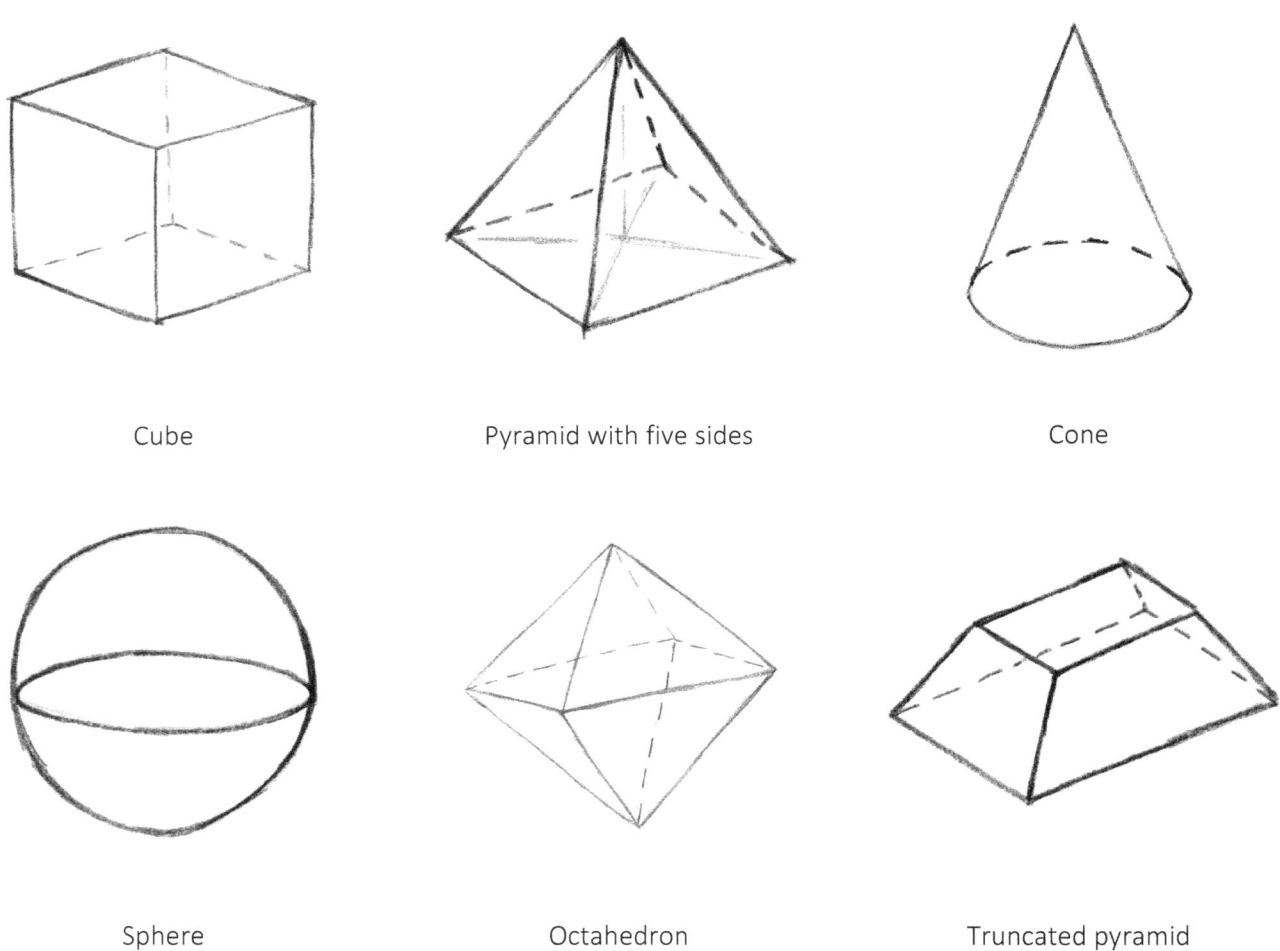

Cube     Pyramid with five sides     Cone

Sphere     Octahedron     Truncated pyramid

# Basic Principles of Drawing

## Transferring from the Surface into Space

The difference between two-dimensional shapes and three-dimensional bodies has already been described. However, to emphasize the meaning again, a descriptive example follows.
With the following drawings you can understand how a drawing gradually leaves the two-dimensional space and transforms into a completely spatial representation. We use a truck as our motif.

**Step 1:**
Pure two-dimensional drawing

**Step 2:**
Simple expansion of the drawing into depth – but only on one side.

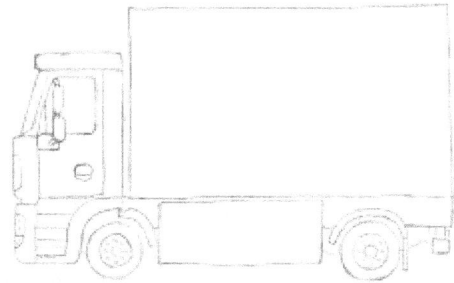

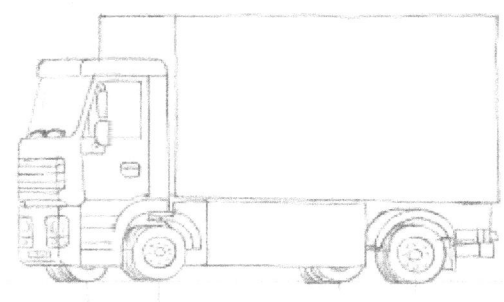

**Step 3:**
More complex expansion of the representation into depth

**Step 4:**
Perspective representation from the front oblique perspective

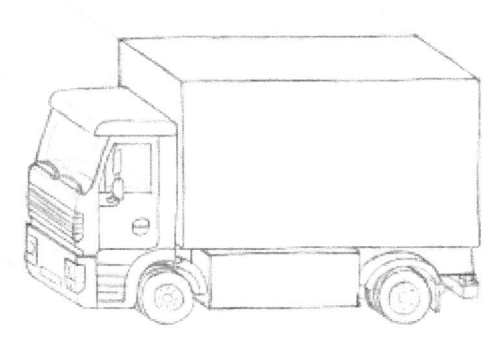

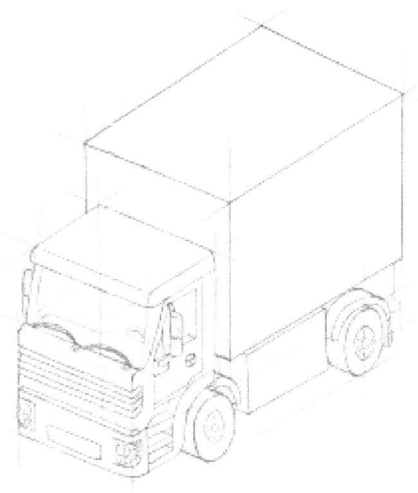

Even more realistic, albeit more complicated, is the three-dimensional representation of objects applying the so-called vanishing-point perspective. Using this method of drawing, the perspective distortion is represented, which we actually perceive in reality.
A drawing of the truck utilizing vanishing-point perspective can be seen here in the following image.

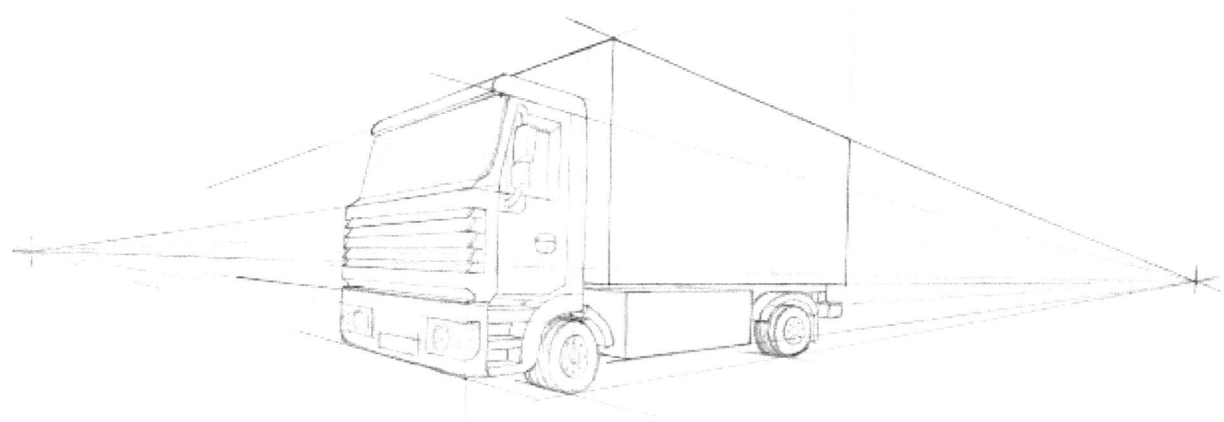

We will take a look at the method of representation using vanishing points in one of the succeeding chapters in this book. In the event that you would like to learn more about this, I recommend my book:
"Drawing Perspective and Space: The Basic Principles of Drawing in Perspective"

The example of the truck demonstrates quite well what it means to illustrate three-dimensional bodies. Knowledge in this area can also be logically applied to landscape representation, since motifs within a landscape are also spatial bodies.

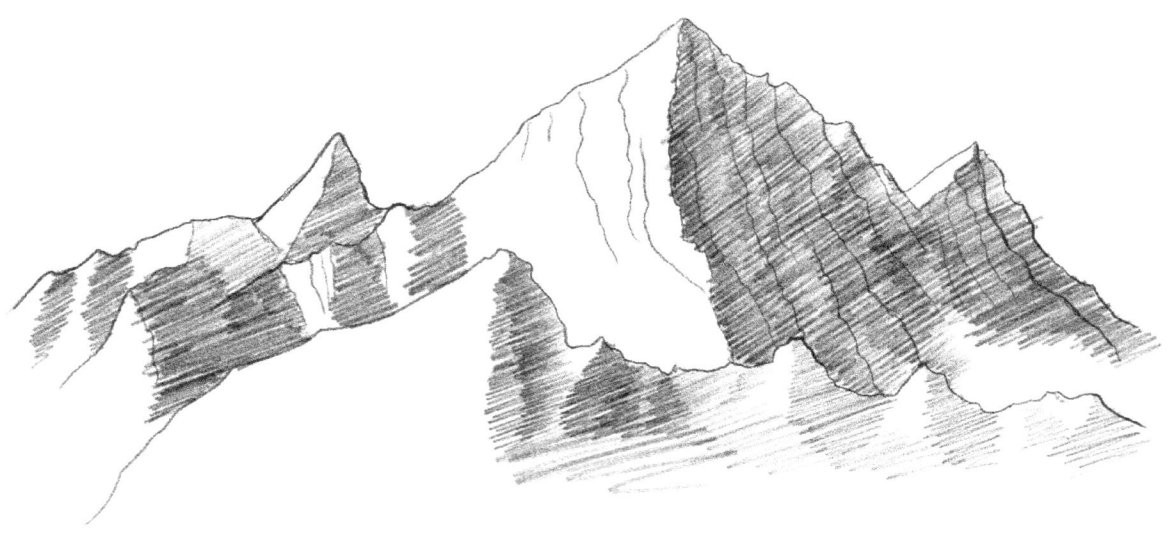

This sketch of a mountain landscape illustrates an example of spatial bodies within a landscape. One can achieve the best three-dimensional effect by including shadows in the image. You can learn how to draw shadows in one of the succeeding chapters in this book.

# Exercise – Simple Motifs

## Mini-Landscapes

In this exercise you can practice using initial small motifs. By making use of only a few strategic lines, mini-landscapes can be created as seen here below.

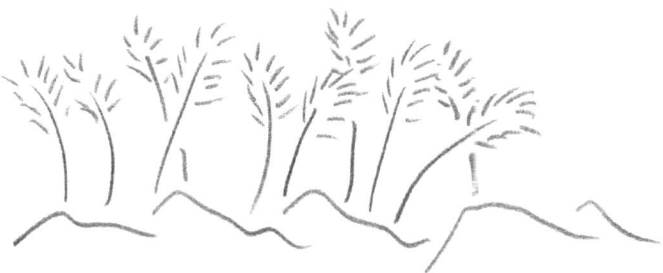

*Field with wheat*

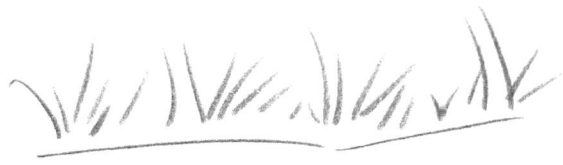

*Field with wheat*

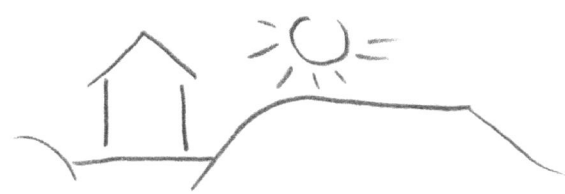

*House in a hilly landscape*

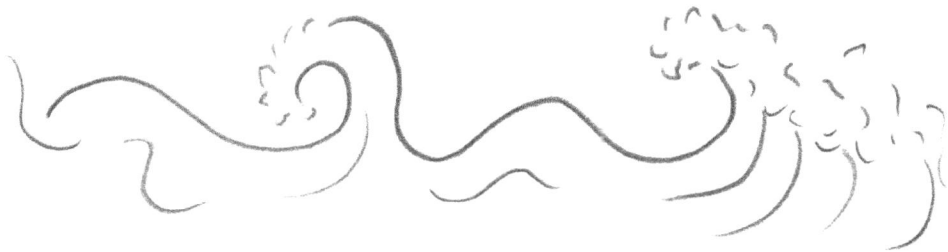

*Surging ocean waves*

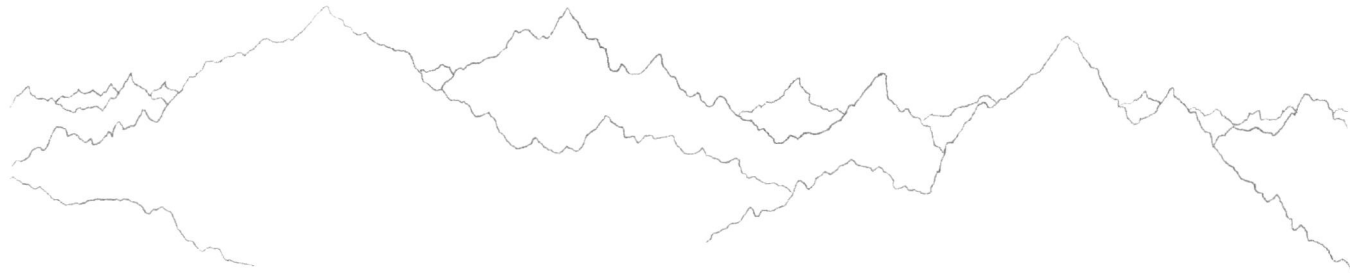

*Mountain range*

## Exercise: Buildings – Constructing Objects in Perspective

And now try drawing a building from a perspective point-of-view. Your goal here is simply the depiction of the contours – and if you like, you can use a ruler to make straight lines. We will proceed in four steps, whereby we first of all make a rough sketch; then we work out the form in two steps and, finally, add a few more details.

Drawing motifs that are geometrically simple and rigidly constructed is an excellent exercise, since you can acquire, in this manner, a better feeling for the representation of space and form. However, these challenges are not meant for everyone, since intuition is rarely required here – this exercise more likely involves a technical approach to drawing.

# Basic Principles of Drawing

**Step 1:**
An initial rough draft of the form

**Step 2:**
More detailed development of the form

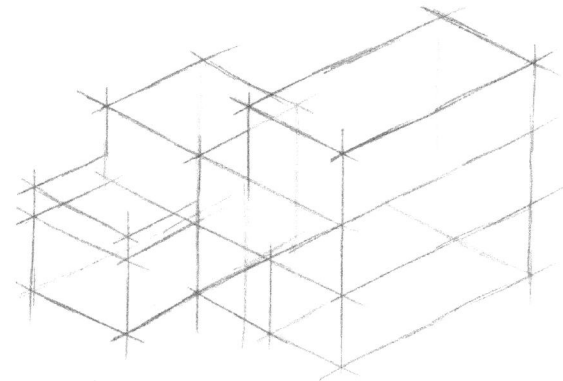

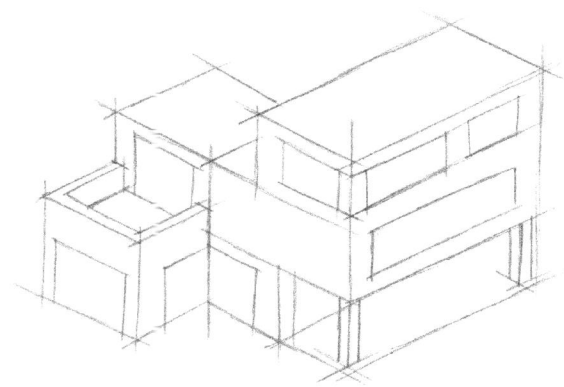

**Step 3:**
Completion of the geometric body

**Step 4:**
Detailing and completion of the drawing

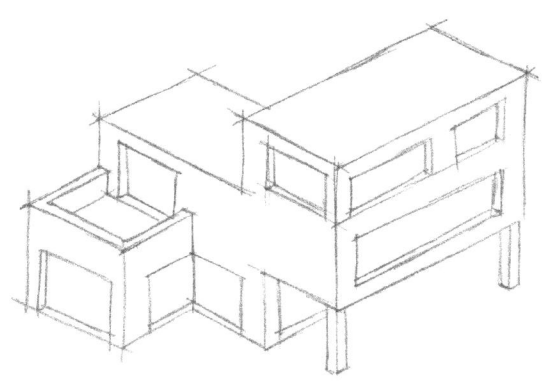

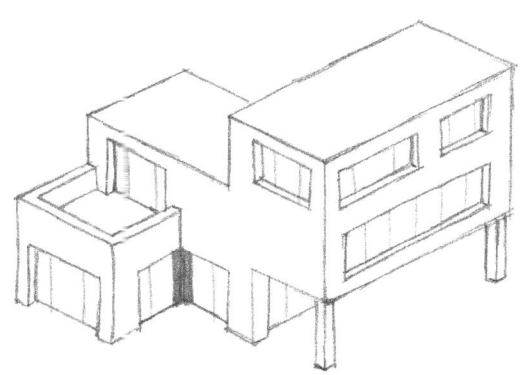

The technique behind three-dimensional drawing is not limited exclusively to geometric representation; illustration of the shadows is also important. Only through shading are motifs able to display their full, spatial effect.

# Drawing Tools

At this point, the various drawing tools will be described. When one is aware of the different material means and their characteristics, it is easier to predict when a certain tool would be most suitable or which ones will be personally more preferable.

## Lead Pencil / Graphite Pencil

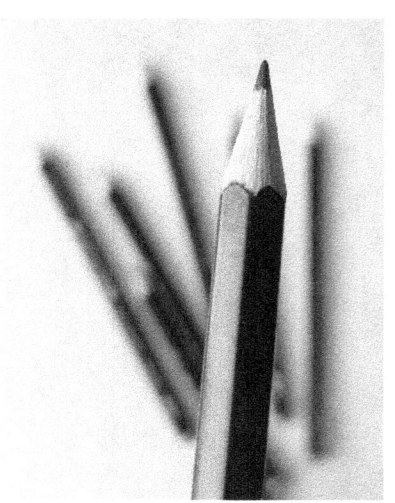

One of the most important tools for drawing is the "lead", i.e., graphite pencil. The designation lead pencil is historical and false in reality, since a pencil core actually consists of a mixture of graphite, clay and water and not of lead.

Pencils have many advantages: one can draw varyingly strong lines by controlling the hand pressure while drawing, and also erase previously drawn lines. Also, by choosing different degrees of graphite hardness in the pencils, various shades of gray (tonal values) can be achieved.

## Indian Ink and Ink

When we refer to Indian ink or ink, we are talking about liquid media for drawing. Artists have traditionally drawn with either quill with Indian ink (bottled ink) or they have used pens. The quill has the disadvantage that one has to dip the quill into the bottle again and again, which can easily lead to splashing. With pens we are offered a broad palette of various products. Examples are fiber pens that utilize Indian ink as well as ballpoint pens, fineliners and drawing ink pens.

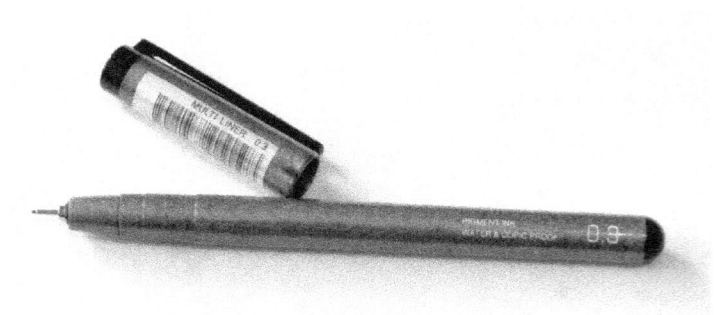

*Fineliner with a 0.3mm point*

These pens have the advantage that it is not necessary to always refill the India ink or ink by hand, since the drawing medium is contained inside. Once the ink reservoir is empty, it can be exchanged, or a new pen has to be used.

Basic Principles of Drawing

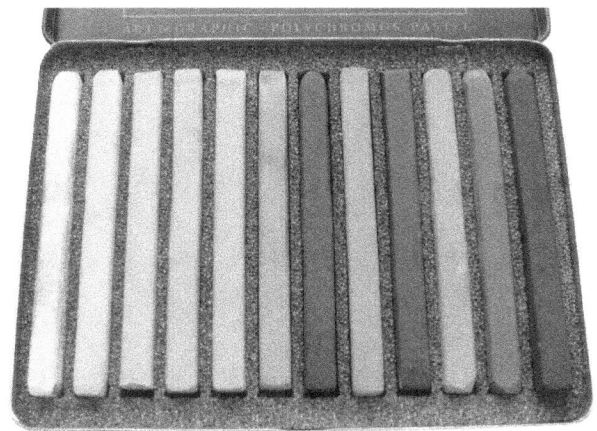

## Chalk / Pastel chalk

Pastel chalk is suitable primarily for color drawings and/or paintings with large colored surfaces and soft color gradations. Application of the color can be either soft or robust. Typical for pastel paintings are, however, the soft color gradations. These colors can easily be blurred with a finger or a swiping tool.

## Charcoal

We can also draw using charcoal. The so-called drawing charcoal consists of carbonized wood. The drawing charcoal is available in either stick or charcoal pencil form. A considerably robust, dark color application can be achieved here, with which highly expressive and contrast-rich drawings are created. One can draw thin lines and uniform surfaces. It is also well-suited to the technique of smearing, which can be used to draw on a large scale.

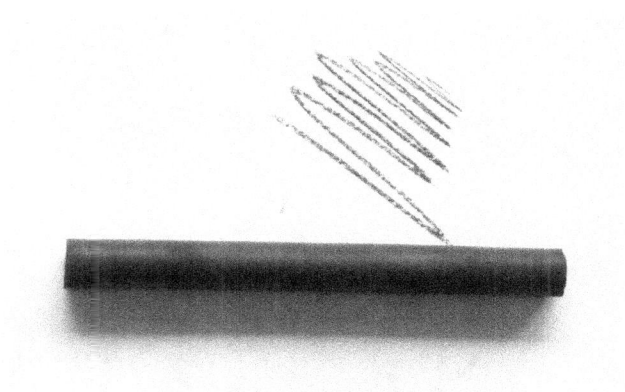

## Colored Pencils / Crayons

A colored pencil is a pencil with a colored core which is – as is the case with a lead pencil – encased in wood. The colored core consists of a mixture of colored pigments, fat, wax, a binding agent, talcum and kaolin.

Colored pencils can be qualitatively quite varied. It is better here if one does not necessarily select the cheapest product, since qualitatively inferior working materials can easily diminish the joy of drawing. Furthermore, among artists colored pencils are preferred over crayons because a reference to crayons reminds one of rather low quality materials from primary school.

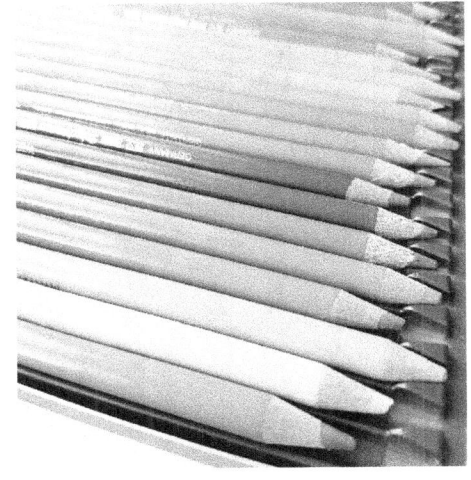

# Further Material for Drawing

## Paper

After the pencil, the second most important thing is the drawing surface – that is, the paper or cardboard. The drawing surface is essential for the achievable quality of a drawing.

Important characteristics of a drawing surface are, in addition to the paper format, the roughness and the relative weight (gram per square meter). In reference to the weight it can be said: the higher the better, since the paper becomes thicker and more stable. The roughness of the surface depends on personal preference.

*Various forms of drawing paper*

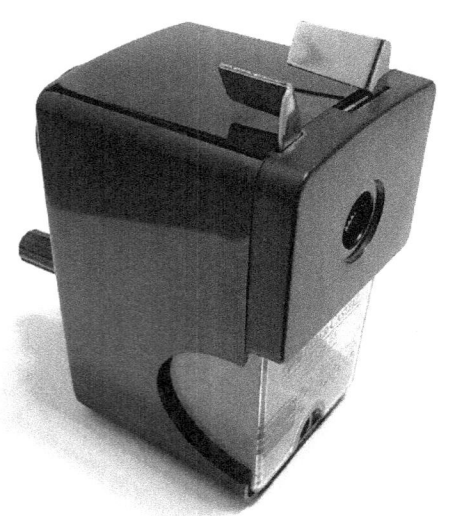

## Pencil Sharpener

With the sharpener you can keep pencils and colored pencils pointed and thus draw thin, fine lines. It is available in different versions and sizes.

A hand-operated sharpening machine is recommended for drawing. Working with it is more pleasant than with a normal sharpener. Moreover, it occurs less frequently that, while sharpening the pencil, the point breaks off. Some artists alternatively use a sharp knife to sharpen their points.

# Erasers

The eraser is not to be underestimated as a valuable tool for drawing. The function of an eraser is of course to remove lines that have been drawn with a graphite pencil, colored pencil, chalk, etc.

During the drawing process, an eraser is frequently used specifically to implement small details – for example, small points of light or light-catching contours. Another function in drawing could also be intentional smudging.

The various kinds of erasers are: rubber eraser (hard), vinyl eraser (soft), eraser pencil ("erasil") and kneaded eraser.

## Rubber eraser

You can remove strong drawing lines and, in part, Indian ink. It has the advantage of a relatively sharp edge that can be used to erase details. The main problem with a rubber eraser is that it can damage the structure of the paper. It thus becomes difficult to erase on roughened paper. However, the removal of color cannot be achieved so readily.

## Vinyl eraser

A vinyl eraser is considerably gentler on paper than the hard variety. A soft eraser is much easier on paper than a hard one. But the removal of color, which can be achieved with the vinyl eraser, is also reduced.

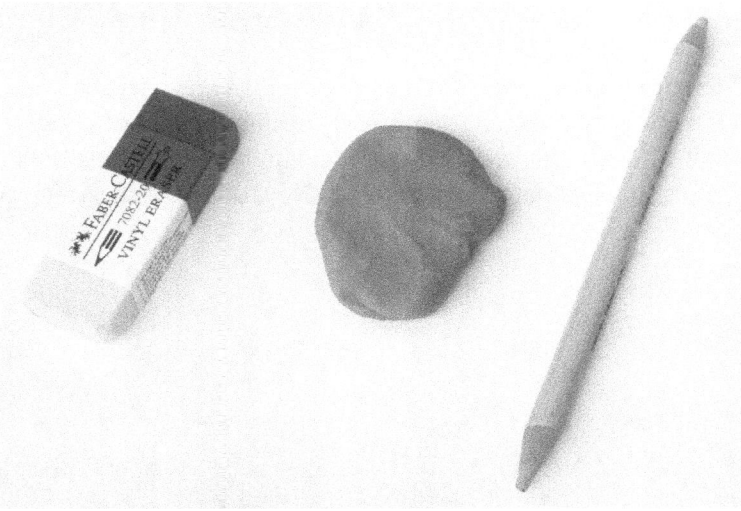

*Two-sided eraser (hard & soft), gum eraser & eraser pencil*

## Eraser pencil

With the eraser pen you can work out fine details in drawings. The eraser pencil can be sharpened. There are pencils with a hard and a soft end. The soft end is also suitable for using the smudging technique.

## Kneaded (art) eraser

The unique characteristic of the kneaded eraser its formability. It can remove sections of the drawing by simply being pressed onto the paper. This can best be achieved with loose drawing methods such as charcoal or pastel chalk as well as pencil. The formability is of great advantage here in particular. The kneaded eraser is soft for the paper, but is not able to remove all of the drawing details.

# Drawing Technique Methods

What are the *methods of drawing technique* and what do you need them for? Both questions can be explained in one answer: simply put, one uses a specific method of drawing technique as soon as one begins. Especially if you want to fill an area with a grey tone, you have to decide on a method. You have the choice between techniques such as shading, hatching or wiping. Grey tones are also referred to as tonal values in technical jargon.

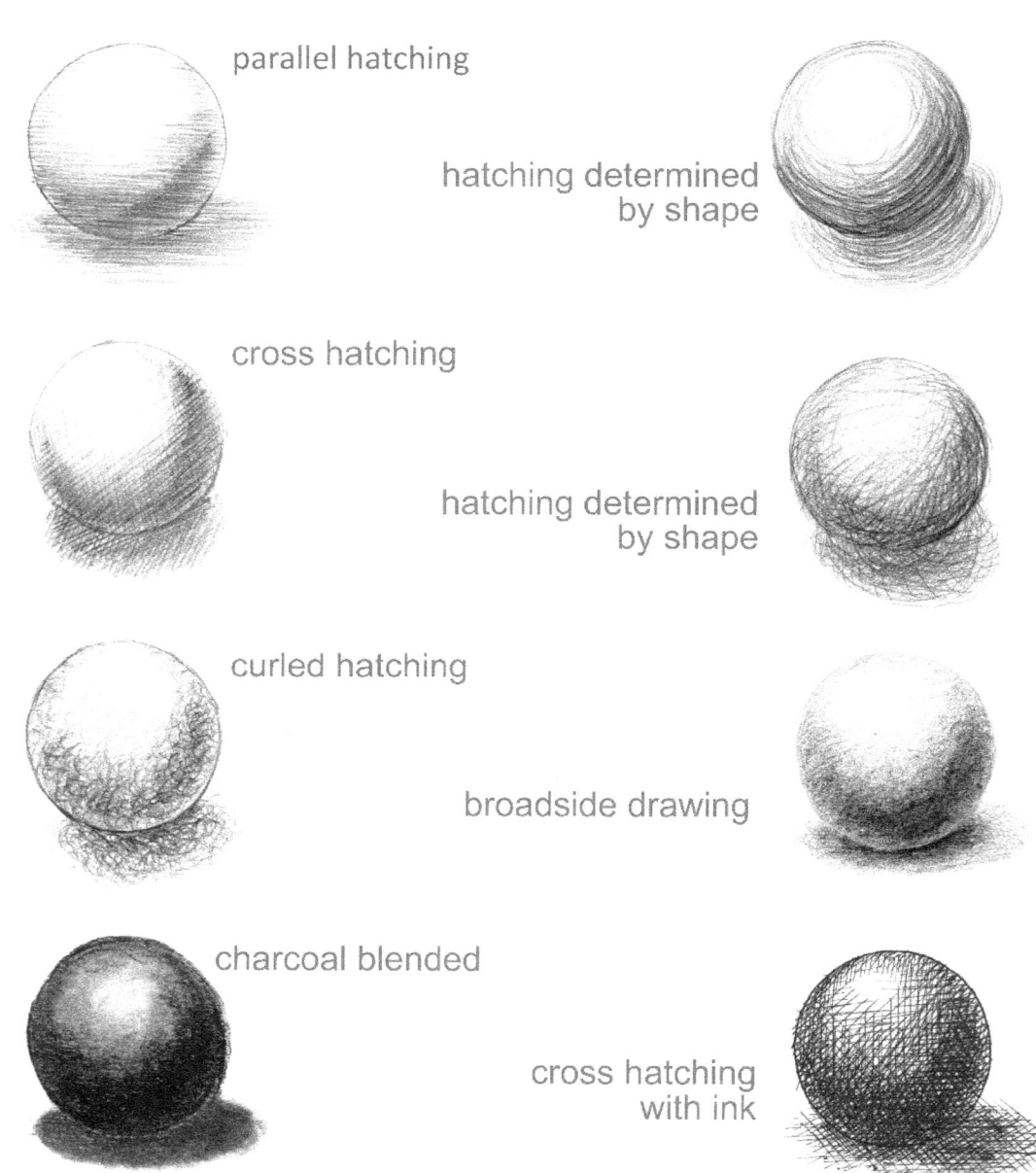

# Basic Principles of Drawing

The most important and probably most frequently used drawing technique - besides the line itself - is hatching. In this book we will therefore deal with this drawing technique in particular. Other important drawing techniques you will learn in this book are the following:

- Hatching
- Shading
- Wiping
- Washing

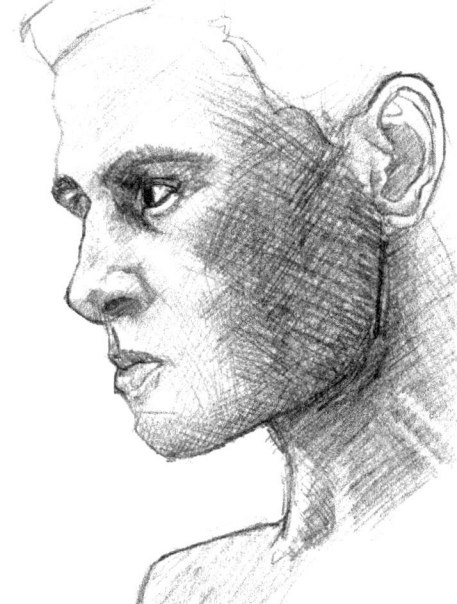

*Hatching in a portrait drawing*

## Drawing Technique 1 – Hatching

In hatching, a row of lines is usually drawn parallel to each other at the same distance apart. It is also possible to draw several hatches at different angles on top of each other. If lines are drawn in only one direction, this is referred to as parallel hatching. If hatches are drawn at least two different angles, this is called cross hatching.

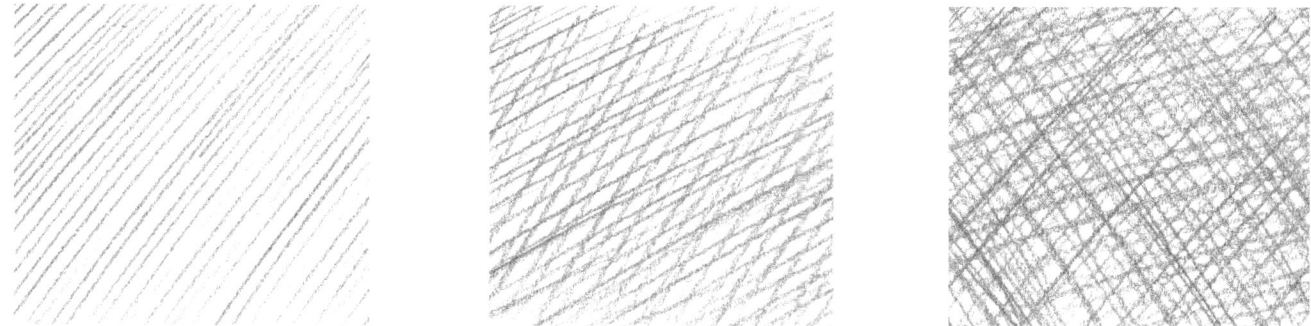

*Parallel hatching, cross hatching in two directions, cross hatching in three directions*

The aim of hatching is to generate a specific tonal value. The tonal value is obtained by mixing the lines with the white paper that appears between the lines. For the observer, lines and background mix to form a uniform grey tone.

# Producing Tonal Values with Hatching

There are different possibilities to draw lighter and darker surfaces using hatching. All methods will be described here in the following.

## Method 1: Line density

By compressing the lines of a hatch, the tonal value can be made darker. You can also darken the overall tonal value by overlaying the lines of a hatching with a different orientation. If, on the other hand, you want to make a hatch brighter, you have to draw the lines at a greater distance from each other.

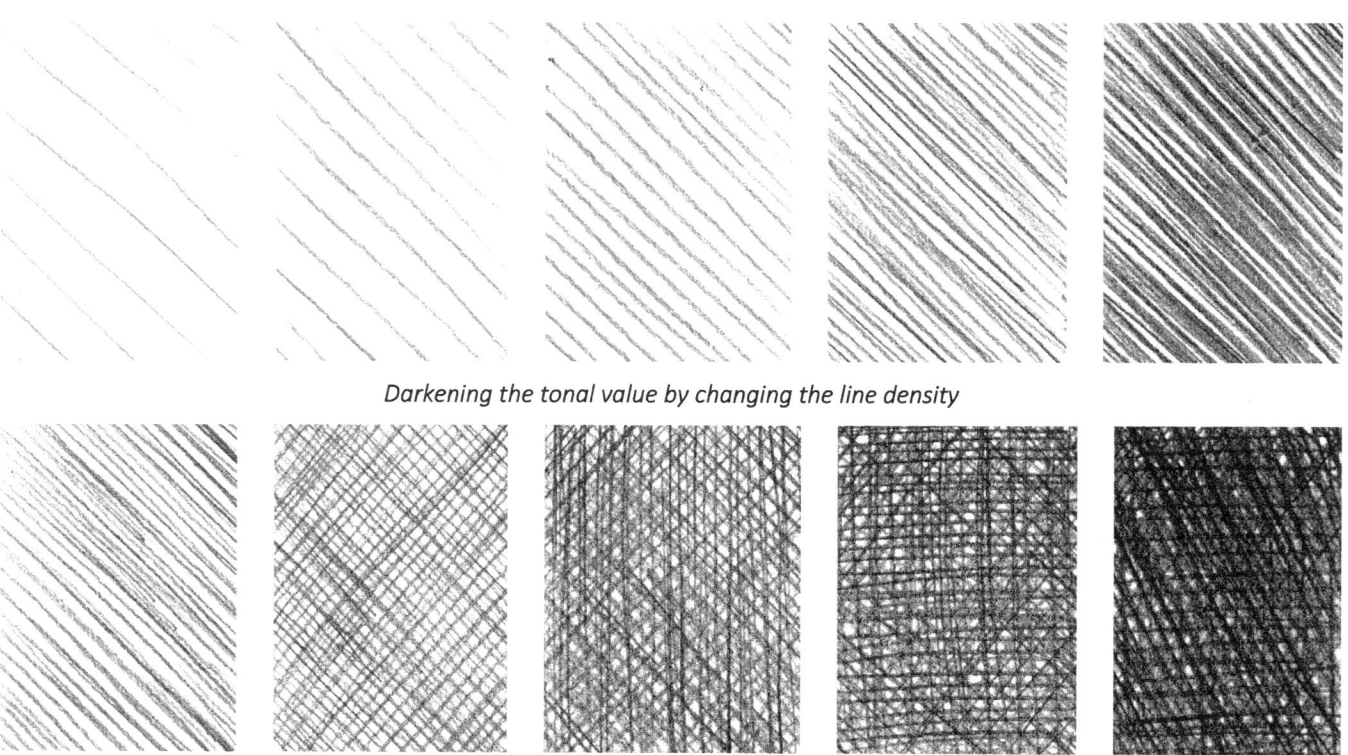

*Darkening the tonal value by changing the line density*

*Darkening the tonal value through additional hatches with a different orientation*

If you are drawing with ink, this method is mainly used. The only alternative would be to dilute the ink with water to draw lighter lines.

## Method 2: Downforce of the Pencil

If you draw with a pencil, you also have the possibility to control the downforce of the pencil. If you press more strongly, the lines become thicker and darker, which automatically results in a darker tonal value. If, on the other hand, the hatching is drawn with little downforce, the lines become thinner and lighter. In this way, dense hatchings can be drawn that still correspond to a light shade of gray.

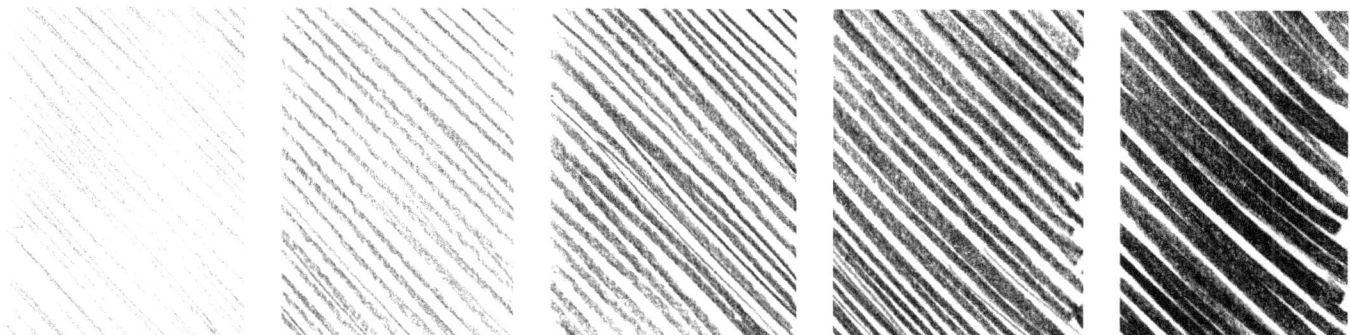

*Different hatchings drawn using varied downforce*

## Method 3: Hardness of the Pencil

You can also use pencils of different hardness to draw lighter and darker hatches. Hard pencils produce a light gray shade, while soft pencils produce a dark gray shade.

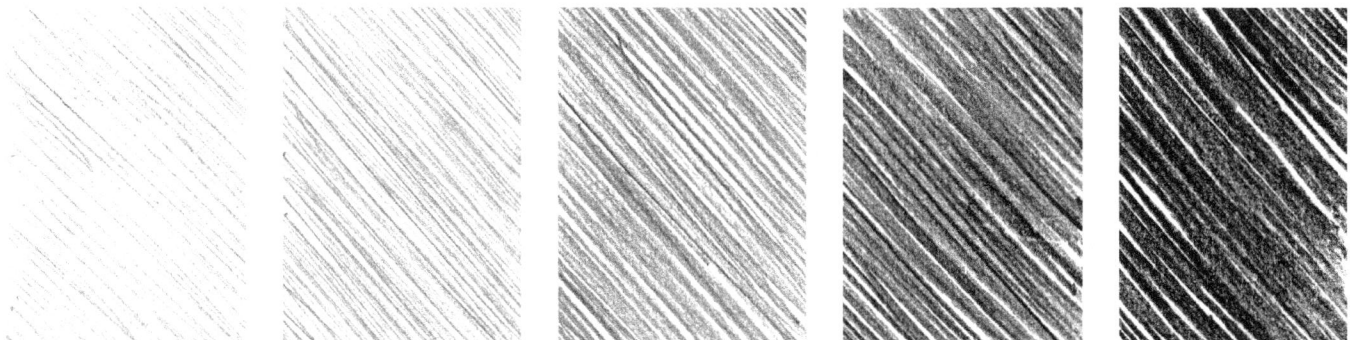

*Hatchings generated using the pencil hardnesses 2H, H, HB, 2B and 6B (from left to right)*

# Special Hatchings and Styles

### Shape-determined hatchings

The shape of a body can also be made clear by means of hatching. The hatching follows the shape of a body. This so-called shape-determined hatching is particularly suitable for objects with convex or concave geometry.

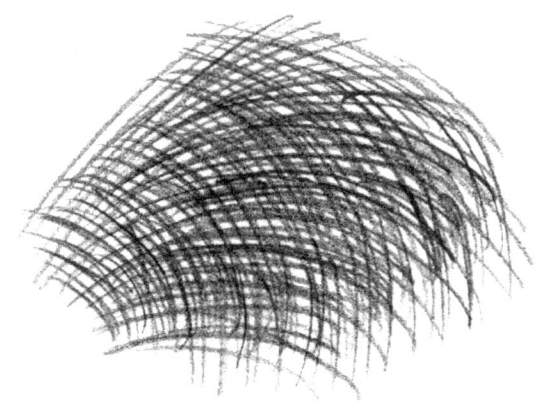

### Curled hatching

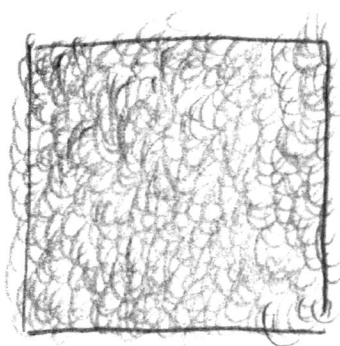

Another variant is, for example, curled lines, with which a certain structure or surface texture can also be conveyed by hatching.

### Hatched groups

Very interesting and lively hatching can be obtained by drawing small groups of parallel lines in different orientations.

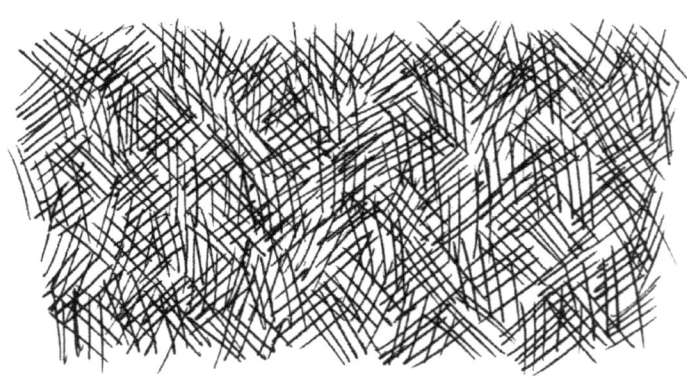

### Scribbled lines

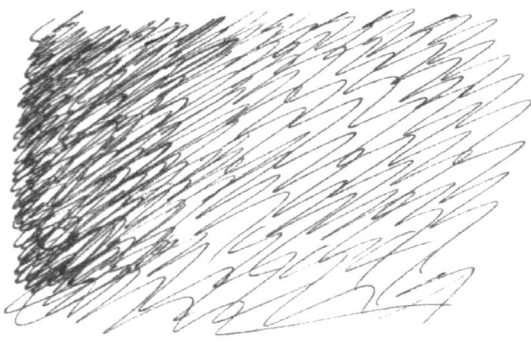

A drawing can impart a certain dynamic through scribbled lines. The hatchings appear more spontaneous and disorganized, which makes the respective image particularly unique.

Basic Principles of Drawing

## Drawing Technique 2 – Broadside Drawing

When drawing with the broad side of the pen, you work back and forth by holding the pen at a relatively flat angle to the paper. You can use this technique with a pencil/graphite pencil, colored pencil, or charcoal and pastel chalk.

By *broadside drawing* you can quickly and easily fill large areas without having to master a particularly skilled technique. Often this technique is regarded as a rather inexact technique. In addition, this is already a drawing technique in which no strokes or lines are visible, which means that the classic criteria of a drawing are no longer fulfilled.

The optical results of hatching are often more impressive than those of broadside drawing and the characteristic handwriting of the draftsman is more clearly visible.

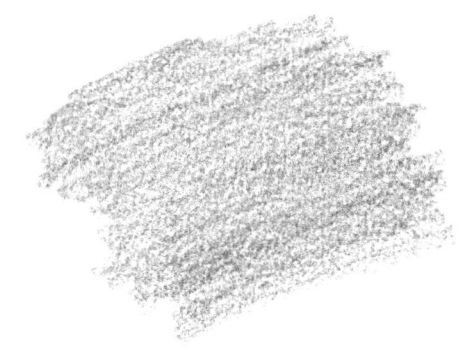

*Area drawn with the broad side of the pen*

*Shaded tone value progression*

## Drawing Technique 3 – Blending/Smudging

The blending technique can be applied with pencil, colored pencil, chalk and charcoal. Especially the loose drawing media - chalk and charcoal - are excellent for wiping.

In the blend technique, a previously drawn surface is wiped with a finger or a wiping tool. In this way you can quickly fill large areas and create particularly soft light-dark gradients.

Please note: When blending, one is already at the border between drawing and painting, as there are hardly any lines or lines to be seen.

*Charcoal hatch blended in the upper right section*

The wiping technique proceeds in three steps: First you draw a surface - for example with charcoal. Then you use a wiping tool such as an estompe to wipe the surface in one direction. In the end you can blur the charcoal even further beyond the drawn surface to create a tone gradient.

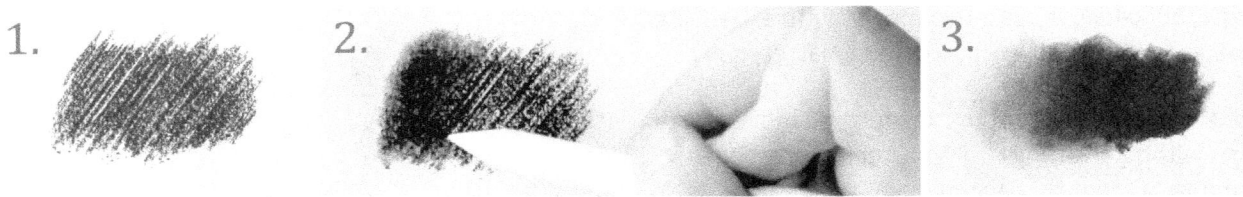

*Smudging in three steps*

## Drawing Technique 4 – Washing

The technique of washing is used in combination with Indian ink and ink. The color is applied with a brush, as in watercolor painting, in order to represent shades and tints. To apply Indian ink or ink transparently, it is mixed with water.

Pen and brush drawings are often combined. In this way, outlines and structures drawn with pen and Indian ink are created, which are then shaded by washing.

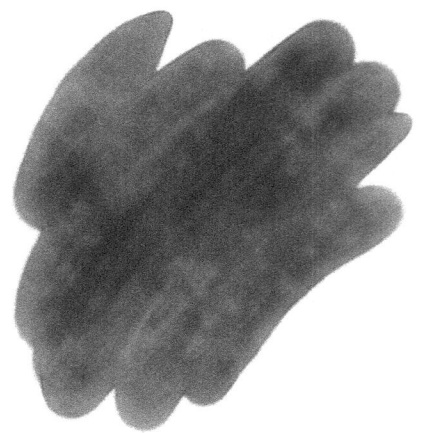

# How to Draw Shadows

In the previous chapters we learned how to draw objects spatially. We also learned techniques such as hatching to display tonal values.

By combining this knowledge, we are able to draw motifs with shadows. Through the representation of shadows one can make objects look really three-dimensional.

## Light and Shade

A prerequisite for the representation of shadows is the corresponding basic knowledge of the interaction of light and shadow. We all know that shadows are created wherever light does not reach. For example, if the sun shines on a wall, it is brightly lit on one side while it remains dark on the other. But not only the wall itself is dark on one side, also a shadow is cast on the floor by the wall.

The sketch shown describes the different types and areas of shadows using the example of a sphere.

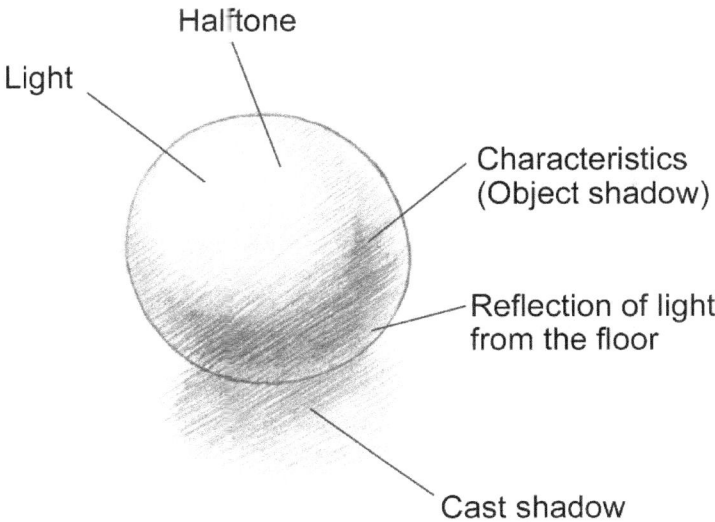

# Various Objects

And now you can draw various basic geometric objects in order to practice. First draw the contours and then shade the object. In the following sketches you can find some examples that you can draw.

**Tip:**

The graphic study of simple geometric bodies is important, because you will find these simple bodies in all complex objects. It is often possible to divide complex shapes into several simple geometric bodies, which is often a great help when drawing.

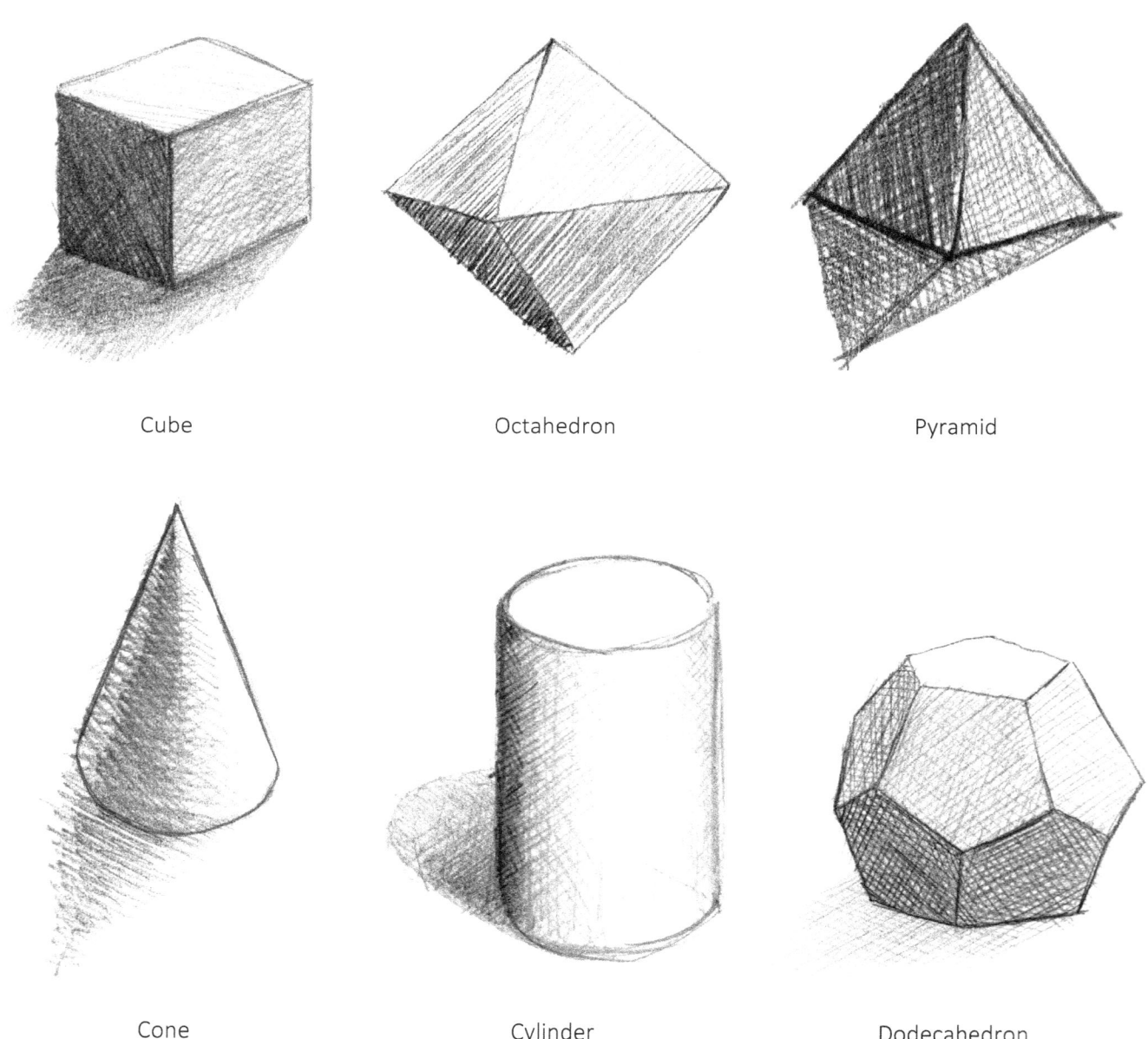

Cube                Octahedron              Pyramid

Cone                Cylinder               Dodecahedron

Basic Principles of Drawing

# Drawing Texture and Structure

Textures and structures are important tools for artists and graphic designers, since they use them to represent various materials and surfaces. The possibilities for application are far reaching: wool, scales, gravel, water, skin, grass and countless other things can be illustrated by means of structure or texture.

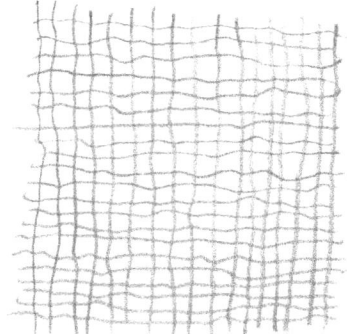
Grid-like lines that recreate a fabric

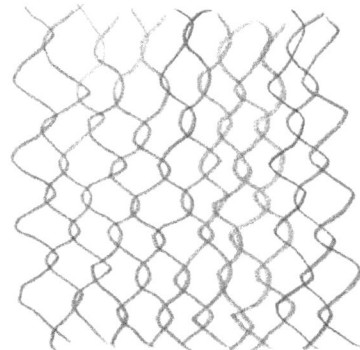
Mesh-like pattern of snake lines

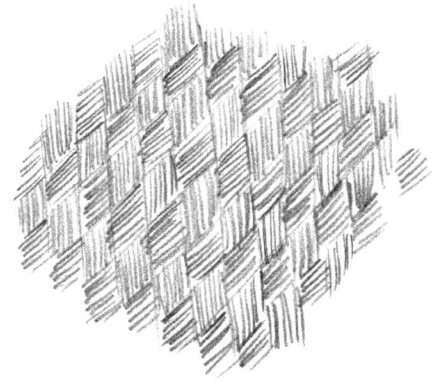
Groups of lines that produce a pattern

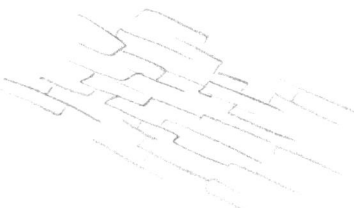
Line structures similar to the wings of a dragonfly

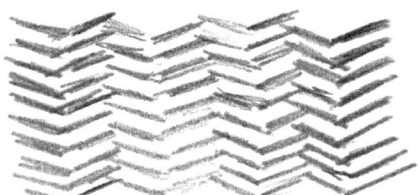
Pattern that recreates the surface of a woven basket

Pattern that looks like a brick wall

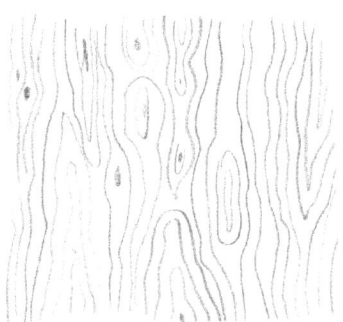
Wood pattern, similar to a board

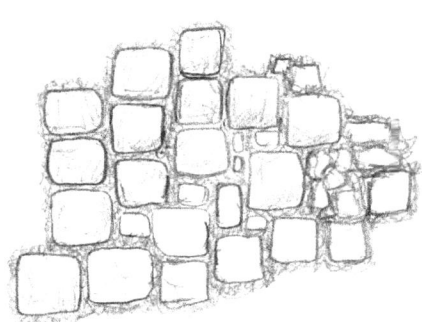
Texture of a stone wall

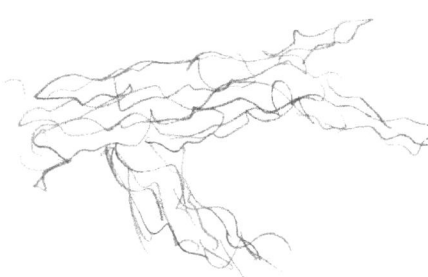
Structure of a branch using scribbled lines

# Exercise – Drawing simple Motifs

In this exercise you may venture into the first real motifs. Find simple objects that you can draw. On the following pages you will find some examples, which you can also replicate.

Start with a simple side view of the motif. Look at the object from the side and draw it. A side view is usually easier to draw than a perspective view that would be drawn diagonally from above, for example. Once you've drawn from the side, you can also draw the object directly from the front. To make it a little easier for you, you can sketch orientation lines to help you transfer the proportions in height. Take a look at the following drawings and you will quickly understand how it works.

## Book

The first object that we'll take a look at is a book. Recreate the book from both sides. With the aid of orientation lines, you are able to transfer the height from one perspective to the other.

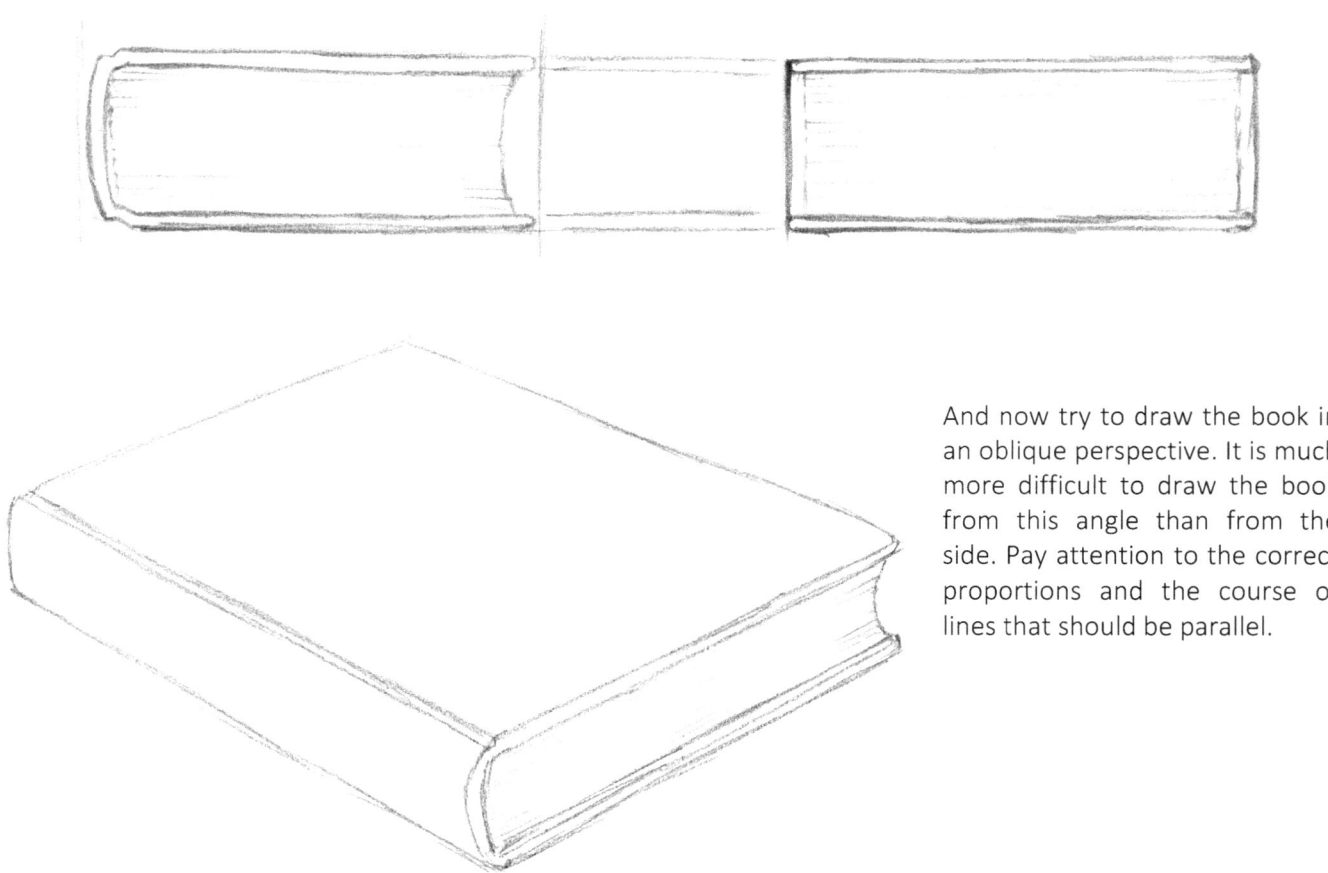

And now try to draw the book in an oblique perspective. It is much more difficult to draw the book from this angle than from the side. Pay attention to the correct proportions and the course of lines that should be parallel.

# Folding Table

In the next exercise we will draw a folding table. A new challenge with this motif is the slope in the table legs. Especially in the perspective view, it gets a bit tricky here.

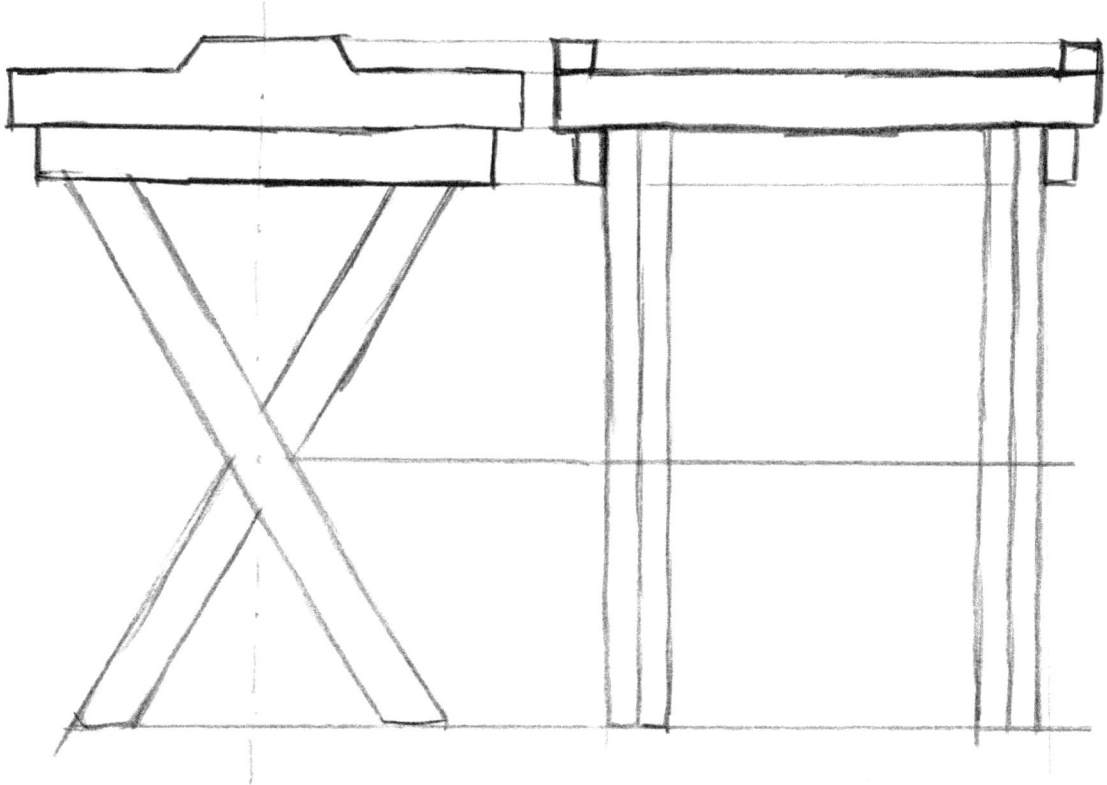

With the diagonal-sided representation, one can start again with a rough sketch. For this purpose, the motif can be broken down mentally into individual geometric basic bodies. In the second step, the sketch is detailed and completed in the final drawing.

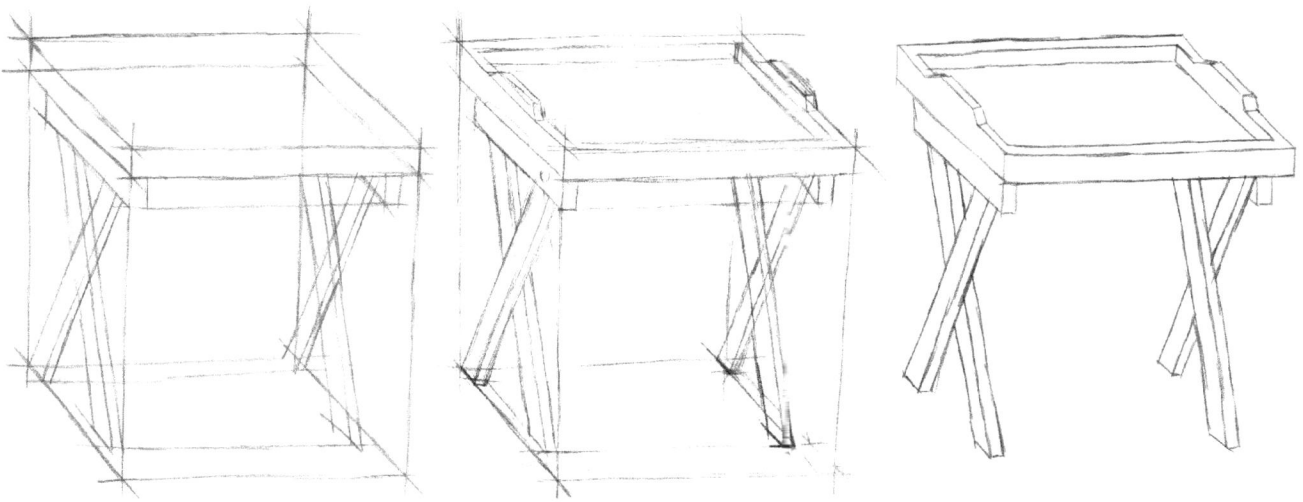

# Spoon

Drawing a spoon is not as easy as one would first assume. Try to re-create the curved form in a manner that is as seamless as possible.

When using perspective, it is once again difficult to represent the spoon. However, for this reason in particular it is an excellent exercise that can help you to improve and expand your skills.

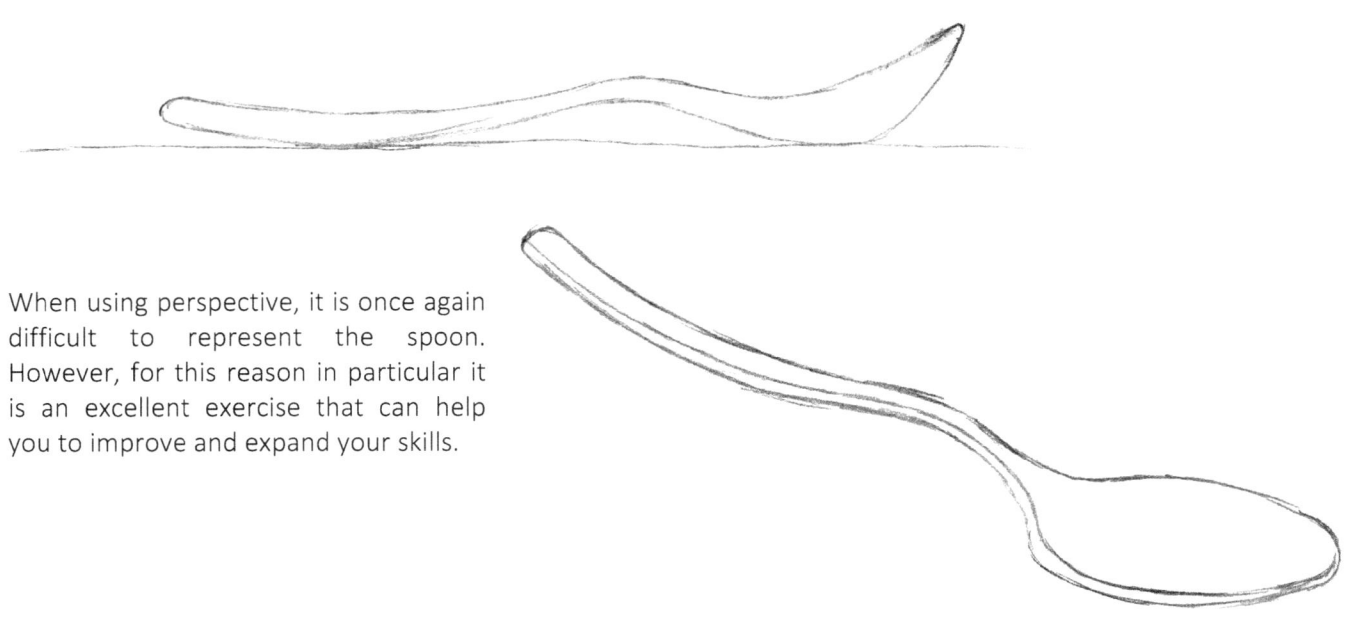

# Bowl

To illustrate a bowl, first draw an ellipse and then extend it downwards with a segment of a circle. You can refine the drawing with a subsection representing the base of the bowl. The inner edge of the bowl can also be represented by a second, smaller ellipse. It is sufficient if this is only hinted at.

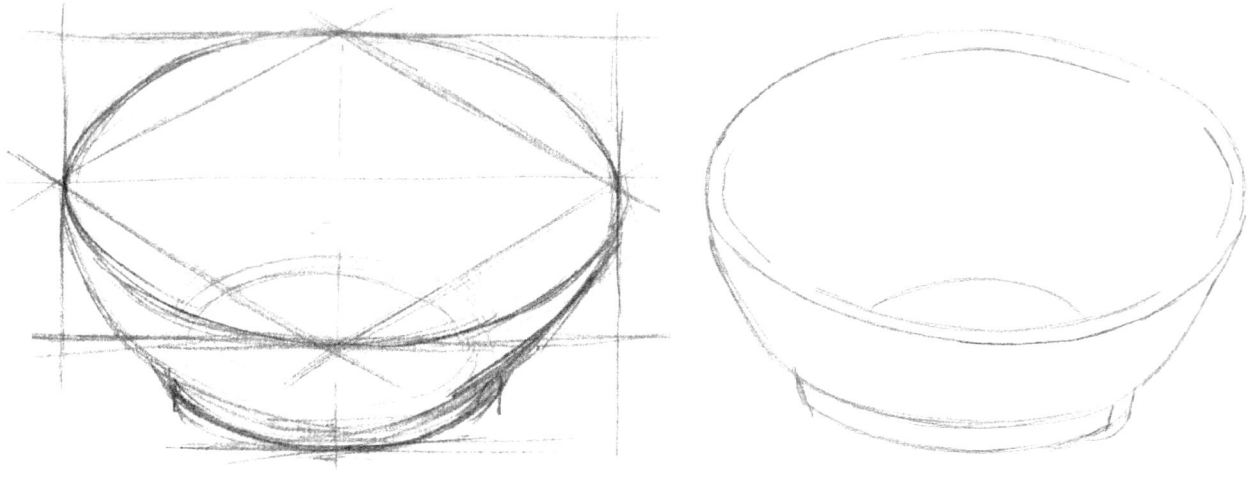

# Camera

The small compact camera in this exercise is actually relatively easy to draw, since it is largely constructed from simple geometric basic shapes. Interesting here are the small details.

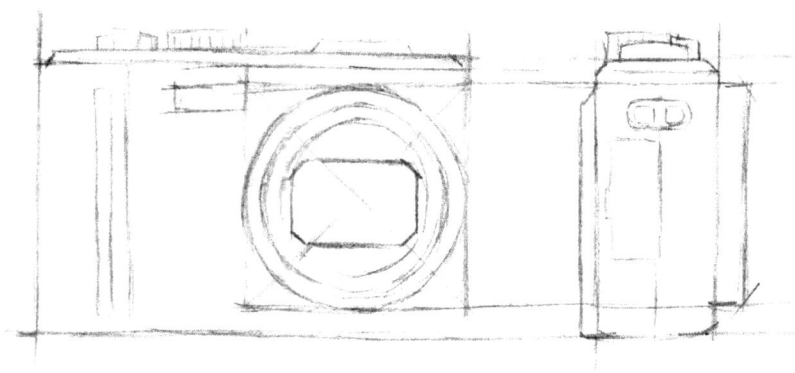

The details such as dials, buttons, shutters, etc. become particularly apparent when the oblique perspective is used.

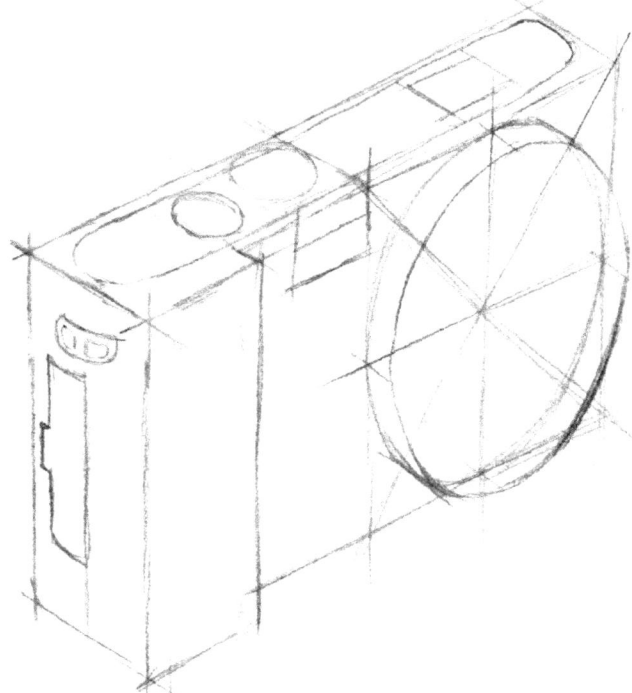

# Lantern

This lantern has a shape that is a bit more complex. It is made of ceramic, but is shaped as if it were woven. The basic shape, on the other hand, is simple because it is a sphere. However, you have to invest a little time in working out the details.

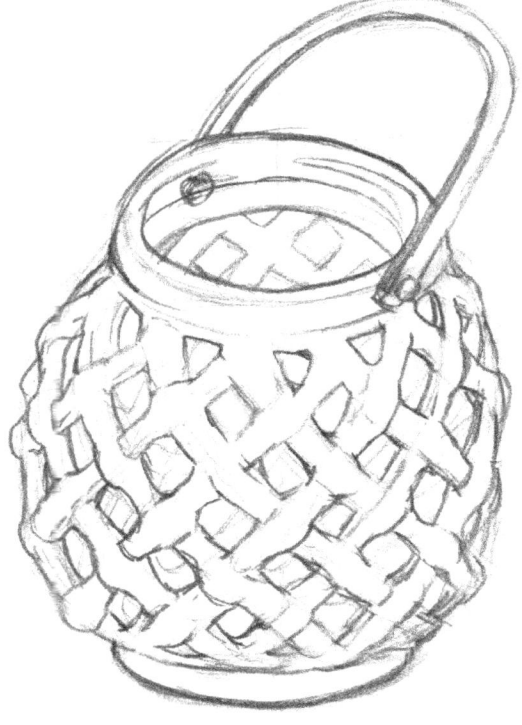

# Teapot

A small teapot has a somewhat more complicated shape. Once you have drawn the side view, you can draw a few orientation lines which can help you to transfer the proportions to the frontal perspective.

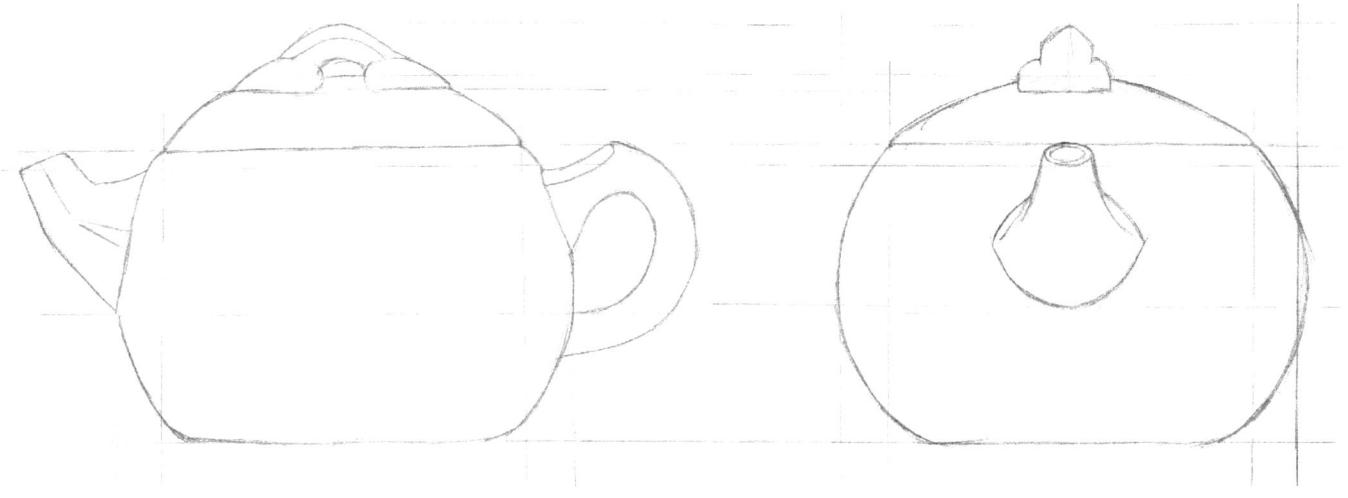

After you have mastered the frontal and side views, you can take up the challenge of the perspective view.

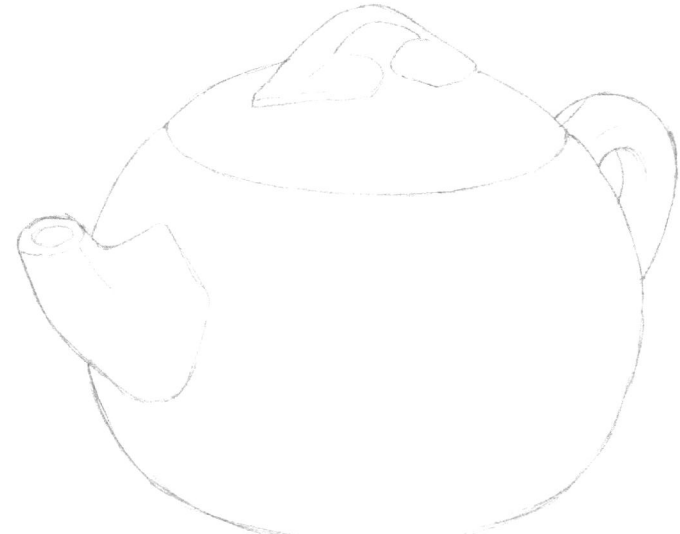

# Constructing and drawing Shadows

In order to reproduce the shadows of a motif realistically, it is best to have a template from which you can draw - be it a real drawing object or a photo template. With simple bodies there is also the possibility to construct the shadows yourself. This is a good exercise to get a feeling for the representation of shadows.

If you want to construct a shadow yourself, you have to define the position of the light source, from which the angle of incidence and the direction of light results. With this you can then construct a shadow yourself, as it is shown in the following drawing.

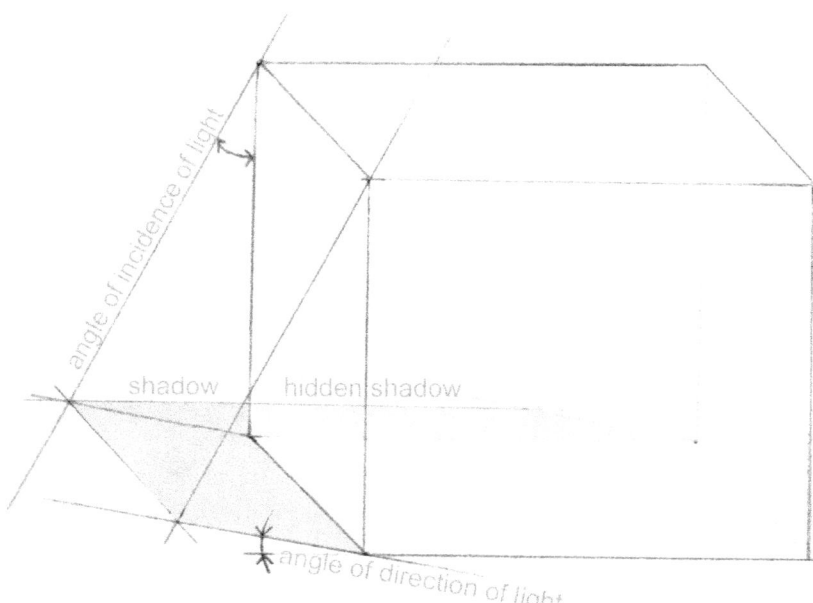

*Construction of a cube's shadow*

If you have enough drawing experience, you can also draw the cast shadow without orientation lines. This also works reasonably well with more complicated shapes. Usually you are not absolutely right with your own imagination and estimation - especially with more complex motives. Therefore it is always better to have a template available.

# Representing Metal

When drawing, one repeatedly encounters objects made of metal - i.e. materials such as iron, gold, silver, aluminum, etc. In this subchapter we will look at the peculiarities of metal in terms of drawing and learn how to represent metal. We will use a metal tube as the subject of the picture.

To draw the tube, you can first break it down into simple geometric bodies. In simple terms, the tube is a cylinder. But this is not quite correct, because the end is flattened. So we have to represent a transition from a round shape to a flat, straight shape.

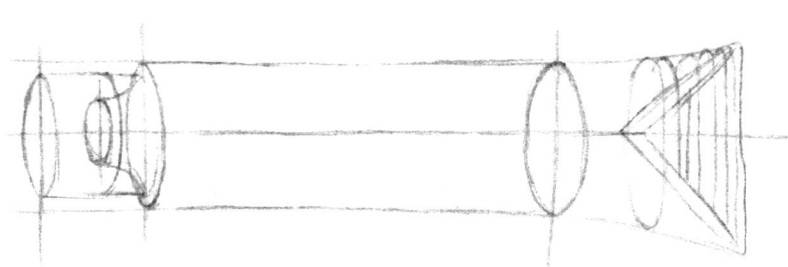

## What consitutes Metal?

The surface of metal can appear very dark and in other places very light. So metal usually also produces very strong light-dark contrasts. Especially those areas in which light is reflected directly towards the observer are very characteristic of metals. This results in highlights and light edges. In addition, the surroundings are also reflected on the surface.

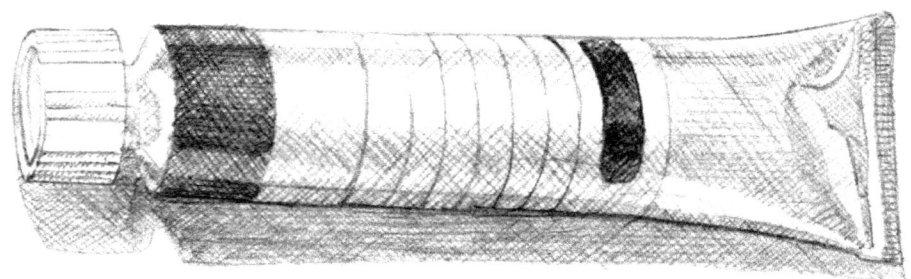

*The completed drawing of the tube of paint*

Basic Principles of Drawing

A good exercise for drawing metal is the illustration of aluminum foil  Slightly crumpled up, it produces interesting light, shadow and reflection effects. An example of a relatively elaborate still life with aluminum foil can be found in the following picture.

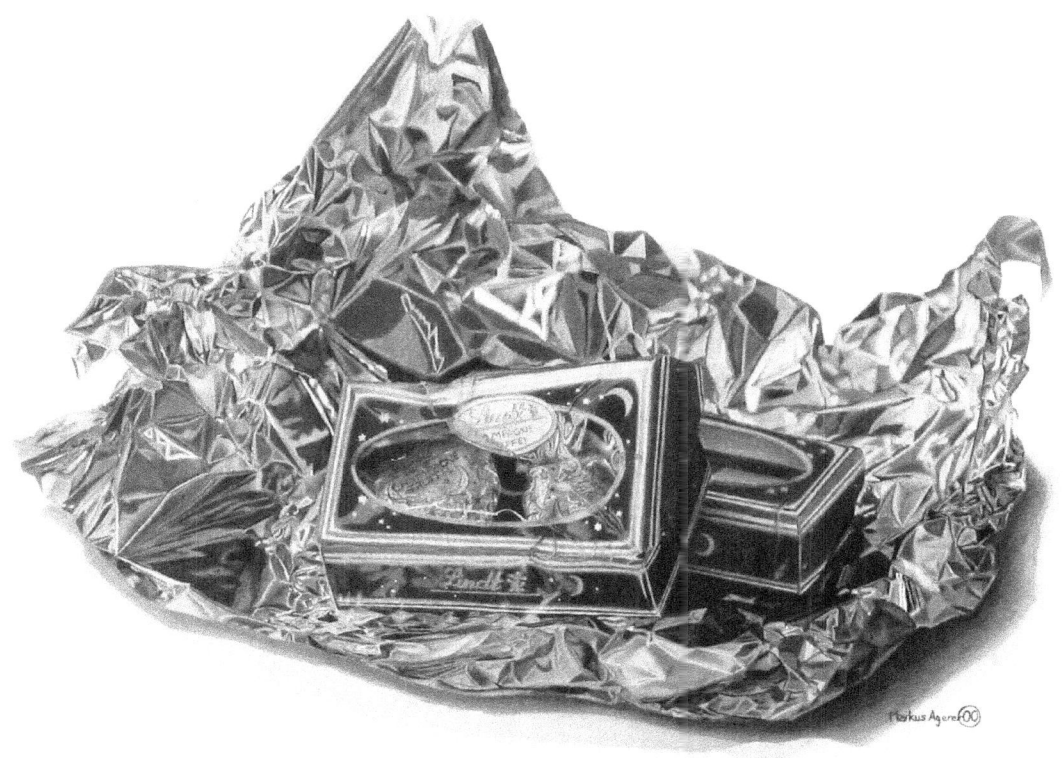

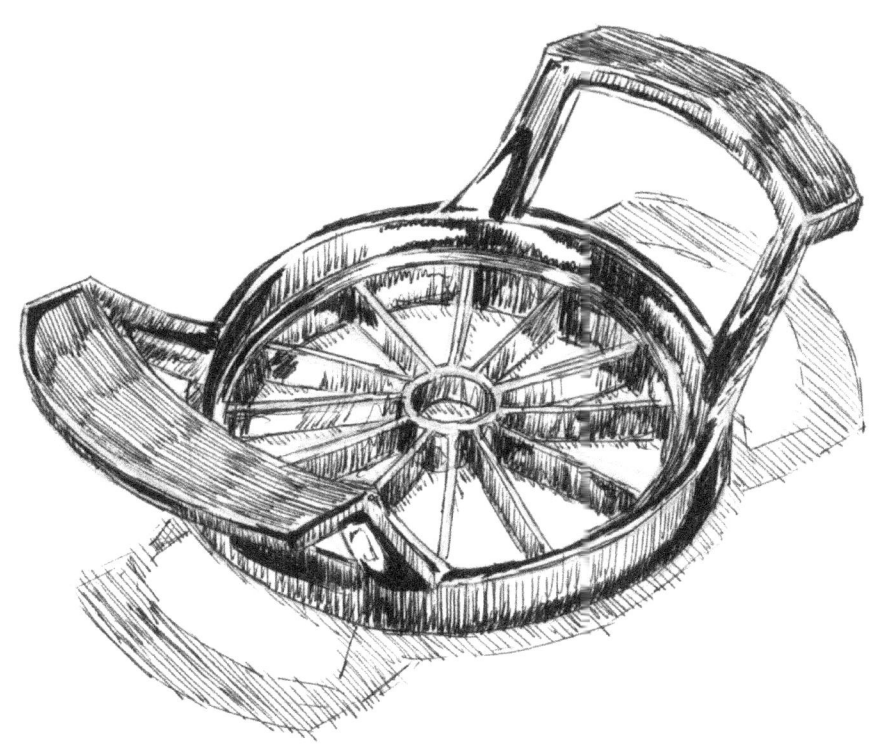

47

# Representing Glass

The special thing about drawing glass is its transparency. But different from what one might think in the first approach, the glass is not transparent in all places. A mistake that is often made by beginners. Here the motto is: Look closely!

From the pictures shown you can already see that there are some places where glass can become very dark and opaque. And this even though the glass is empty and there are no other objects in the surrounding area. With a normal drinking glass you can find this effect mainly at the bottom and partly at the left and right edge. But the areas where the glass becomes so dark are limited to very few spots.

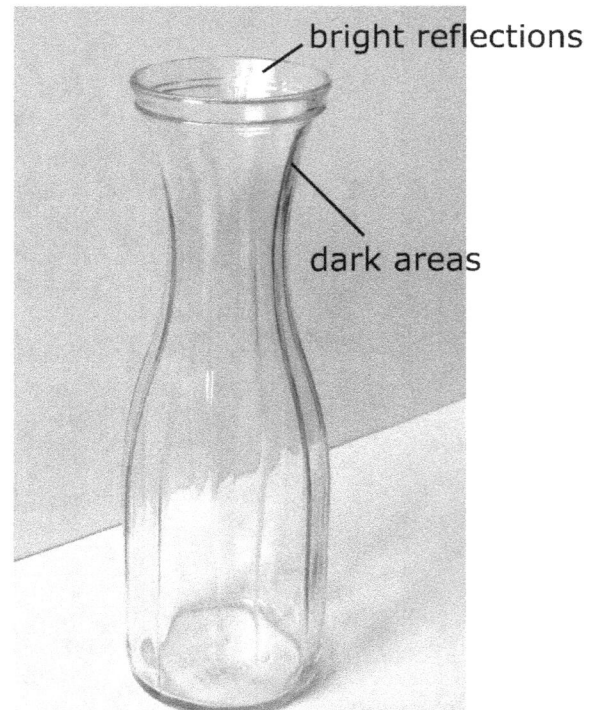

*Light and dark areas in a glass vase*

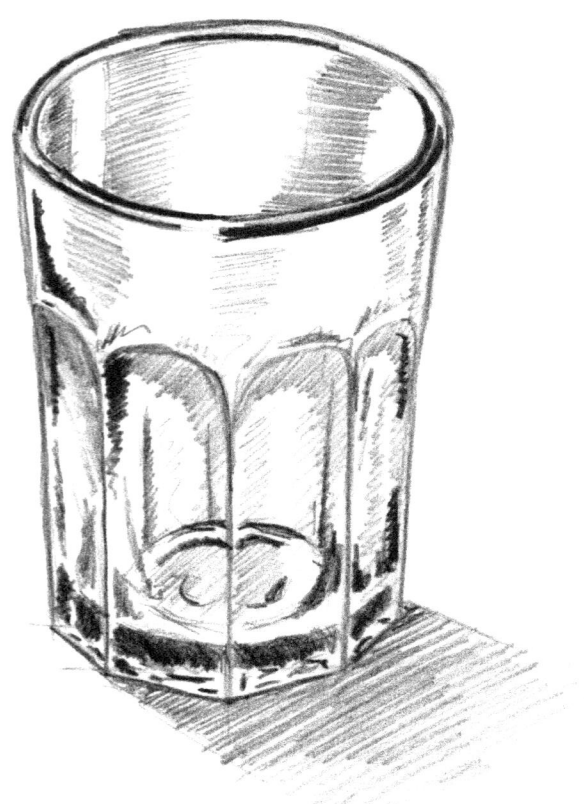

Glass also has a very smooth surface. This means that light is reflected very strongly in some places. In extreme cases, the light is reflected so strongly in our direction that one sees a pure white surface. However, this effect does not make the entire surface of the glass brighter - only certain areas are white.

By skillfully depicting such light and dark areas, one can very specifically convey the impression of glass in a drawing.

# Wooden Surfaces

Wood has a very characteristic and unmistakable structure. In the following example we will look at a wooden bench, which offers us three different types of wood structures.

The seat is a cut tree trunk, where we look at the surface with the bark removed in the frontal view. In the side view we can see the annual rings, whose structures continue on the upper side. The side surface corresponds to the cut across the trunk, while the upper-surface corresponds to the cut lengthwise through the trunk. The backrest also shows the structure when cutting longitudinally through a tree trunk, although some structures from branches can also be seen here.

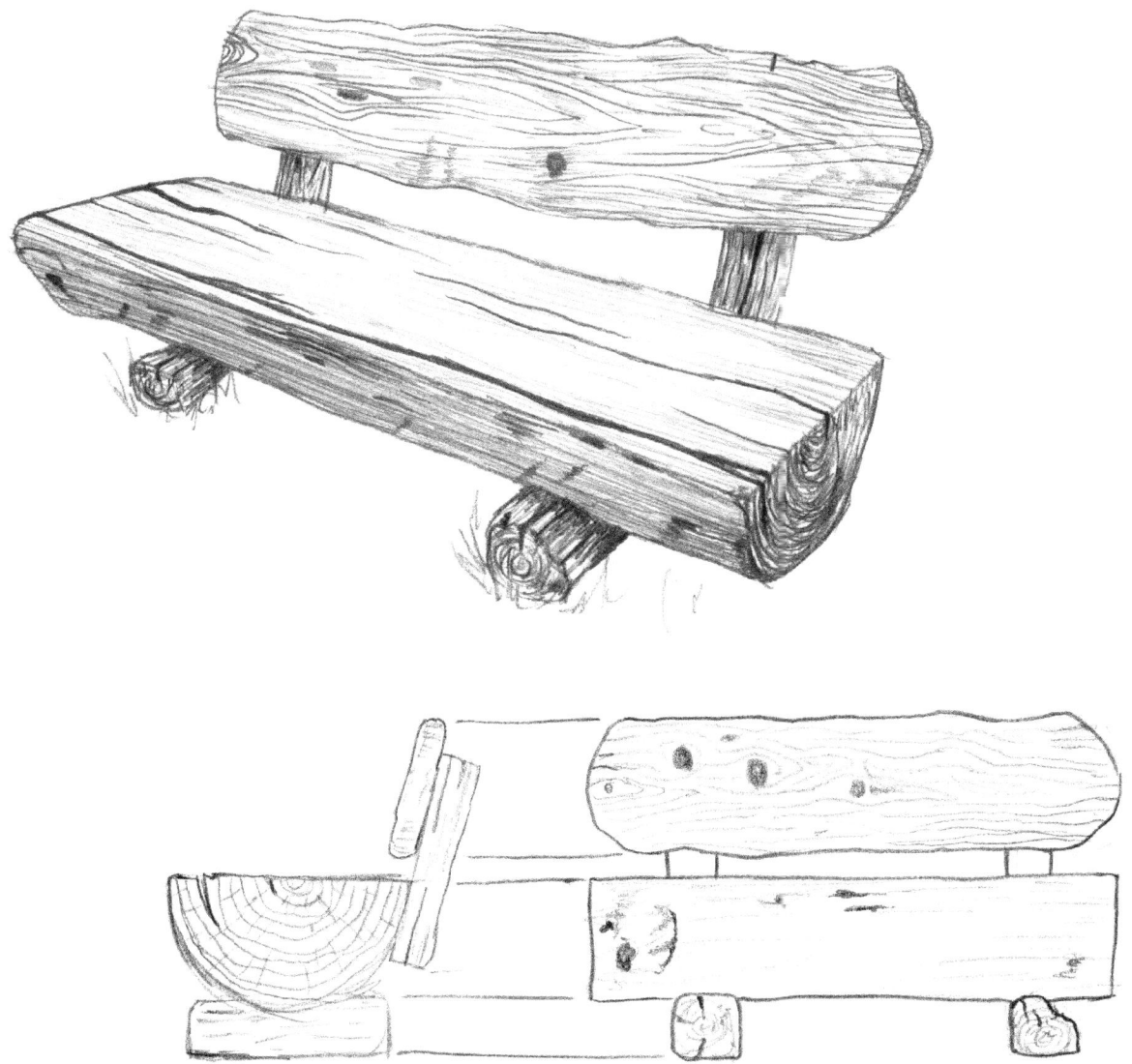

In a representation with perspective, in addition to the structures also forms are able to be recognized more easily. By depicting the structure of the wood, the form of the motif becomes accentuated even more.

# Structured Surfaces

Structured surfaces can be found in cloth, for example. A good example for drawing exercises is a pillow. By using respective hatching, not only the shadows can be depicted; the form and surface can be described as well. And don't forget that the form of a pillow is not simply a rectangle – it also exhibits irregularities and bulges.

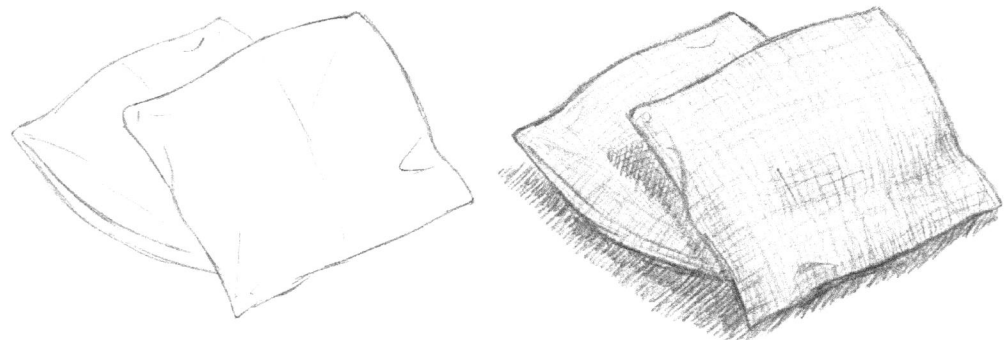

# Exercises – Drawing simple Motifs

In this chapter we will provide objects with shadows and show their surfaces. You will be able to draw on the knowledge of the previous chapters. So we come back from theory into practice. Among the objects to be shaded in this exercise, you will also find some motifs from the previous exercise.

## Book

A book is relatively easy to shade. But note that the cover casts a shadow on the pages of the book – and also that the cover has its own little shadow on the edges.

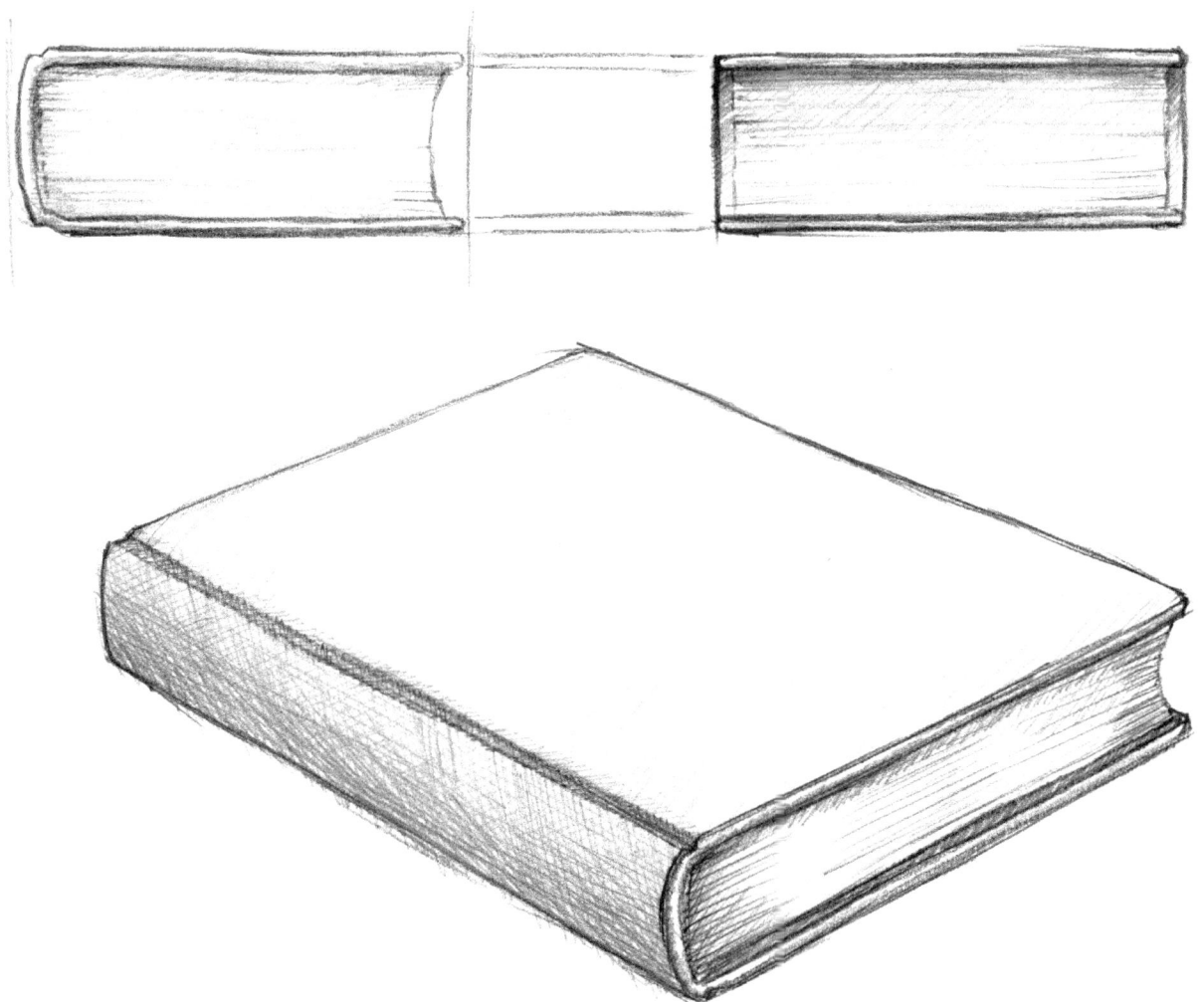

## Folding Table

The folding table, as shown in the illustration, is loosely shaded with the pencil. When drawing, consider from which side the light is shining and on which side of the folding table there are, therefore, lighter or darker shadows.

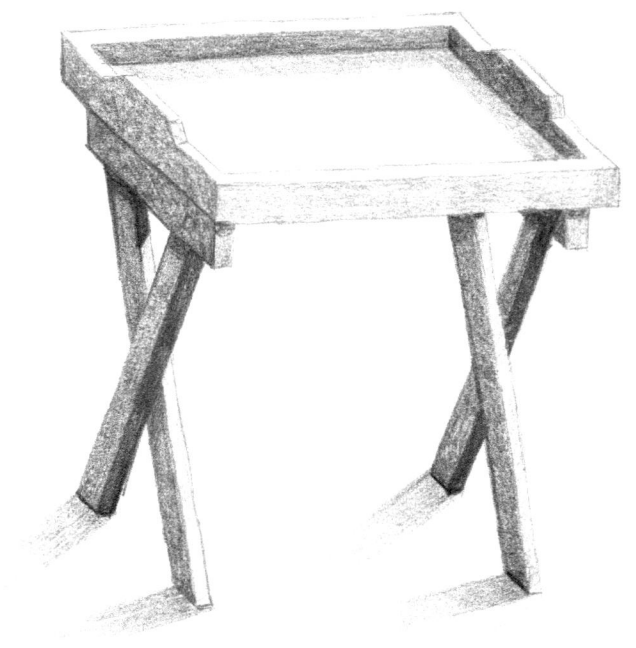

## Bowl

If the light is shining from the right, as in this example, the left inside of the bowl and the right outside are illuminated. This results in corresponding tonal gradients in the opposite direction, through which the typical shape of a bowl becomes recognizable.

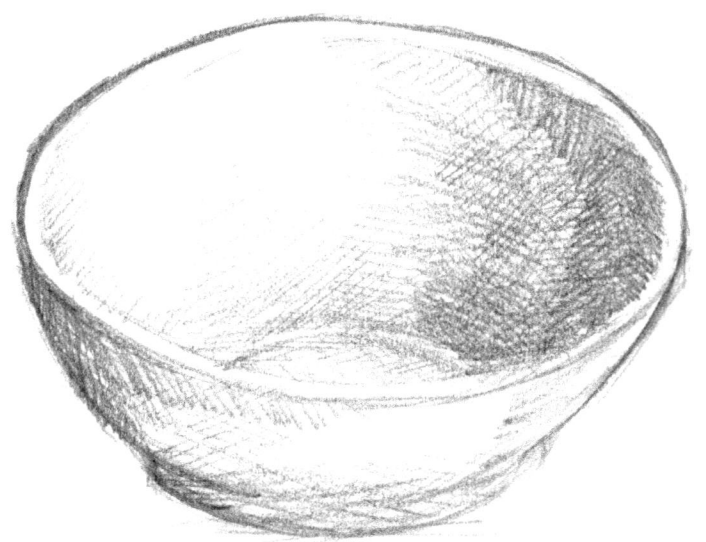

Basic Principles of Drawing

## Scissors

A pair of scissors is an attractive motif because of its shape. In a still life it can be used to create a contrast of form when juxtaposed with closed objects such as boxes, bowls, plates etc., or to connect objects visually.

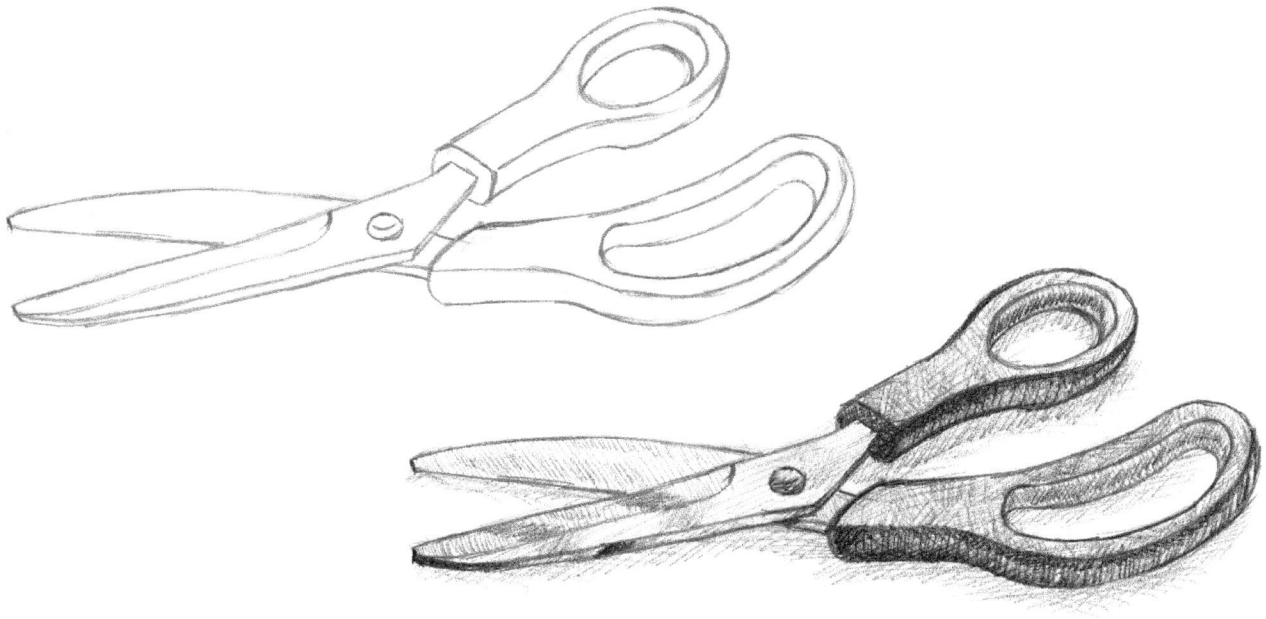

## Spoon

For shading the spoon, it is best to use a real spoon as a direct model; this is because the reflective surface is not easy to reproduce. Bright reflections as well as very dark areas can be re-created.

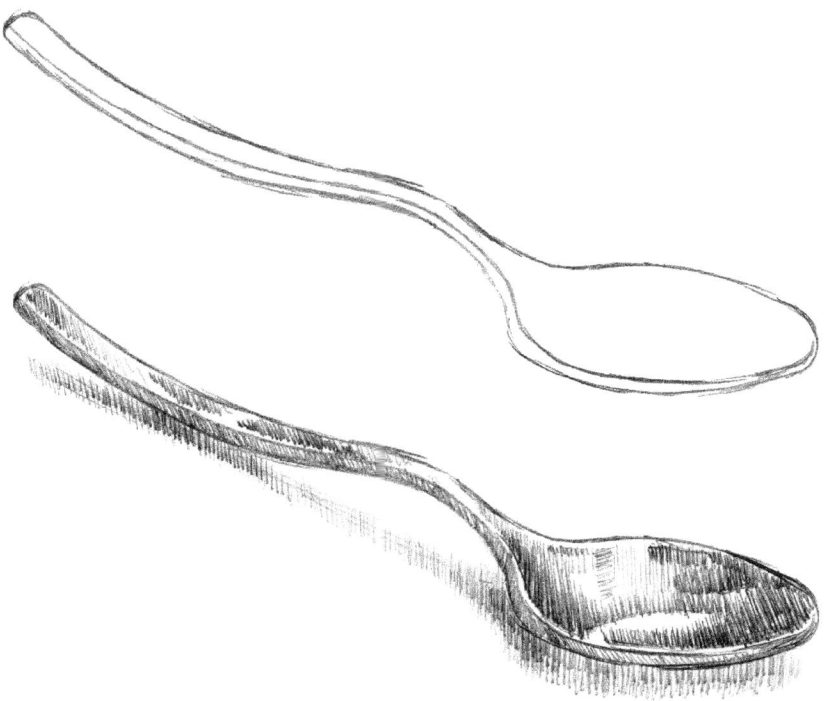

53

# Camera

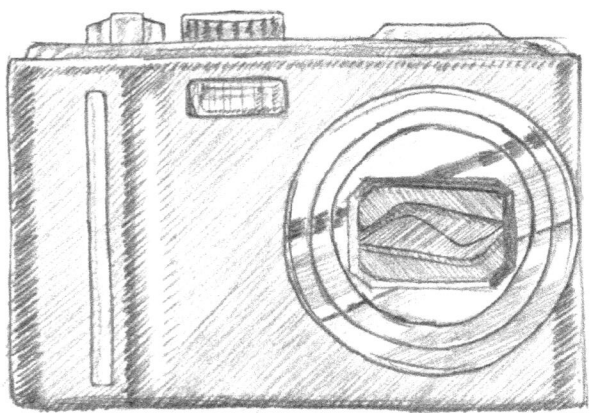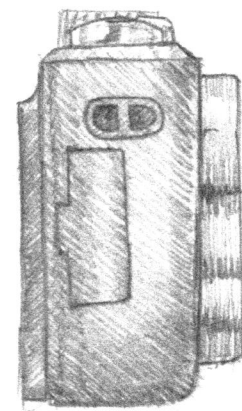

It is a useful exercise to shade the camera from both sides as well as in perspective. Pay attention to the metal parts that shine and try to convey their material properties through the drawing. With sensitively applied hatchings you can also show the slight curvatures in the shape of the camera.

When drawing in perspective, shading is a bit more difficult, but it is also more interesting to draw. There are light reflections on the housing which can be used to describe the shape of the device even better. In this exercise, also work out small details such as, for example, the flash and the switches.

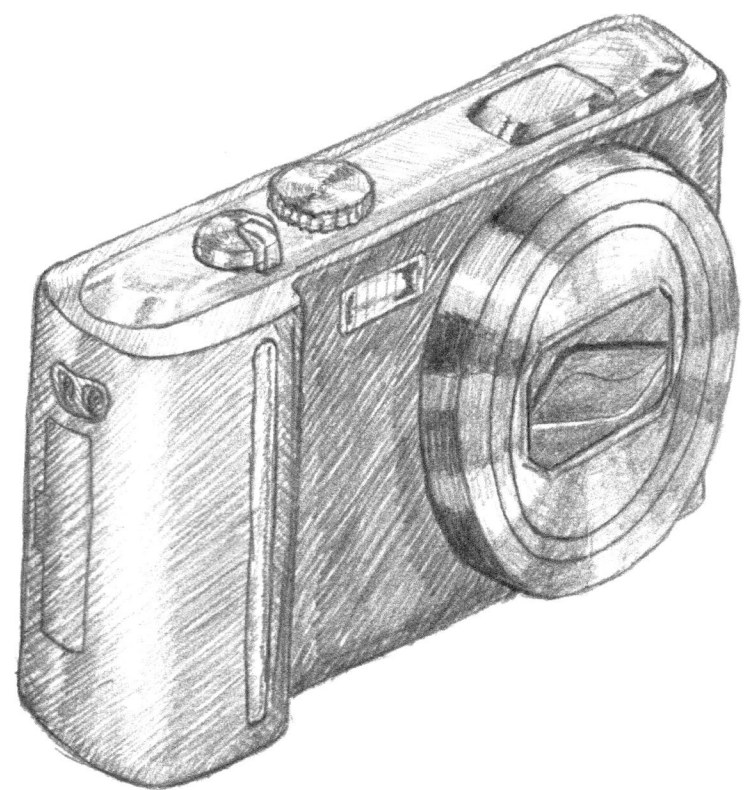

# Teapot

In this example, the teapot was shaded with hatchings in various orientations. First you start with a light tonal value and can already indicate the deeper shadows by applying additional hatchings.

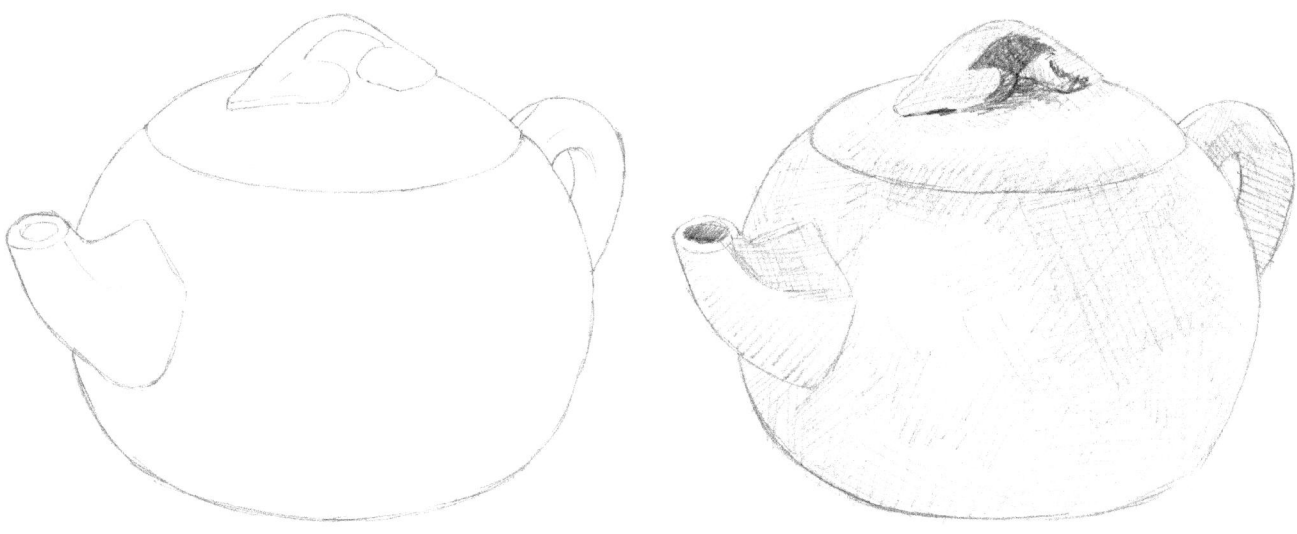

Now intensify the darker areas of the teapot and work out the shape more clearly. In the last step, the darkest areas of the motif are followed by the cast shadow.

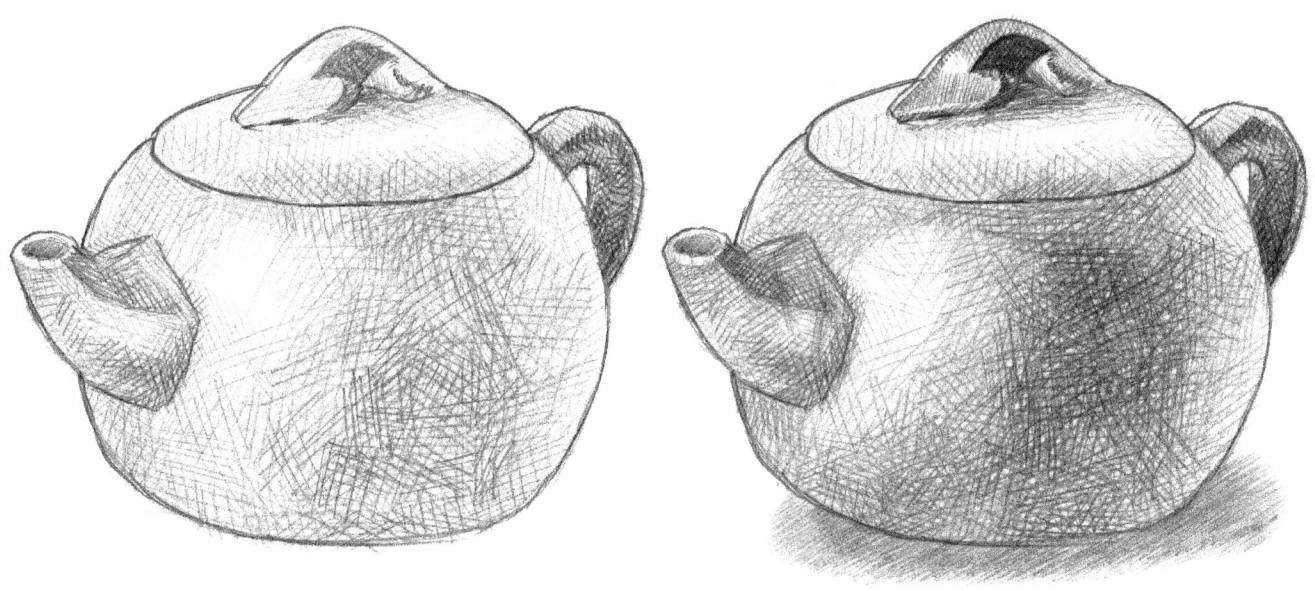

# Crumpled Paper

A classic among drawing exercises is the crumpled paper. This simple motif is particularly suitable for training the eye of the drawer and learning how to study an object. You have to look carefully so that you can reproduce the individual folds and creases correctly and authentically.
Similar to drawing are also objects such as blankets and cloths, which appear again and again in still life.

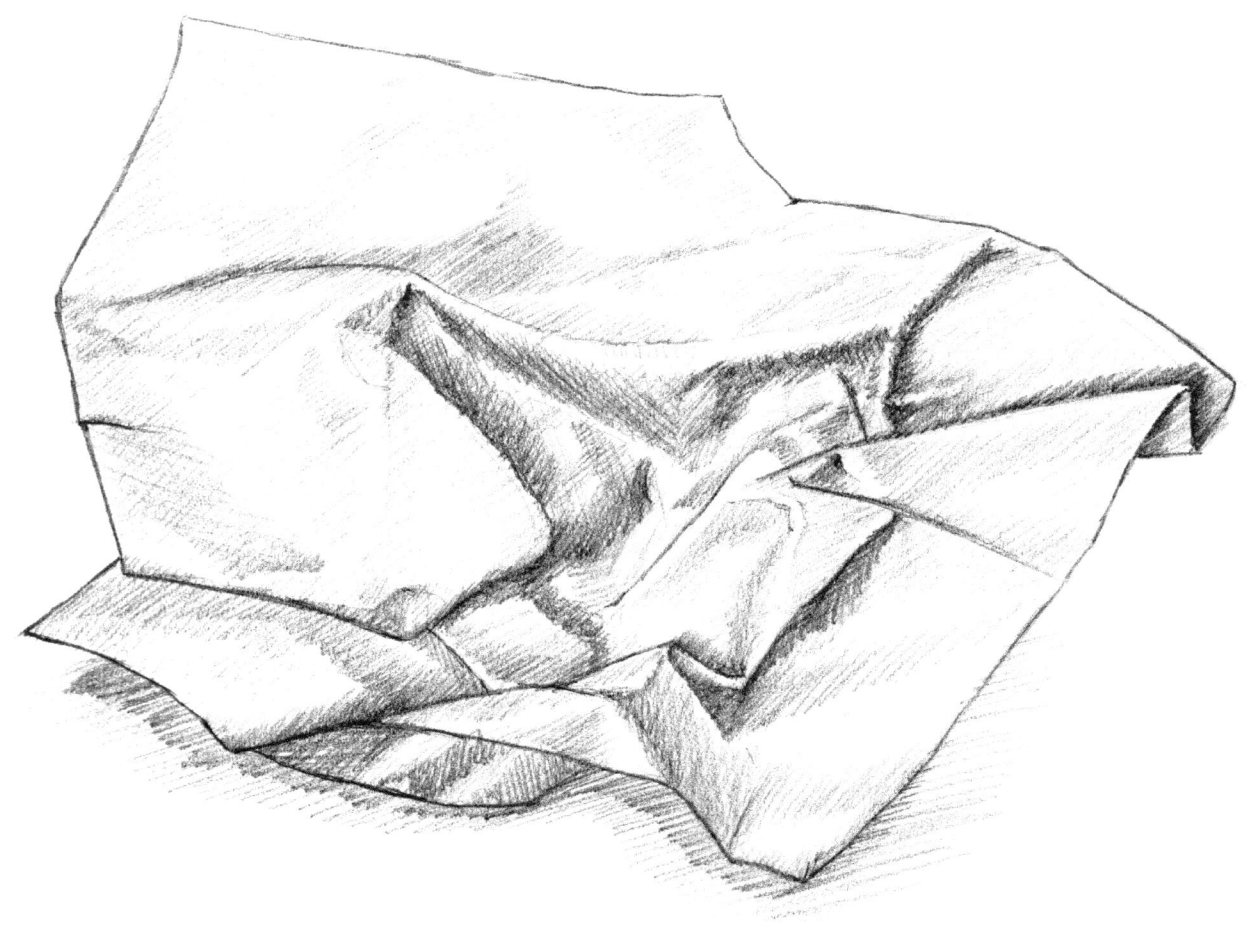

# Vase with Flowers

In this exercise we find a nice combination of artificial and natural forms. On the one hand we have a jug and on the other hand some flowers which are inside. The jug is still a rather simple geometric shape. The flowers consist of a multitude of small details. In this case, one does not have to draw everything completely perfect. It is actually sufficient to only hint at the details and to represent them in a simplified way. This skill of simplification should definitely be acquired by an artist, as one has to fall back on it again and again.

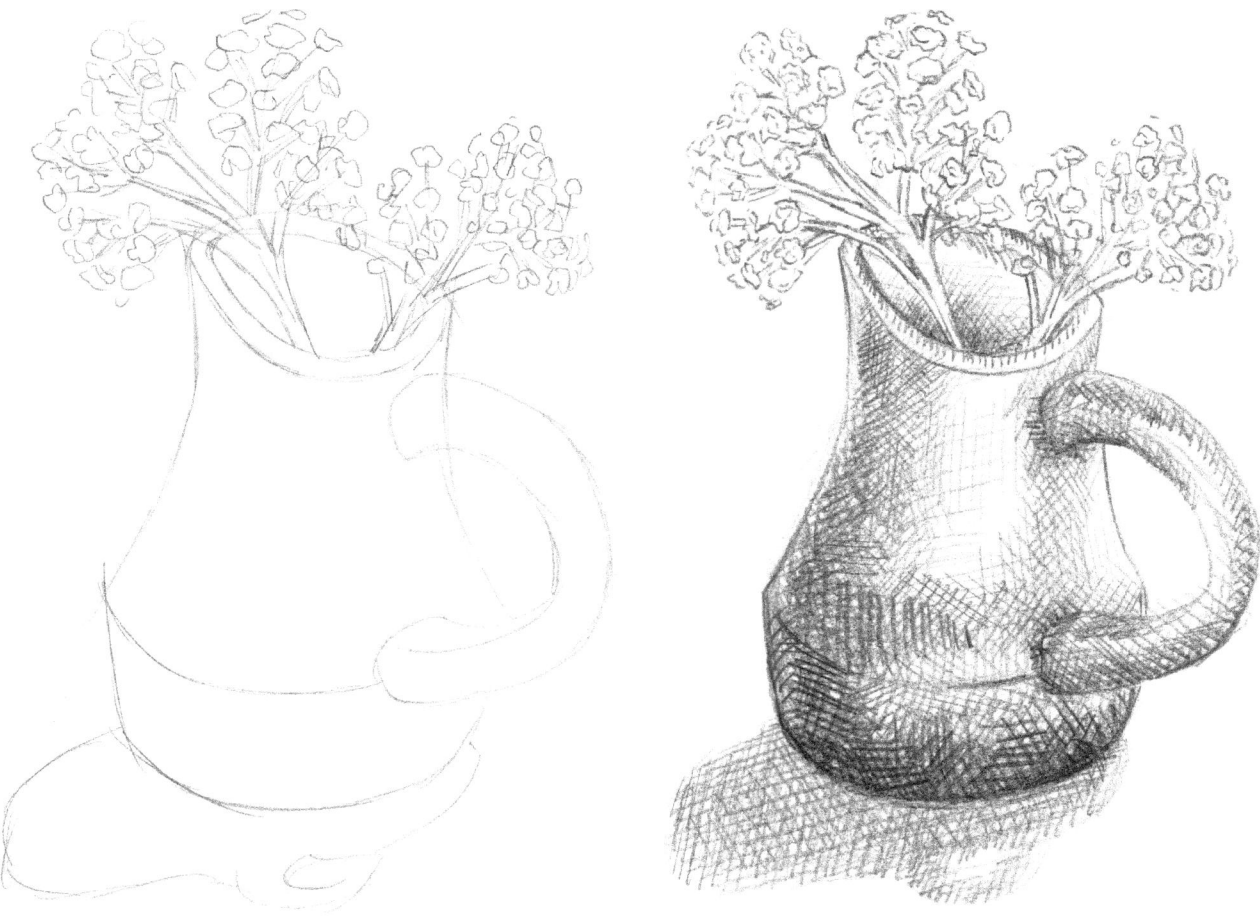

# Simple Arrangements

*» Simplicity is the highest form of sophistication. «*

- Leonardo da Vinci -

# Simple Arrangements

Now that you have learned how to draw bodies and can also illustrate simple objects with the pencil, you can now take on new challenges. Through the combination of several objects, simple arrangements and small still lifes can be created.

## Combination of several Objects

Combine a few simple objects that are easy to draw. It is best to use objects that have a very simple shape, for example a few boxes. Arrange the items in such a way that the result is a composition that you like. Then sketch the objects loosely with a few strokes on the drawing paper.

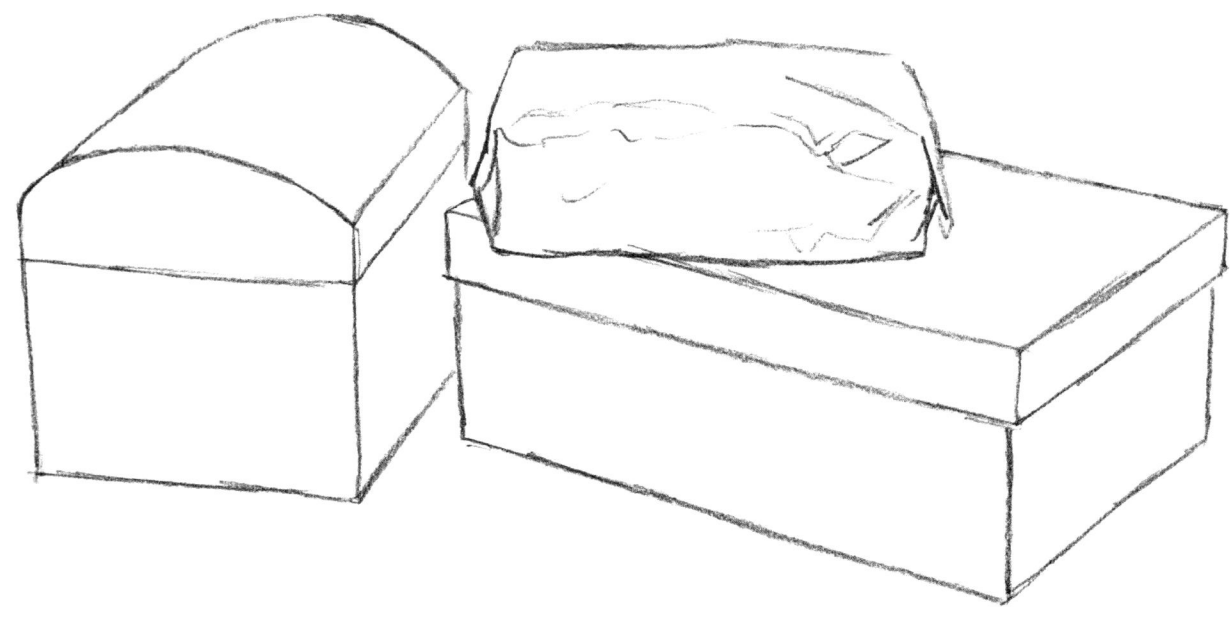

*A composition of two boxes and a package of coffee beans*

Now you can draw the shadows to make the subjects look spatial. You can use the hatching techniques you have already practiced in the previous chapter.

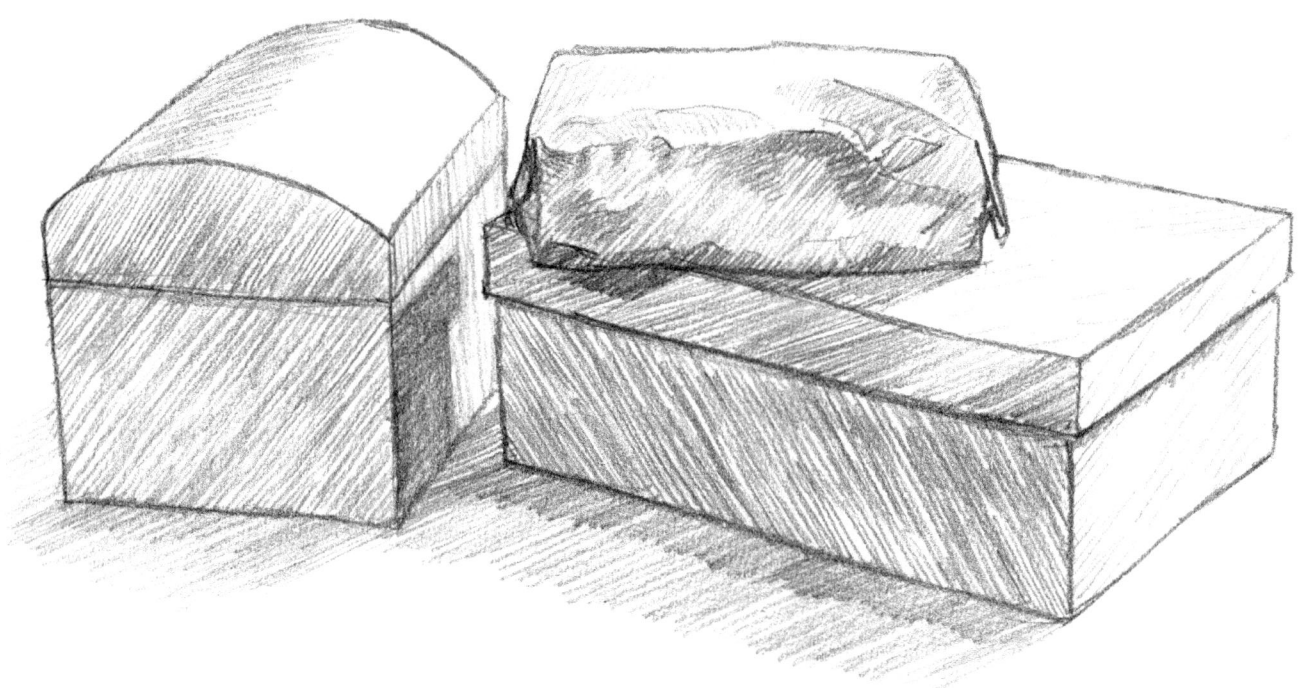

*Motifs shaded with hatching*

Once your drawing is finished, it is time for a short evaluation of the result. Compare the picture with the real objects. Are all proportions reproduced reasonably correctly? Do the tonal values of the shadows match the real objects?

Self-criticism is always important on the way to success. But don't be too hard on yourself either.

# Combinations of various Objects

Now combine a few objects that have different shapes and dimensions. It is best to use objects that are round and square, large and small or bulky and slim. For this, find objects that do not have a complicated shape.

In the example here a box was used and combined with three vases, which are round and have different sizes.

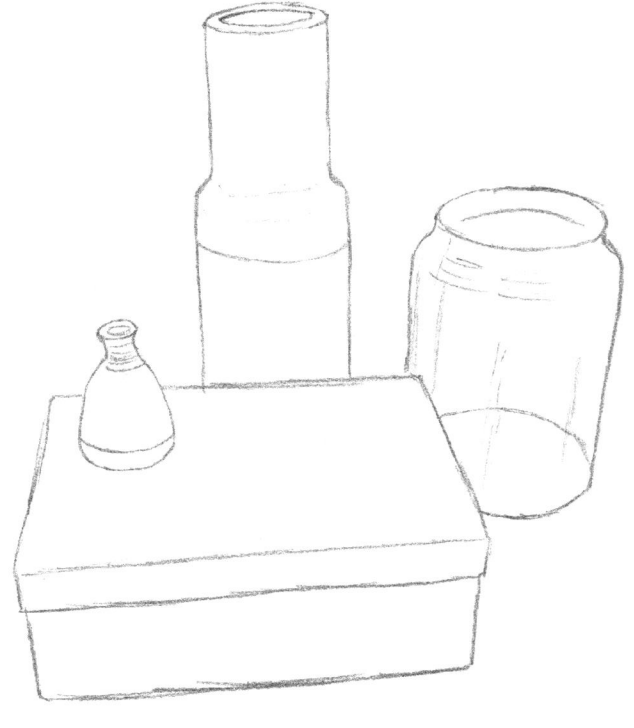

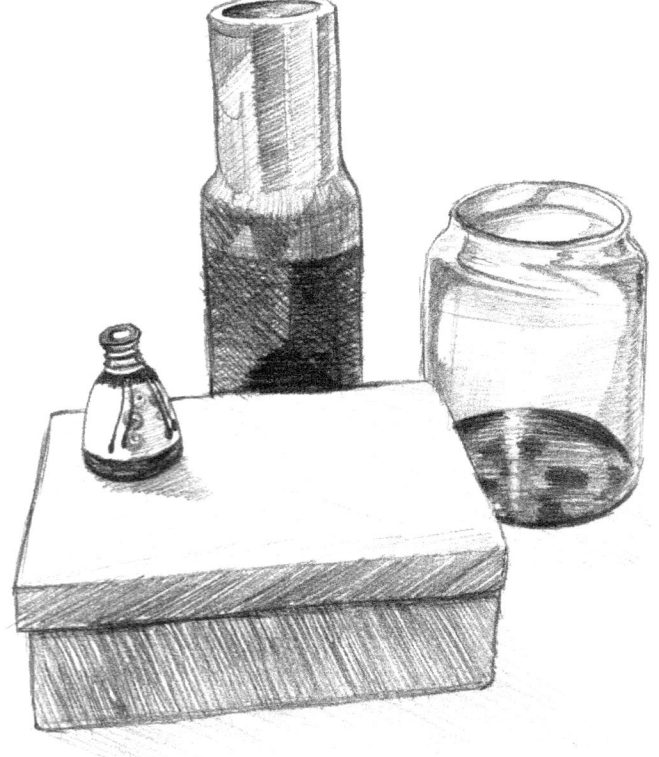

Afterwards, you can shade the motifs again. Pay attention to the different materials the objects are made of. The vase on the right is made of glass. You have learned in the previous chapter how to represent glass.

# More complex Forms

You can also try more complex shapes, such as the two vases in the example picture. If you are not yet proficient enough, you can start by grouping only two or three items. This keeps the effort low and there is no frustration in the early practice phase.

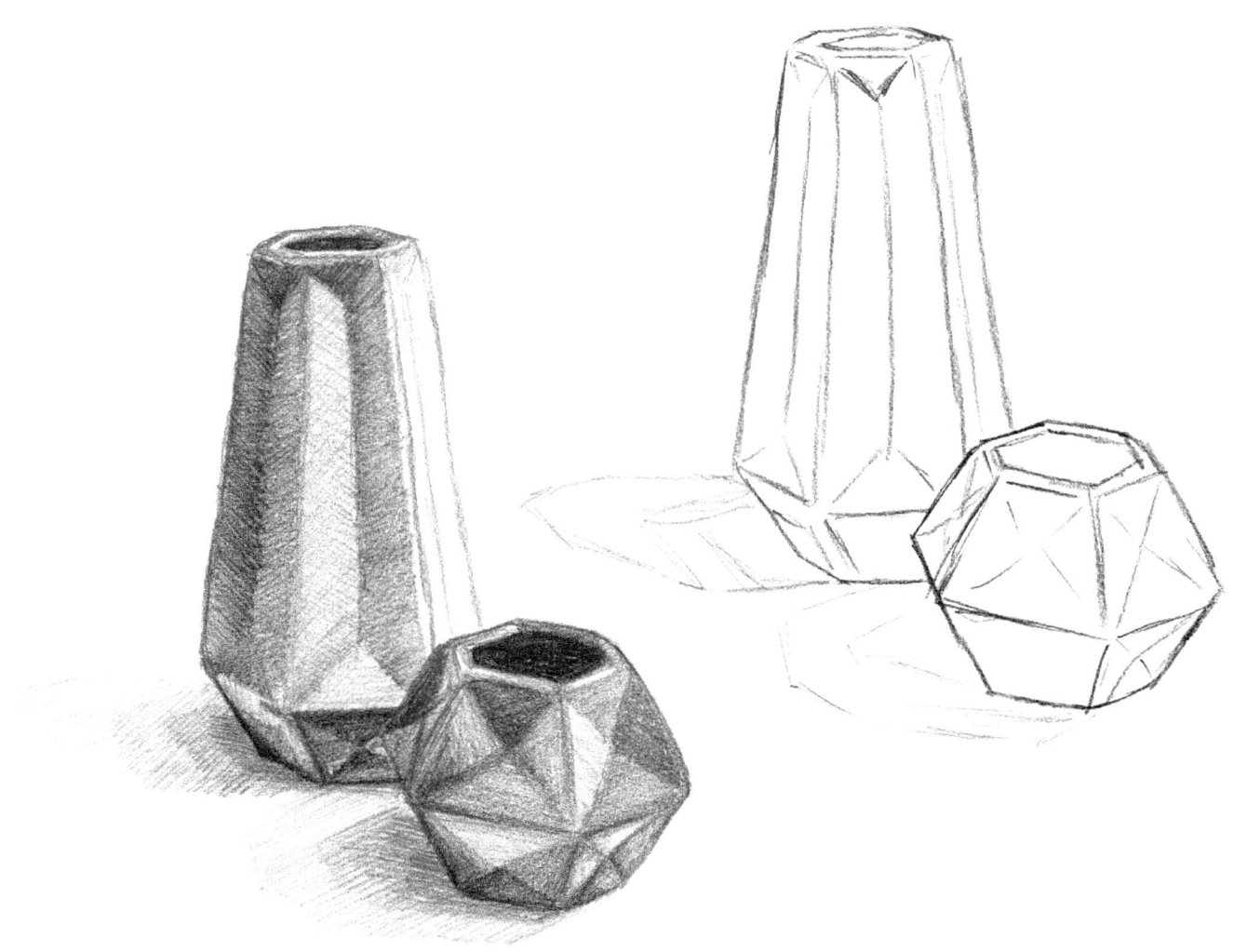

# Drawing Your First Still Lifes

*» The best thing is to have talent, but the second best thing is to practice. «*

- Epicharm (about 550 - 460 b.C.) -

# Drawing Simple Still Lifes

If you want to draw your own still life, it is best to choose objects that are related to each other in terms of content. Here you can learn from the artists of the past, because they too had arranged objects thematically. The different types of still lifes have already been described in this book.

Once you have selected some items, you can group them. Try out different arrangements. You can move one or the other item over and over again until you are satisfied with the arrangement.

Artists often orientate themselves to geometric forms, according to which the objects are arranged in a still life. Different types of triangular designs are particularly popular. The methods of picture design are also referred to as picture composition, about which we will learn more in a later chapter.

## Still Lifes in a triangular Composition

In this exercise we will arrange several objects in a picture composition using an isosceles triangle. We start with a small sketch to plan the picture.

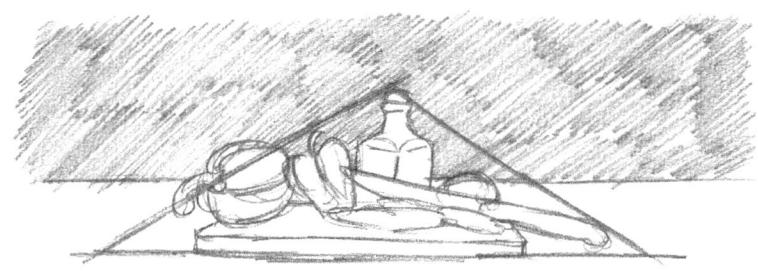

As far as the choice of objects is concerned, this still life is primarily intended to depict various foodstuffs. It is therefore a mealtime still life. To match this, we will add a snack board and a knife.

The exercise is also about drawing different materials. In the picture we find a wooden lunch table, a metal knife, a glass oil bottle, a smooth surface with two peppers and a rough surface with two carrots.

### Drawing the Still Life

Now you can use a pencil to draw a sketch of the still life very gently on the paper. If you like, you can first sketch the basic geomorphic form of your composition as an orientation aid.

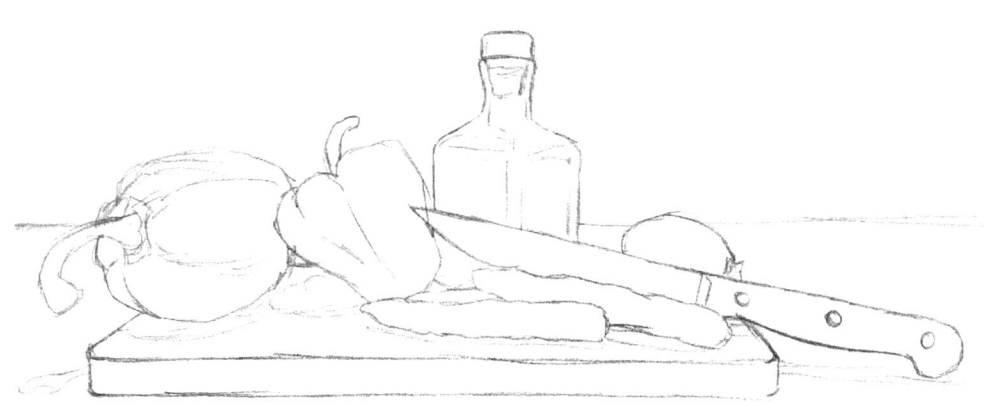

Drawing Your First Still Lifes

After the rough sketch of the still life, one can now begin to draw the shadows. Do not draw the shadows too much at the beginning. For the bottle and the knife you can use the knowledge you have gained from the previous exercises.

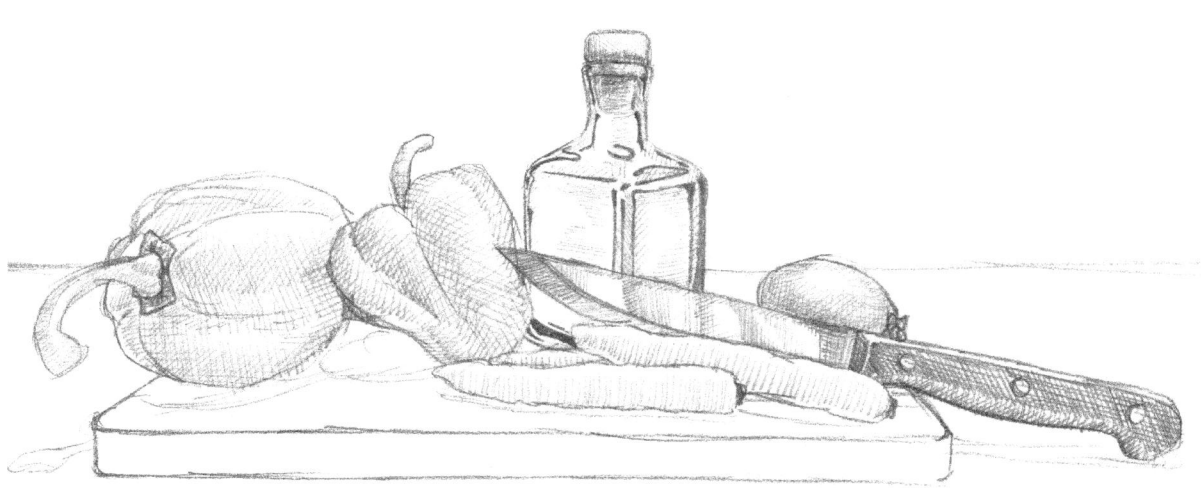

The next step is to work out the darker parts of the still life and draw the cast shadows. The wooden board on which the objects lie can be given a wooden structure.

Draw the objects as detailed as you like. Don't be afraid to use strong contrasts - they make the picture more interesting. Dark areas may also have pronounced dark shadows, while especially light areas are best left completely white.

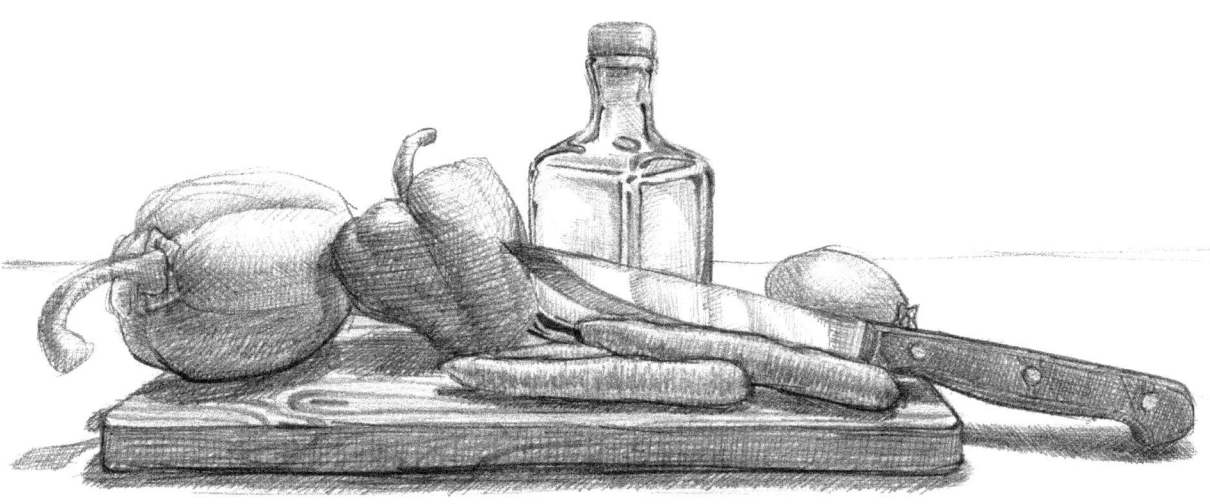

# Still Lifes drawn with Charcoal

In this exercise we turn to another drawing technique: drawing with charcoal. As an example we will try a still life in which a composition of mandarins and dried mandarin slices is shown.

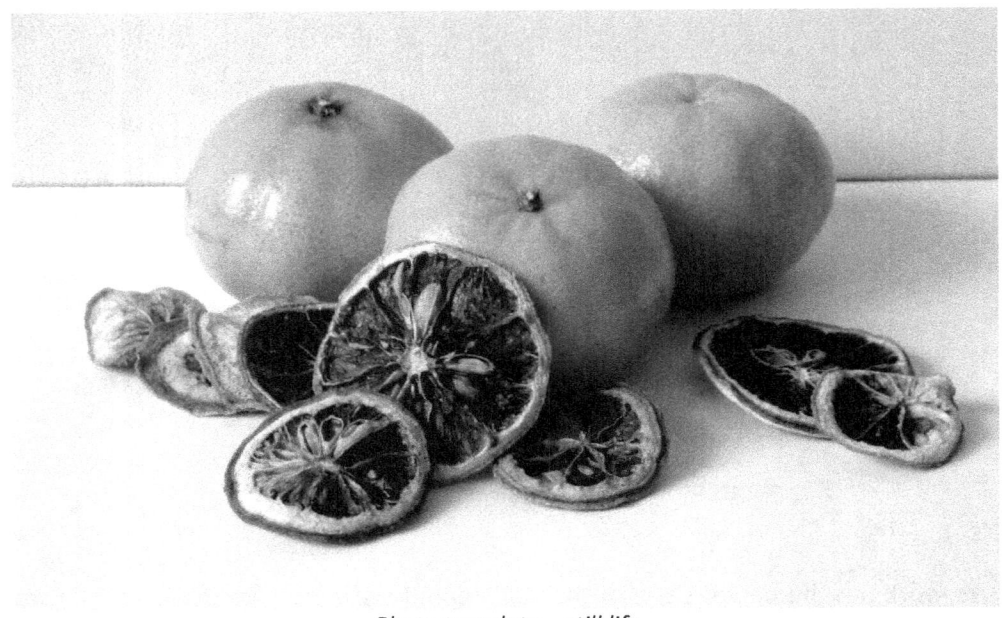

*Photo template – still life*

## Step 1 – Preliminary Sketch

As always, we start with a preliminary sketch in which the contours are drawn.

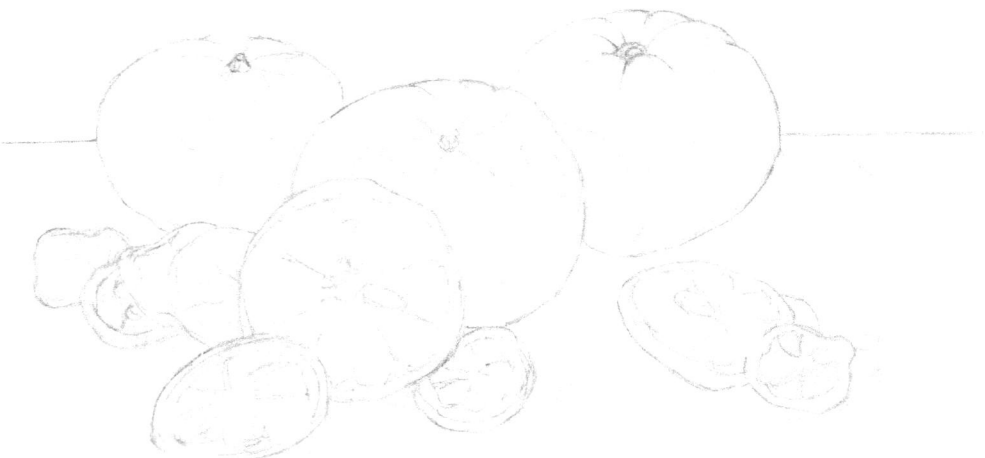

*Preliminary sketch of the still life*

Drawing Your First Still Lifes

## Step 2 – Shading the light Areas

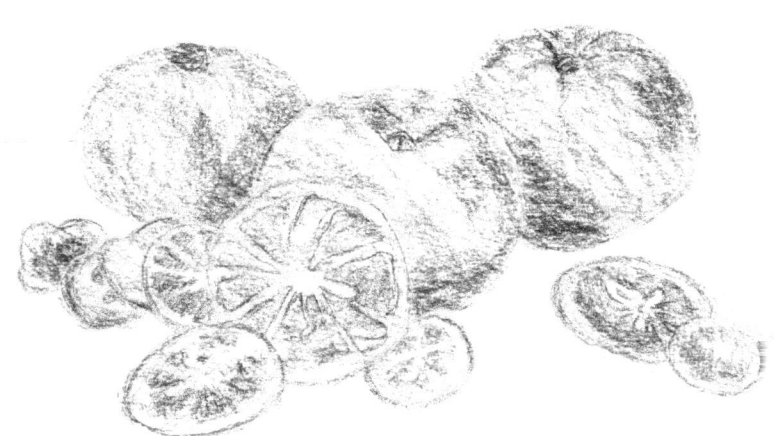

Now we take a piece of charcoal and carefully blacken the mandarins and the mandarine slices. You can already suggest some structures.

But don't press too hard with the charcoal pencil; otherwise the drawing will become too dark too early. Dark areas are drawn later.

## Step 3 – Using the Wipe Technique

When drawing with charcoal, the wipe technique is the best drawing technique. We will try it out in this exercise.

You can use a washcloth for wiping. With this you carefully blur the charcoal until you get a smooth tonal value or a soft light-dark gradient. Usually you can't see the paper structure after wiping, which makes the drawing look even softer.

In the picture you can see what the drawing looks like after wiping.

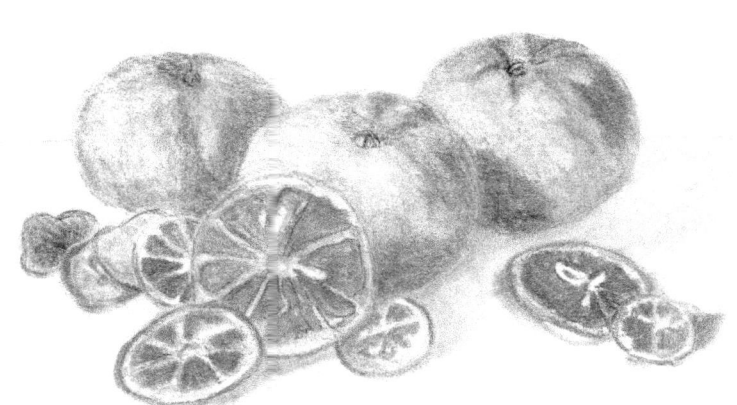

69

# Step 4 – Working out the darker Areas

In the following picture you can see how the darker areas are worked out. I have already drawn structures in the mandarin slices, which create a very plastic effect.

You then continue in this manner. You can blur the coal again and again.

With a kneading machine you can carefully lighten areas that have become too dark. Also structures can be worked out with it.

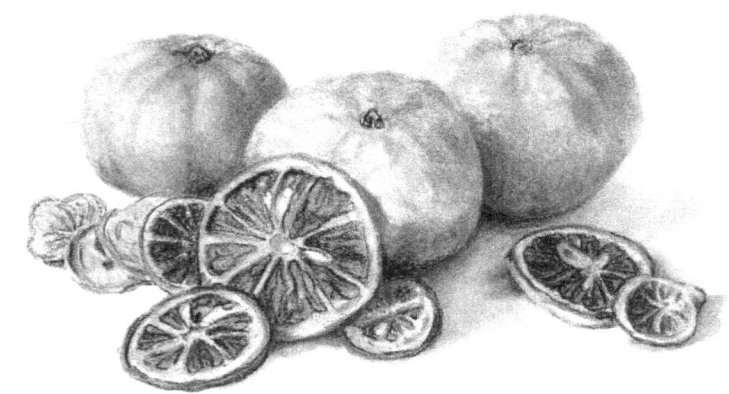

After that the drawing is given a dark background. With this last step the still life is complete.

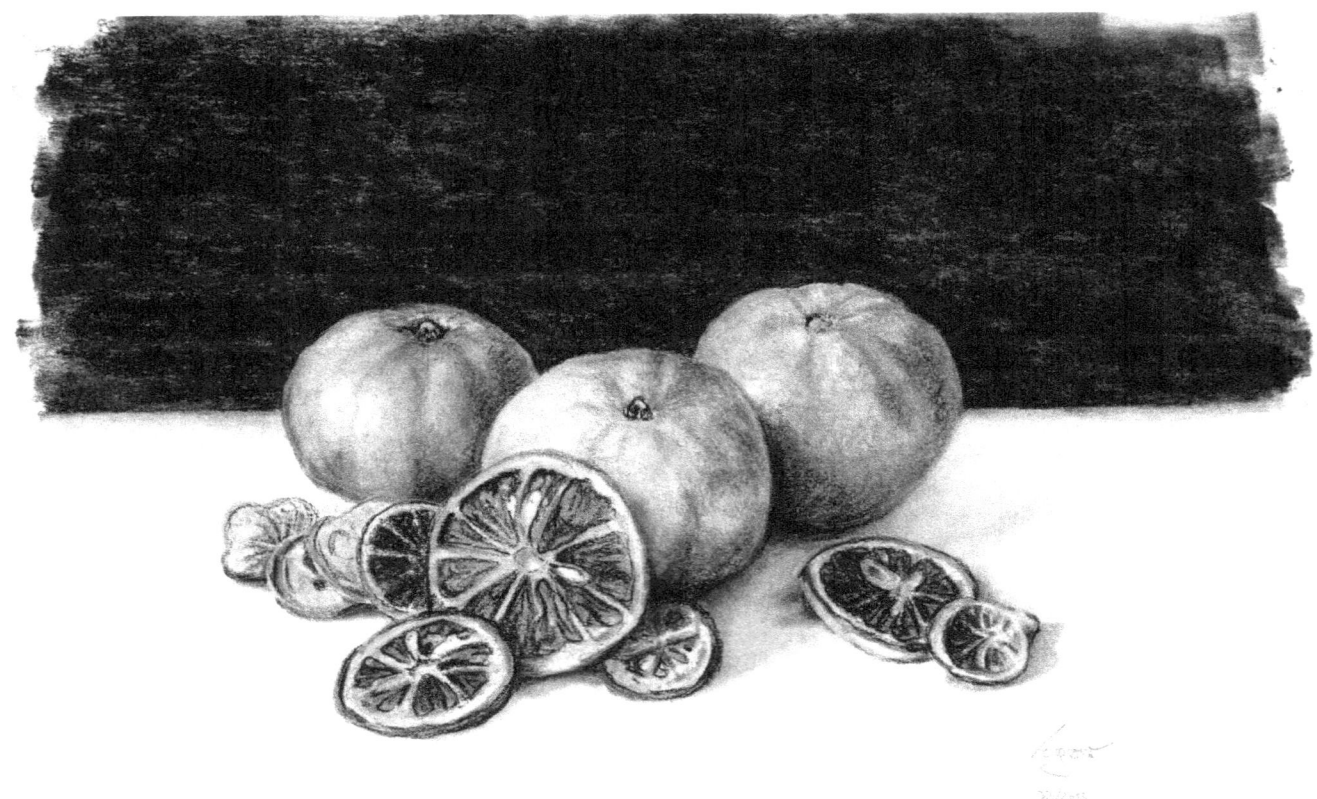

# Representing various Materials

This exercise is mainly about representing different materials. Each material has its own character, which has to be conveyed with the pencil onto the paper. In this example we will draw a woven basket containing a roughly woven linen cloth and several cups. The basket is leaning on a wooden beam. These are therefore four different materials, each with its own unique surface texture.

The different materials must be taken into account already at the preliminary drawing stage. However, the preliminary drawing in the picture shown is already very detailed. It took a lot of work until the sketch was available in this quality.

Analyze the different objects carefully and try to recognize what makes up the special and typical characteristics of their materials. The basket, for example, is very roughly woven from willow rods. The linen cloth has a structure that can be depicted with small strokes that are alternately turned 90° to each other. You don't have to show every single detail of the cloth here. It is enough to draw some braids and to indicate a part of the structure here and there. Also try to show the deformation of the cloth due to the structure.

The cups that lie in the basket, on the other hand, have a very clear shape and a smooth surface.

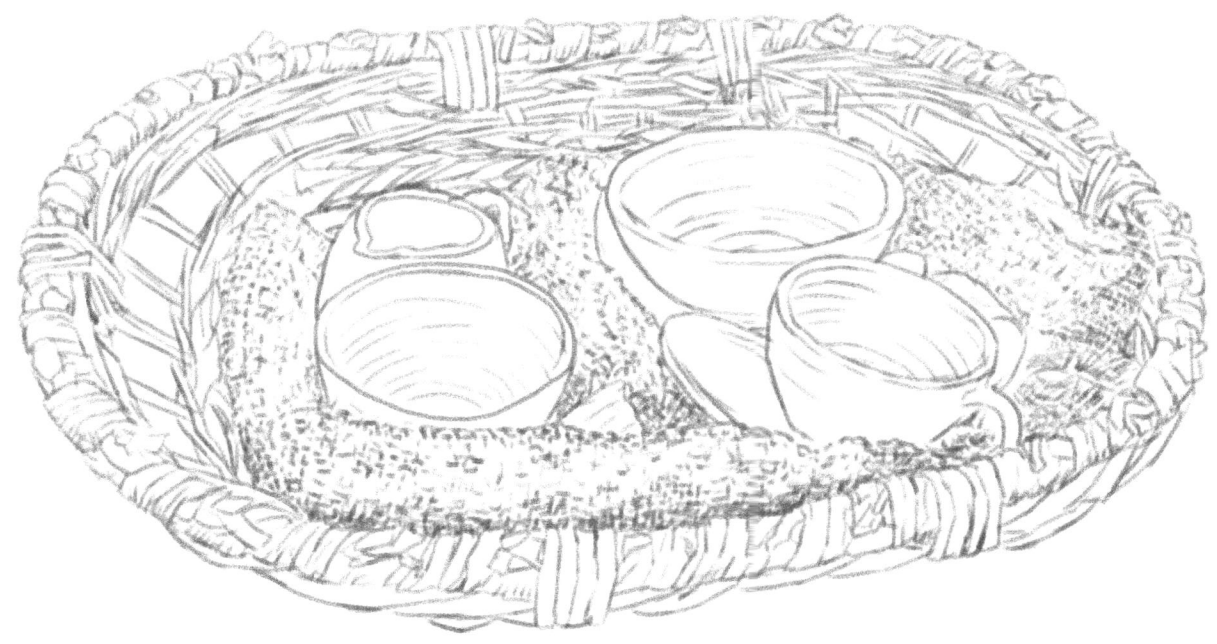

After completing the preliminary drawing you can start shading the objects. An important aspect of this work is to convey the smooth surface of the cups through drawing techniques. For this purpose, shadow areas can be drawn relatively dark, while the places where the light is reflected are depicted very brightly - in extreme cases white.

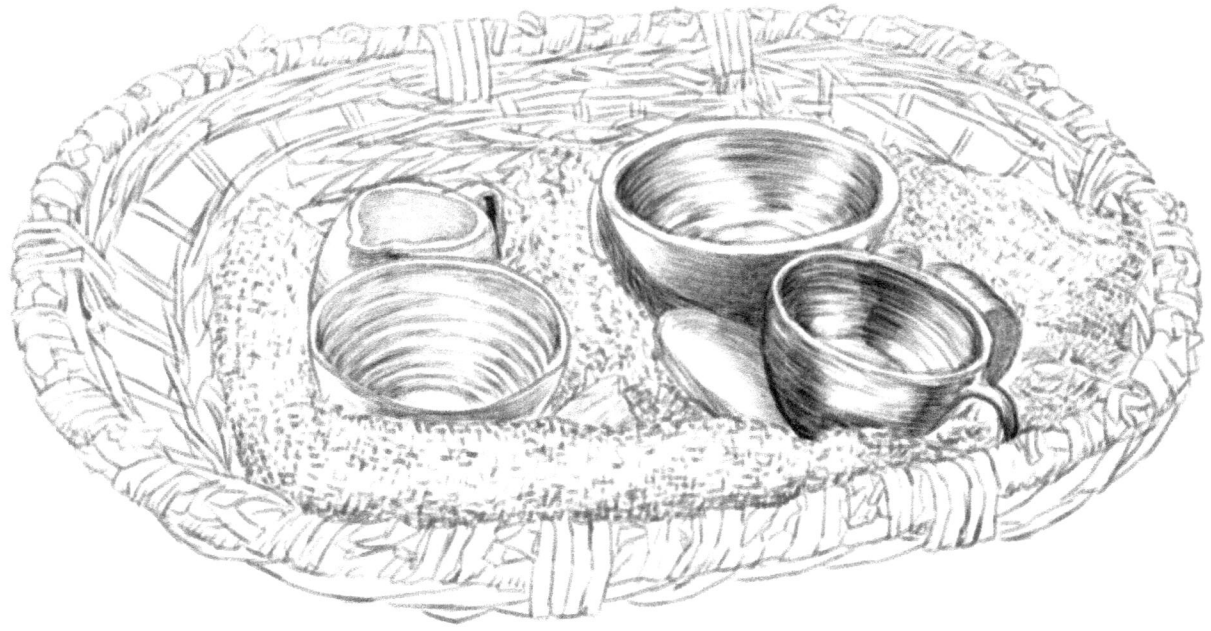

As far as the wicker basket is concerned, the most decisive part of the work has already been done with the depiction of the contour. Because by displaying the contour, the structure of this object was also drawn. When shading, mainly the shape of the basket is thus reproduced - less so the structure.

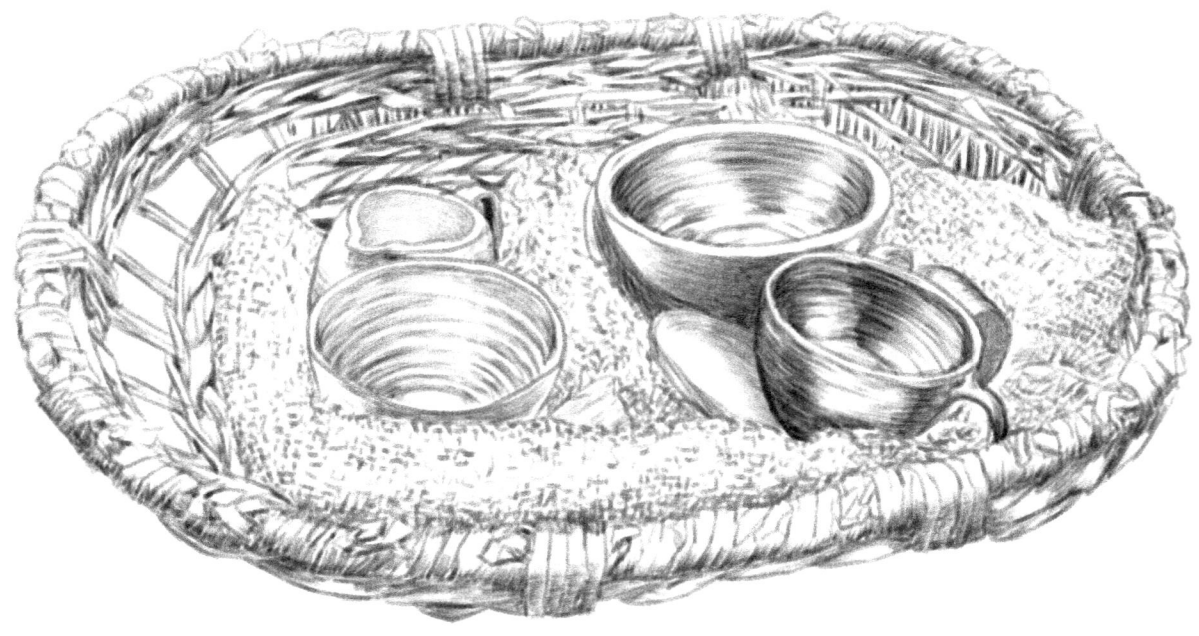

To get even more out of the drawing, it is often worth your time and effort to amplify the darkest tonal values. Corresponding areas can be drawn darker with a soft pencil. This sets accents and increases the plasticity.

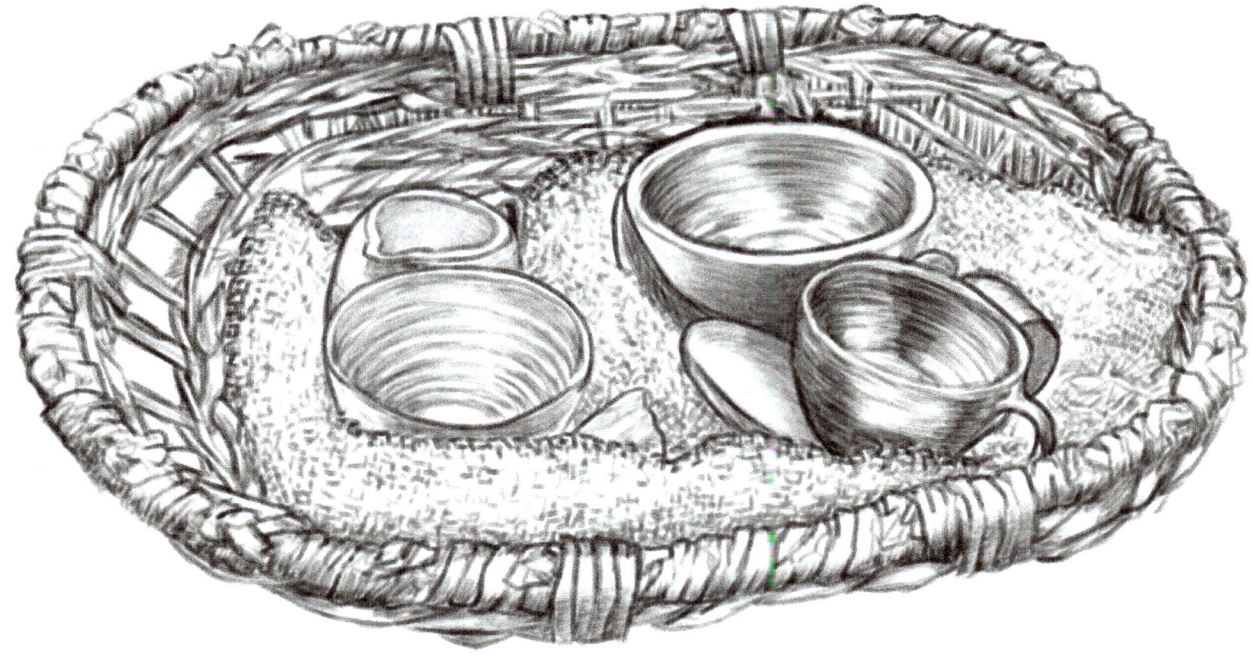

Now you can devote yourself to the wooden beam upon which the basket is leaning. The structure of the wood is hinted at by means of the grain in the wood and cracks. The effect is intensified by hatching in the direction of the wood grain. At the left end of the bar you can see the typical annual rings of the tree.

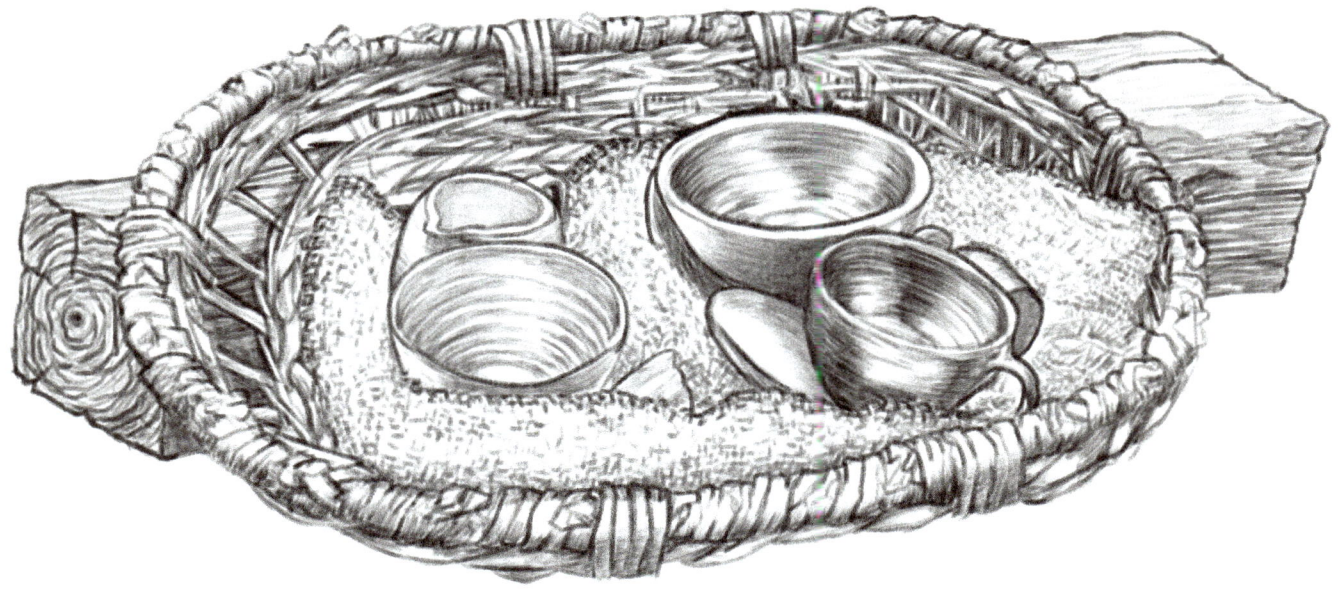

The last step is to add the cast shadow of the objects on the ground and draw the ground and background. A dark background is especially useful for still lifes, as it does not distract from the motifs and produces a very high light-dark contrast, which clearly highlights the objects in the foreground.

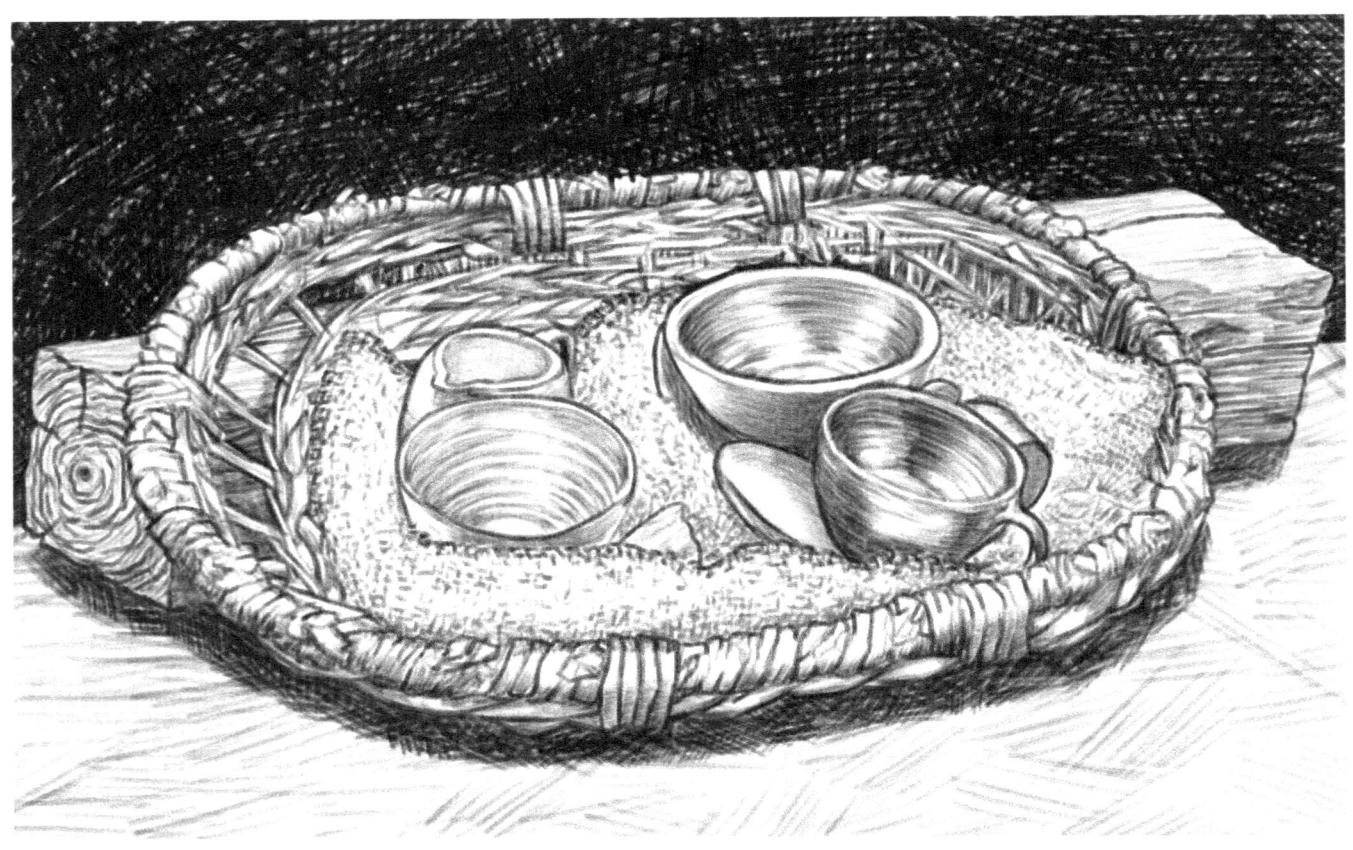

# Drawing a floral Piece

A classic motif in the field of still lifes is the flower piece. It is actually easy to find objects that fit together, because flowers and a vase belong together. But more challenging is the task of arranging the flowers into an attractive bouquet.

In this exercise we will draw a flower still life by Hans Memling, a German painter of the Dutch school who lived in the 15th century. A main focus is the drawing of natural shapes, but also the representation of patterns on the vase and tablecloth.

A large part of the work, however, consists first of all in sketching the contours. Try to make the shape of the flowers and leaves look as natural as possible. The leaves in the lower part of the bouquet do not have to be drawn down to the last detail. Try to capture the structure and reproduce it with pencil.

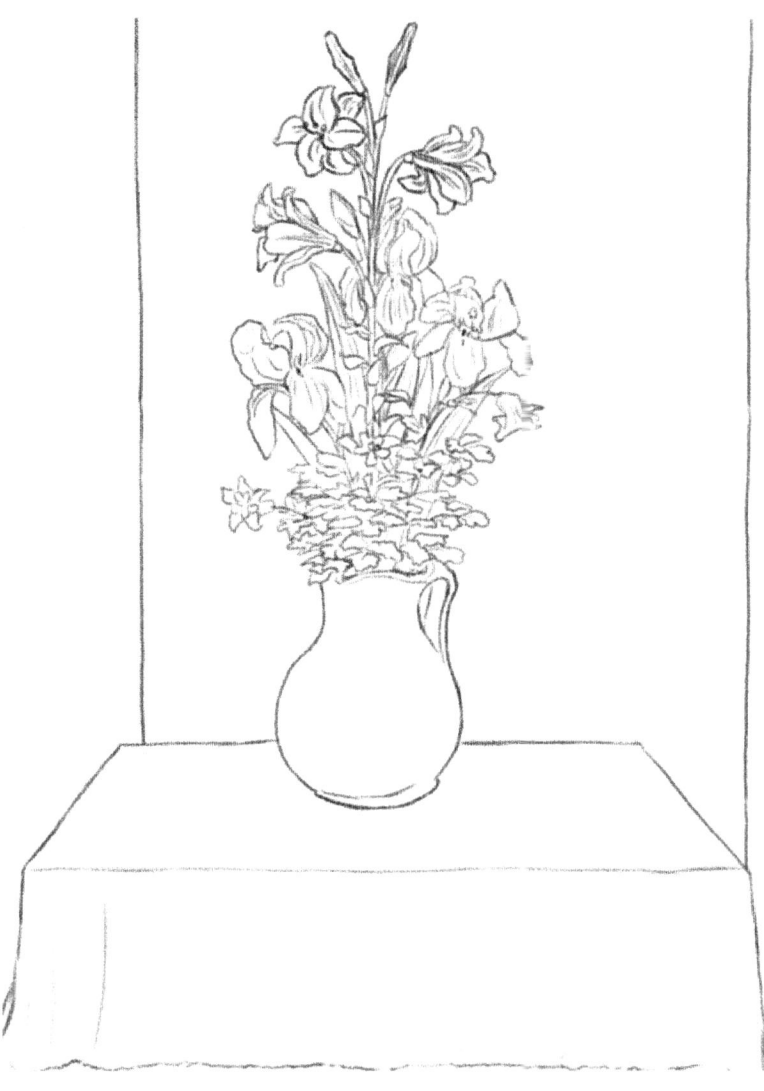

Once the preliminary sketch has been made, you can already start drawing the patterns on the vase and tablecloth. Use different tonal values for the pattern on the tablecloth. Three different tonal values will suffice.

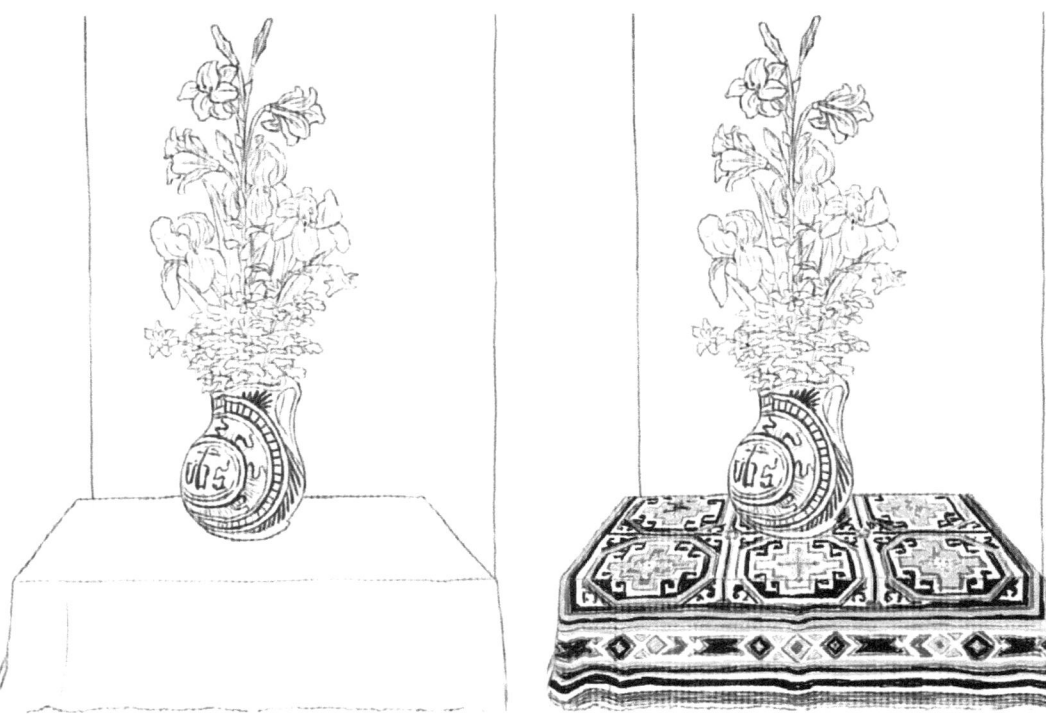

Next you can shade the bouquet. You can use a drawing technique of your choice. Try to imitate the shape of the flowers and leaves with the strokes. You can also shade the vase in this step.

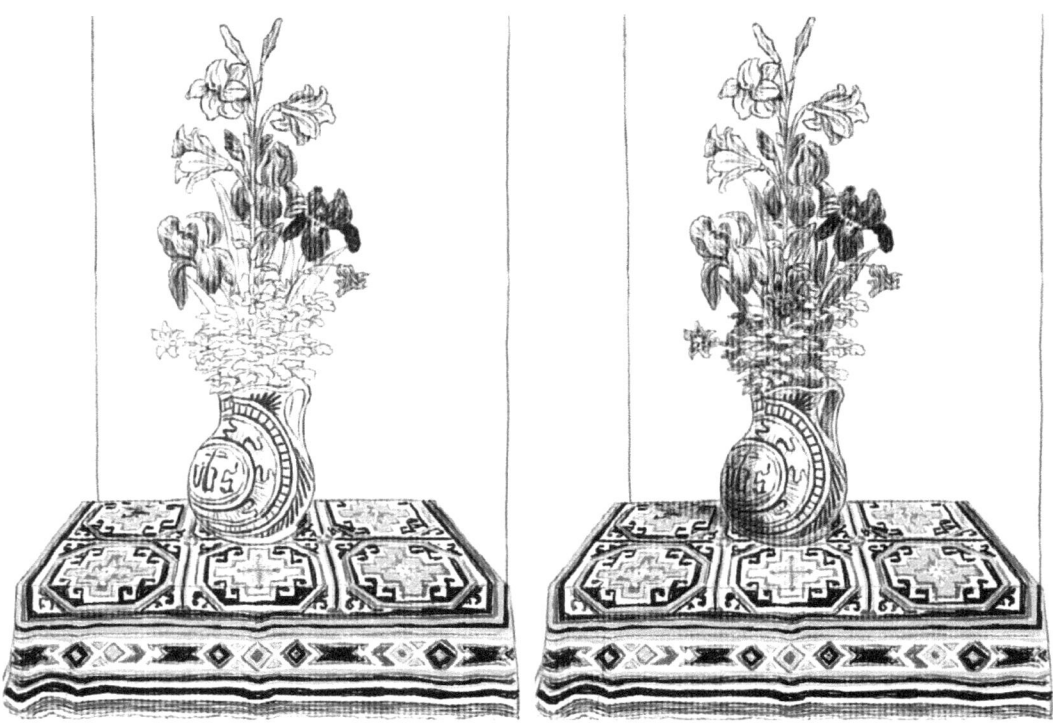

Now that the main motif has been shaded, the next step is to start designing the background. In the original painting, the light falls into the room from the top right, causing the flowers to cast a shadow on the left side of the wall. As it is a niche, a shadow is created on the right side and on the upper part of the walls.

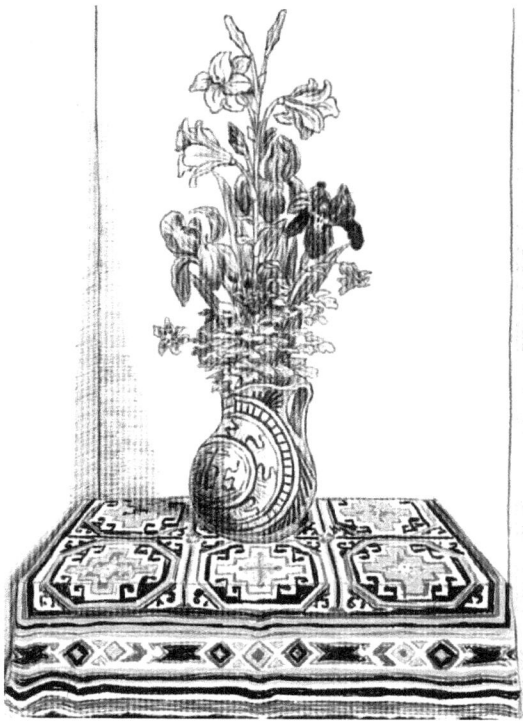
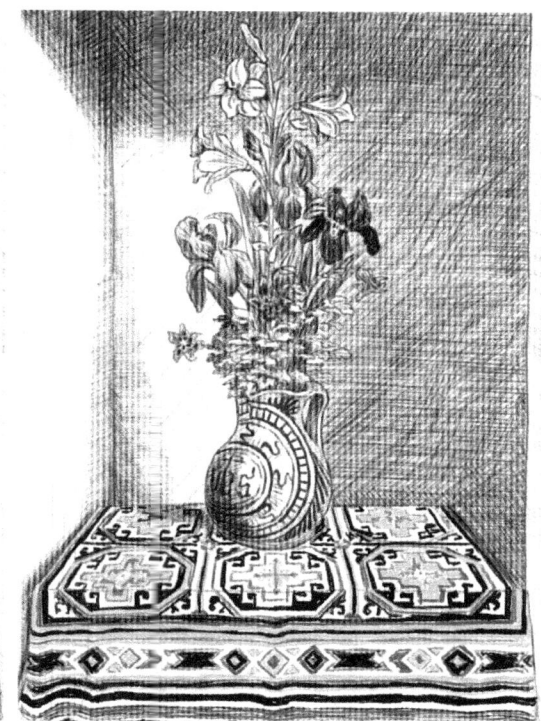

The darkest areas on the wall can be worked out even more in the last step. Also on the side of the tablecloth that hangs down from the table a slight shadow is still missing. After these last optimizations the drawing is complete.

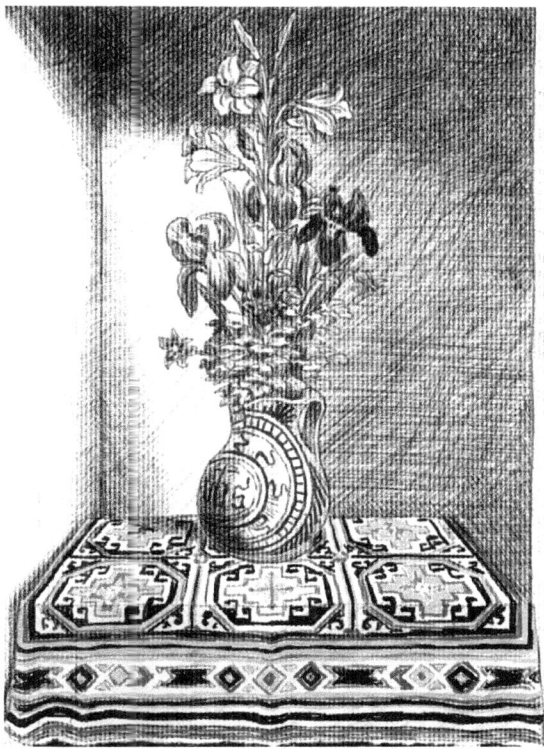

# Representation of Space and Perspective

*» He who changes his perspective, sees things in an entirely different light. «*

- Engelbert Schinkel -

# Representation of Space and Perspective

## Introduction

This book is dedicated to the topic "Drawing in Perspective". Primarily, it involves so-called vanishing-point perspective. By making use of vanishing-point perspective, it is possible to realistically display objects, landscapes and architecture. A persuasive illusion of reality is thus created on paper.

The depth of space becomes visible the clearest from a larger distance. Therefore, the depiction of depth plays especially with landscape pictures a major role. In order to allow this sense of space to emerge upon a two-dimensional drawing surface, diverse graphic aids are frequently deployed. In the following pages you will become acquainted with the most important methods.

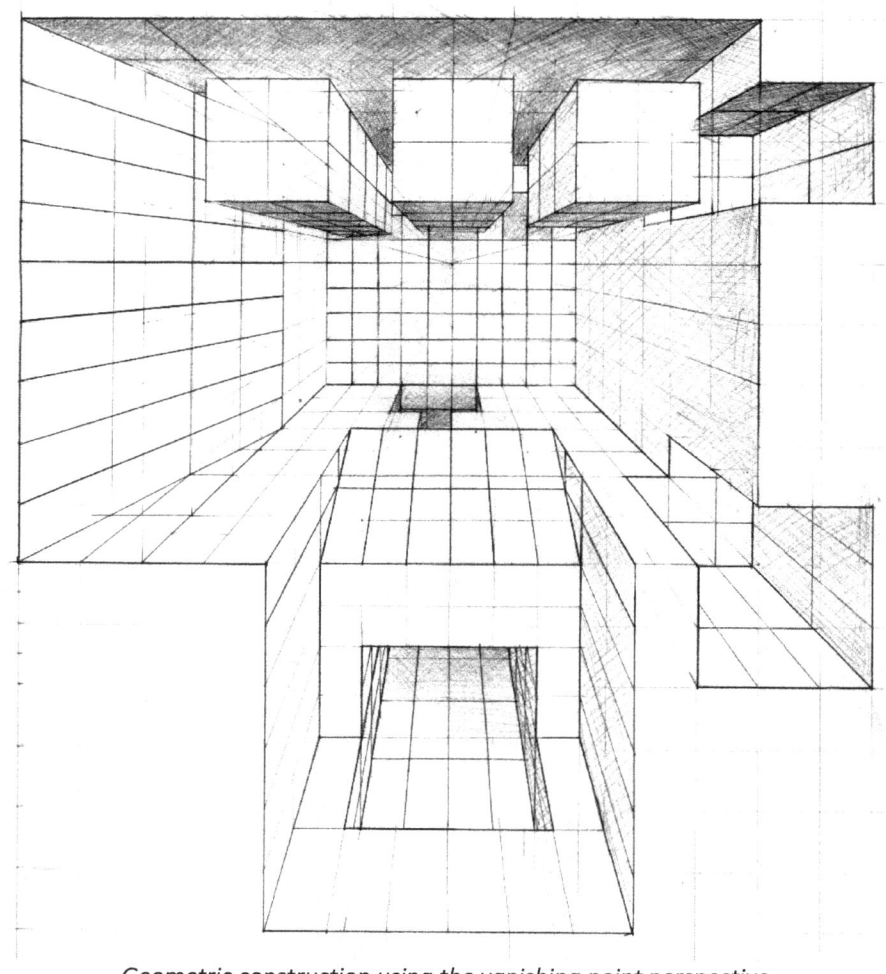

*Geometric construction using the vanishing point perspective*

# Proper Composition of an Image

A simple principle for achievement of the effect of space and depth is to fulfill the expectations of the observer. This means that we represent the space in the manner that he is accustomed to and anticipates according to his own experience. Specifically: those objects that lie on the ground, i.e. in the lower area of the drawing, are located in the foreground, and those objects that are in the upper section are more likely located in the background. Thus we make it easier for the observer of the drawing to get his bearings within the image, and the impression of a three-dimensional landscape is more readily conveyed in this manner.

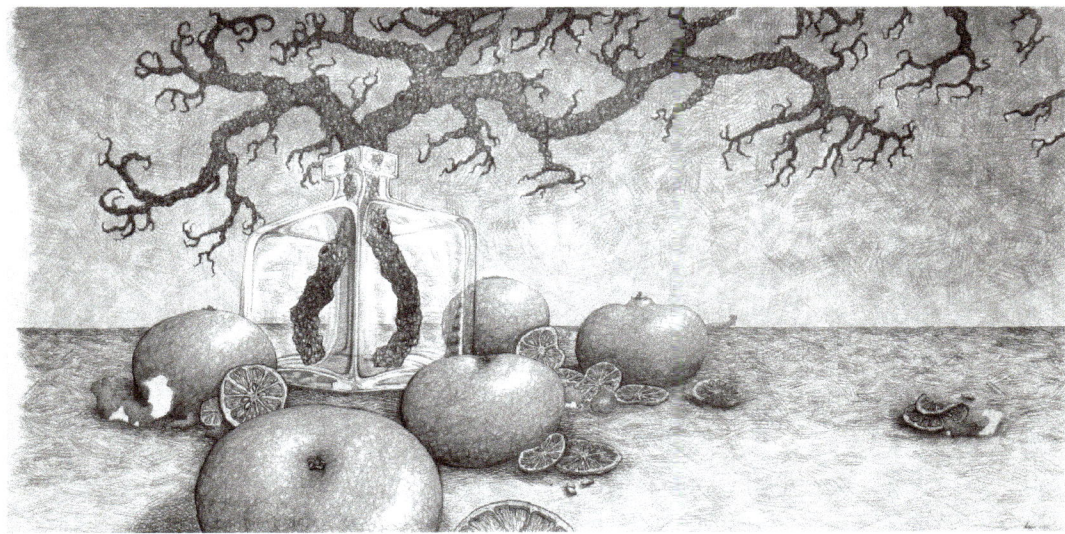

*Still life in a perspective representation*

# Overlapping

The effect of spatial representation is optically reinforced when the image is constructed in several upright planes. These planes can contain trees, a house, a car etc. The planes are laid out at varying distances and overlap one another. Due to the fact that the planes overlay one another, it is immediately obvious to the observer that the various objects in the image are located at different distances.

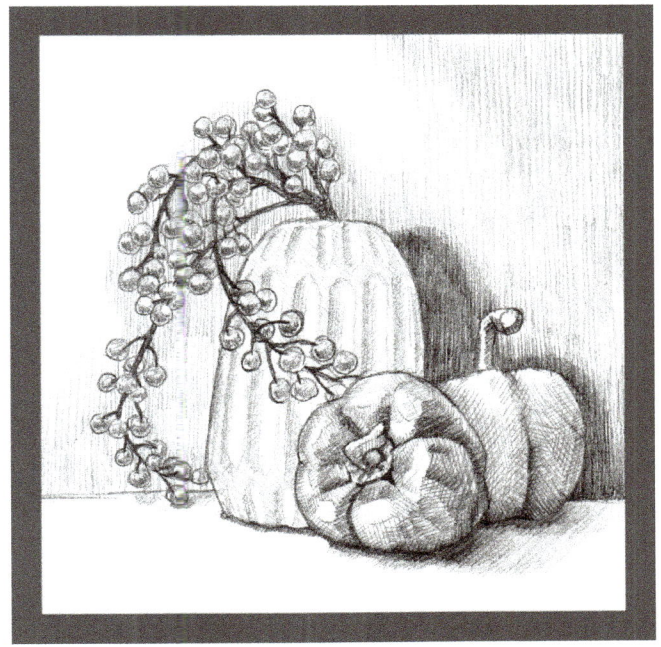

# Levels

The effect of the spatial representation is visually enhanced by building up the image in several levels. These levels could include trees, a house, a car, etc.

In many cases, the overlap method is combined with the level method. The levels are at different distances and overlap each other. As the levels overlap, it is immediately obvious to the viewer that the different image objects are at different distances.

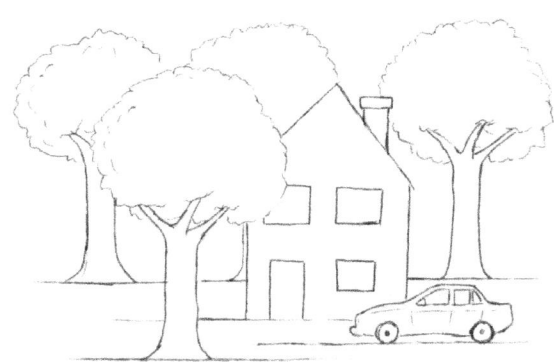

# Perspective Foreshortening

Perspective foreshortening is an effect that becomes particularly distinct when we view, from straight ahead, an object that stretches out into the distance. For example, we look at an outstretched arm or a branch directly from the front.

The graphic problem arises as a lot of "information" is compressed into very little space in this foreshortening of perspective. Such views are not only difficult, but also unusual to draw. They often contradict the experience stored in our brain.

Unbiased seeing and observing are important approaches here. The vanishing point perspective is also a particularly effective method for representing such views.

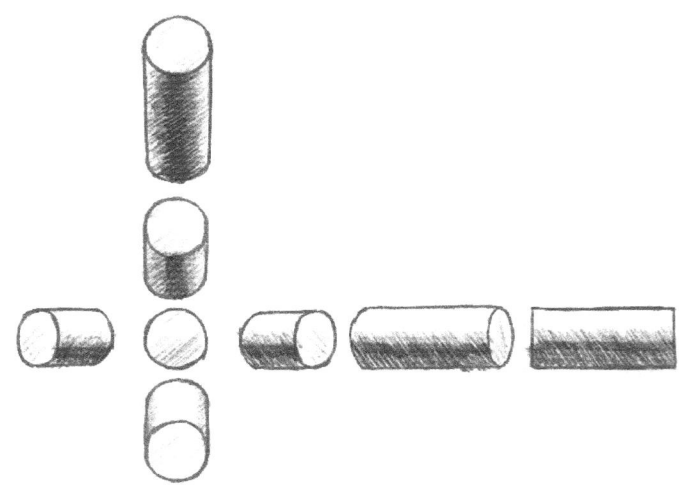

*Perspective shortening of a cylinder*

# Vanishing Point Perspective

The last method of spatial representation to be introduced here is vanishing point perspective. The procedure here is much less characterized by feeling and intuition than the previous methods. Vanishing point perspective is first and foremost a technical method. But more about that in the remainder of the book!

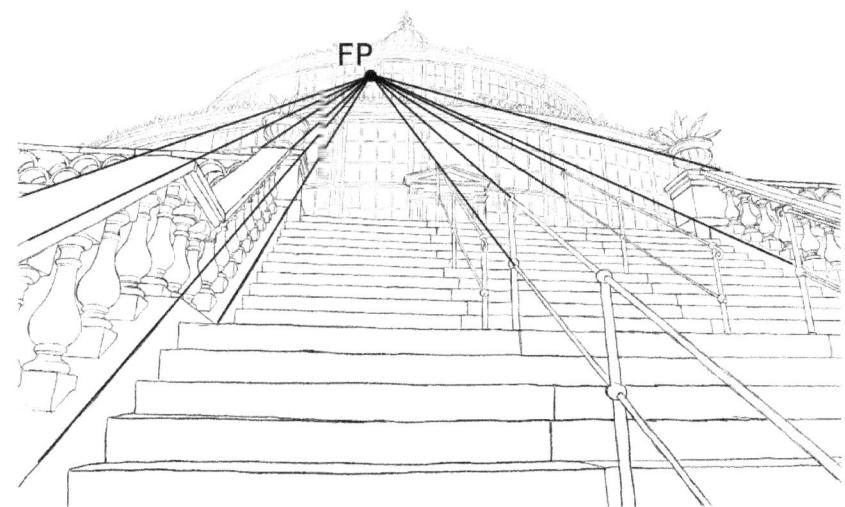

*Example of the perspective representation of a staircase*

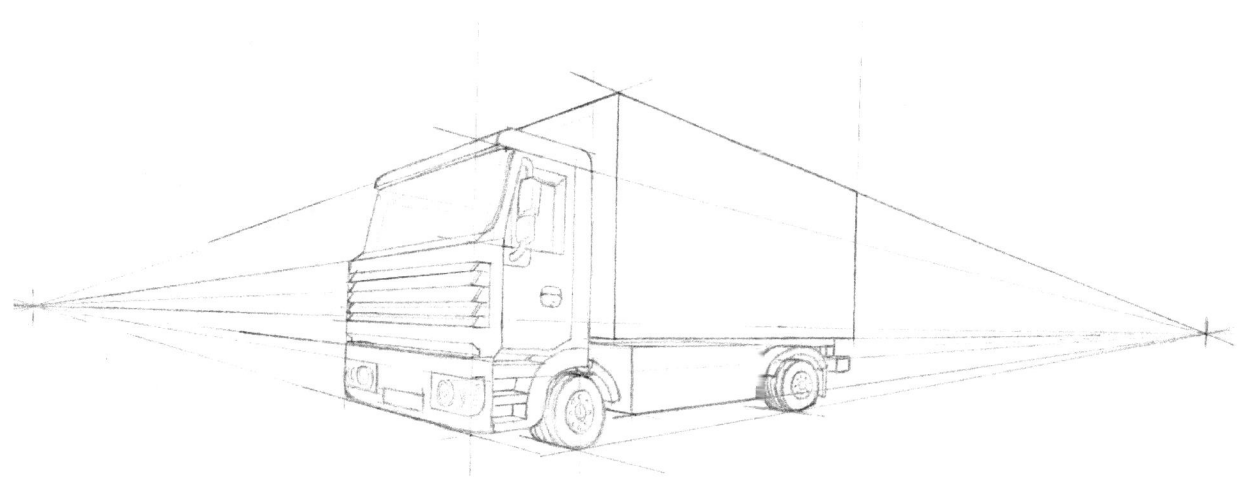

*Perspective drawing of a truck*

# Vanishing Point Perspective – the Basics

## General Information about Vanishing Point Perspective

### Perspective

The term perspective refers to the spatial circumstances of objects in space. Perspective is always dependent on the standpoint of the viewer and describes the relative distances of objects in comparison to the viewer. Perspective only changes when either the location of the objects or that of the observer changes. This means that the perspective does NOT change when only the observed section of the picture is changed (e.g. in a zoom-in using a camera).

### Vanishing Point Perspective

Vanishing point perspective presents a graphic method with which we can represent three-dimensional objects on a two-dimensional surface with the use of perspective. This involves a construction procedure that is both technical and artistic. The objective here is to create the illusion of a three-dimensional space, even though the drawing, i.e. the surface of the canvas, is only two-dimensional.

The perspective perception is characterized above all by the fact that we perceive objects the smaller the further away they are from us. This reduction occurs because the rays of light enter our eyes at a shallower angle when an object is further away.
Another effect of perspective is that we see more objects in the distance than in our vicinity. In principle, this phenomenon has the same origin as the previously described effect of objects getting smaller in further distance.

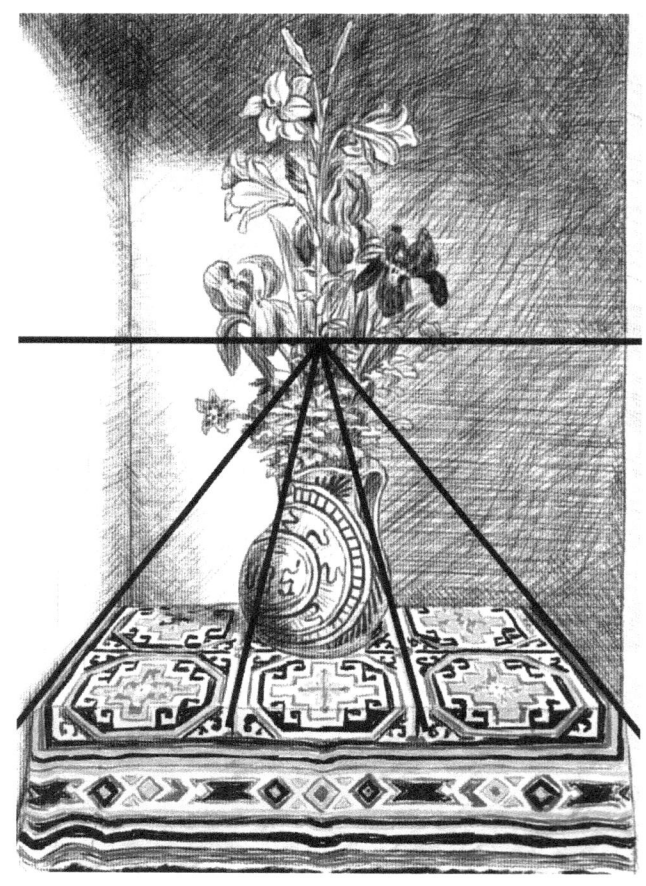

*Drawing after a still life from von Hans Memling*

# Construction of Vanishing Point Perspective

At the beginning of this chapter we will have a look at the individual elements of vanishing point perspective. The simplest form of perspective representation requires a horizon, a vanishing point, vanishing lines and, of course, an object that we would like to draw spatially.

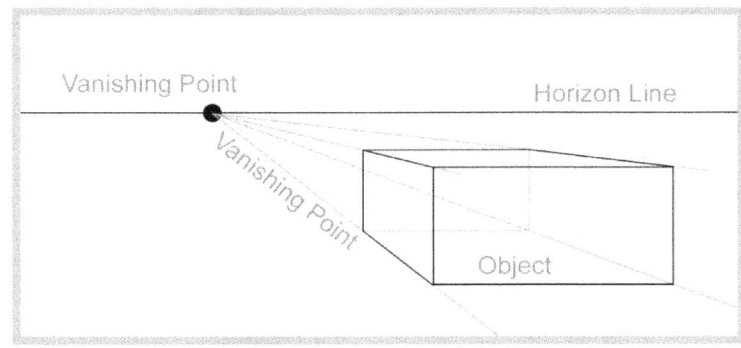

# The most Important Terms

## The Horizon

The horizon is the separation line between the ground and the sky. The technically correct description, however, would be "the line at which the view from below and the top view are separated". This means that one looks down (top view) at everything that is located below the horizon line – one is thus looking at the upper face of the object. Conversely, everything that is located above the horizon line is viewed upwards (view from below) – it is thus seen from below.

Even though the Earth is a sphere, the horizon is always perceived as a horizontal line. Obviously, mountains, hills, canyons and such interrupt the horizon line – in order to execute a drawing in perspective, we are forced to just imagine the horizon here.

It is furthermore important that the horizon is always placed at eye level with the observer! The horizon is the most important element in a drawing with vanishing point perspective, and is therefore drawn first.

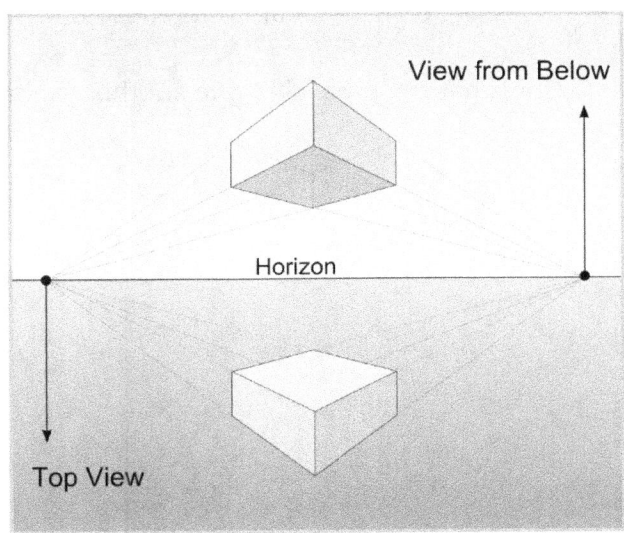

## Vanishing Point and Vanishing Line

After the horizon line, the vanishing point is the second most important element in a drawing in perspective. With vanishing point perspective, all lines vanish into (i.e. are aligned in) one or several points. These points are called vanishing points. The aligned lines are also called vanishing lines and are frequently extended out to the vanishing point to aid construction of the drawing.

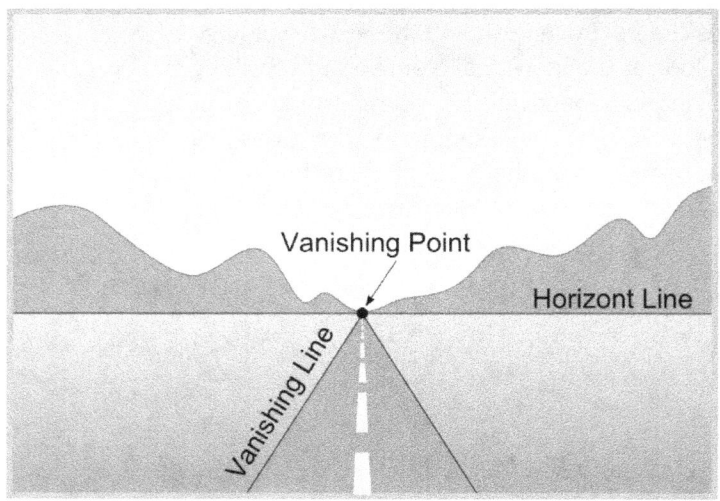

### A few important rules for vanishing points and vanishing lines:

- Depending on the spatial position and the form of an object, an individual vanishing point can suffice for representation, or several vanishing points are required.

- Vanishing points that are referenced underground are always located on the horizon line.

- Lines that run parallel to one another vanish into a common vanishing point.

# Central Perspective with one Vanishing Point

For central perspective with a (main-)vanishing point, the objects to be displayed are situated with their front surface parallel to the picture plane. We as observers are thus looking straight at the frontal face of the objects.

It can be said that the vanishing point is the point at which the observer's visual axis meets the horizon.

This type of perspective is certainly the simplest form. Only lines that lead back into the depth of space disappear into a vanishing point. Vertical lines are always vertical. Horizontal lines that run parallel to the horizon remain horizontal and do not align/disappear. The entire frontal face is thus not distorted through perspective.

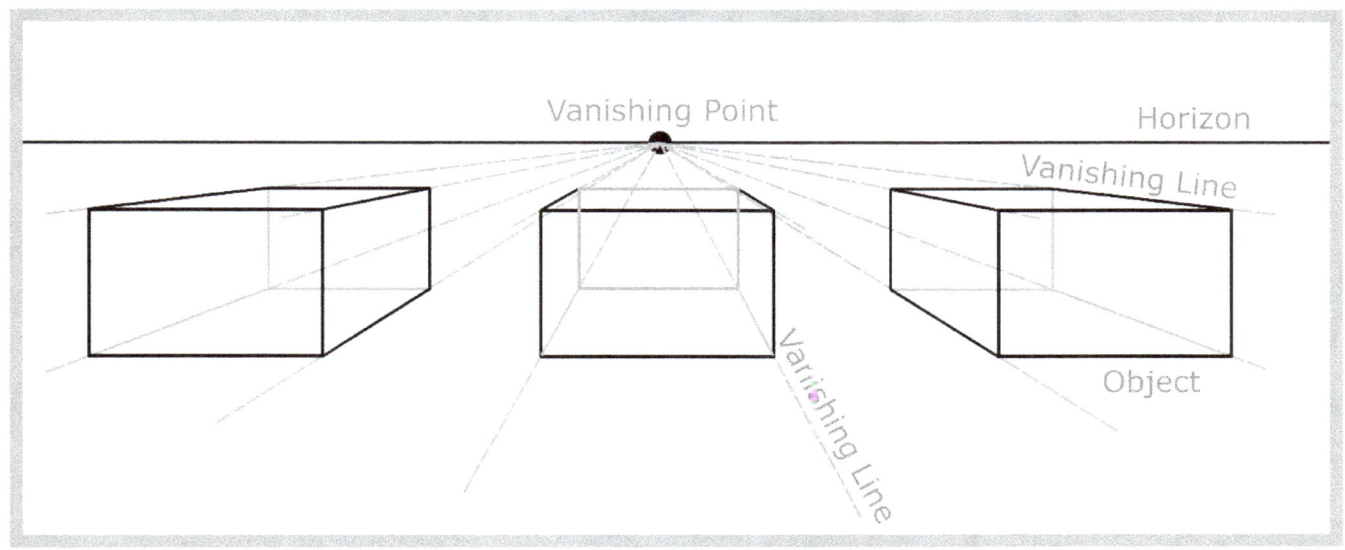

*Three cubes in central perspective with one vanishing point*

Central perspective with one vanishing point, however, can only be used when the represented objects stand vertically on the base plane and stand with one surface head-on to the observer, i.e. the front is parallel to the picture plane.

# Exercise – Central Perspective with one Vanishing Point

And now we would like to translate, with a small exercise, the theoretical principles from the previous chapter into practice. A box with one vanishing point should be drawn in central perspective. As you proceed, you can view the picture series step by step. A clarification of the individual steps will follow the drawings.

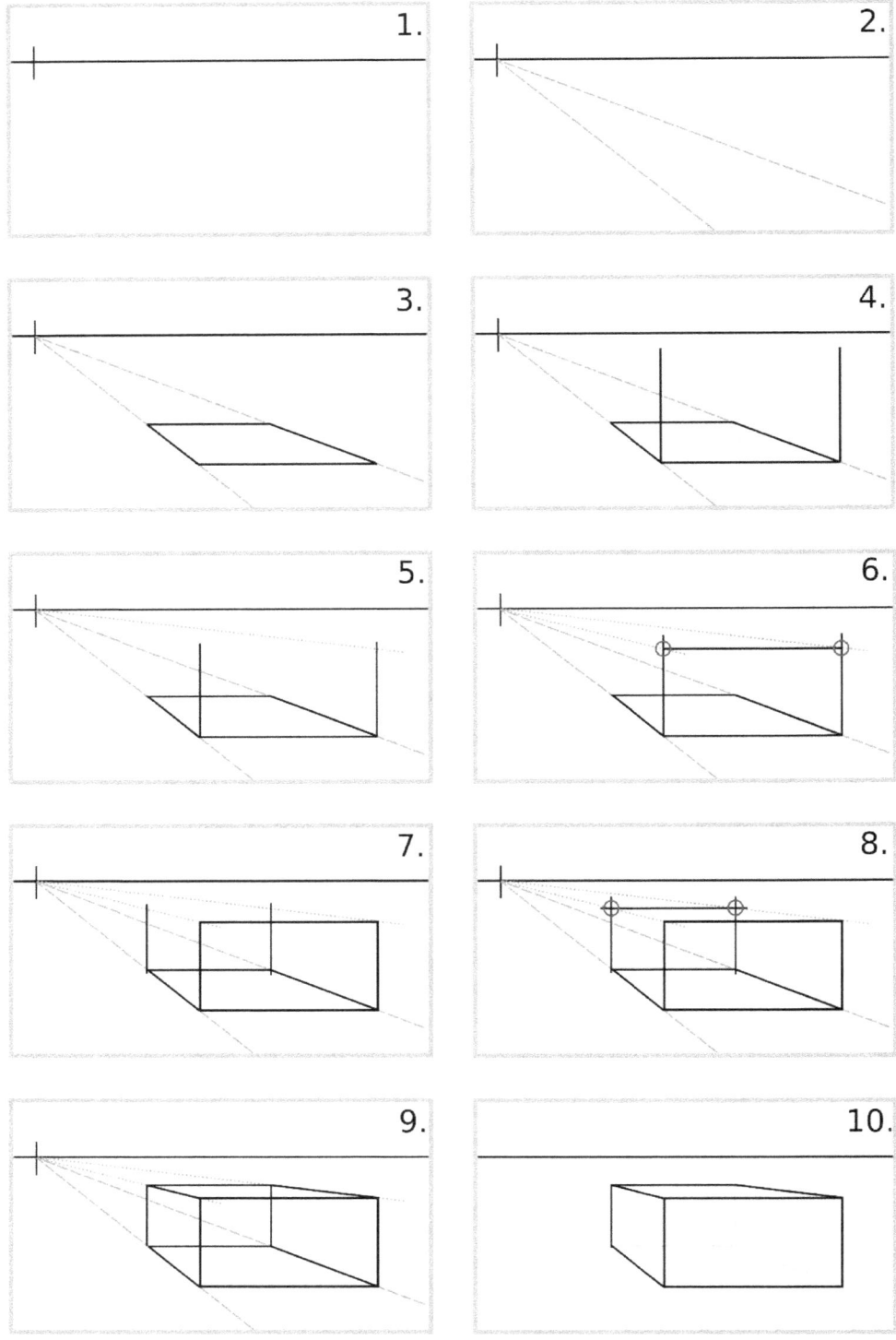

Representation of Space and Perspective

1. As you can see in the first image (upper left), we begin with the horizon line. It is drawn at any desired position. In this step we can also determine the vanishing point at the same time.

2. Now you can draw two vanishing lines that will determine the width of the box. These vanishing lines emerge out of the vanishing point and run in a direction towards the observer.

3. The base of the box is defined by two horizontal lines that intersect with the two vanishing lines.

4. At the corner points of this square, two vertical lines are drawn upwards. These lines represent the edges of the frontal face of the box.

5. Two more vanishing lines are then drawn which intersect with the two vertical lines. The height of the box is determined in this step. The two vertical edges of the box must be intersected at the same height. Step 5 can be executed together with step 6, so that it is a bit easier.

6. In this step, a horizontal line is extended out from one of the two points of intersection – this refers to the two points of intersection between the vertical lines and the new vanishing lines. This line represents the front upper-edge of the box.

Moreover, the point of intersection for the second vanishing line, which we have already drawn in Step 5, would appear due to the horizontal line. Thus one could also proceed in such a manner that one draws only one vanishing line at first, then the horizontal upper edge of the box and, finally, the second vanishing line.

7. In the seventh step, two further vertical lines are drawn on the two back corner points of the floor area.

8. The new points of intersection can once again be connected to each other by a horizontal line.

9. And now you only have to represent the upper face of the box by drawing in the upper vanishing lines.

10. If you now remove the extraneous construction elements (vanishing point and vanishing lines), you'll get the completed box drawing in perspective. The hidden edges are represented in light grey in the drawing.

# Drawing a Cube (Box with equal Edge-Lengths)

Drawing a box in central perspective with a vanishing point is not difficult. And now you will get an assignment that is a bit more complicated: we want to draw a cube.

In geometry we define a cube as a rectangular solid in which all edges have the same length. The difficulty that one runs into concerning this perspective representation involves the problem of initially not knowing how far (deep) the solid object extends back into space.

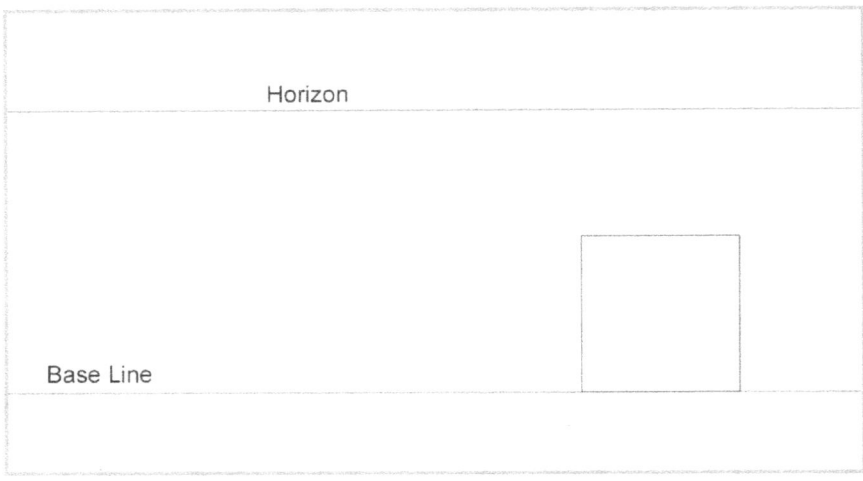

Let's just begin with the perspective drawing. This time we want to proceed somewhat differently compared to before. That is, we first of all draw the complete frontal face of the cube on the base line.

Then we define a vanishing point and extend vanishing lines to the four corner points.

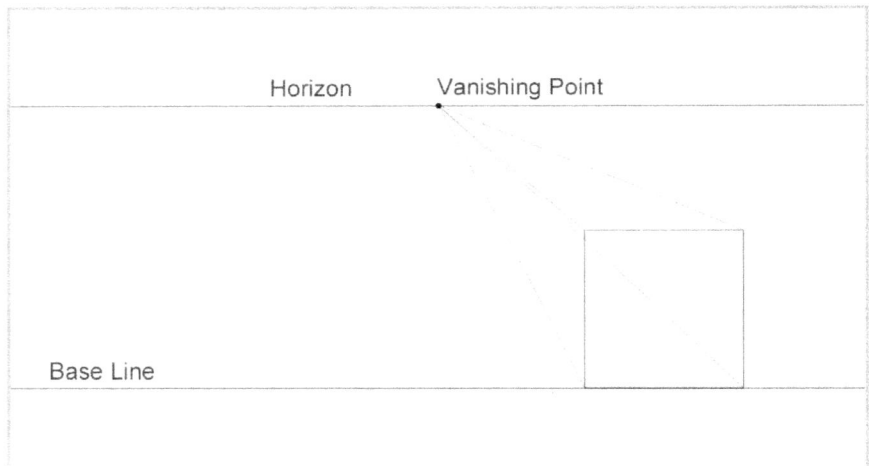

At this point, the problem becomes obvious. How far back in space is the back edge of the cube?

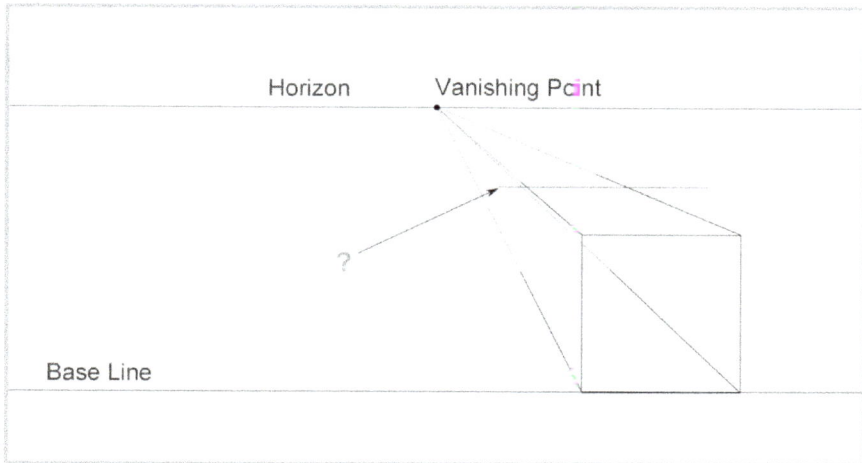

In order to solve this problem, we need two additional vanishing points: the vanishing points of the diagonals. These vanishing points are given this name because we are able to determine with their help the diagonal lines for the upper face and lower face of the cube.

As you can see in the image, it is possible to determine the vanishing points by means of the eye point. This point gives the distance from the observer's eye to the drawing, from which the illusion of perspective seems to be perfect.

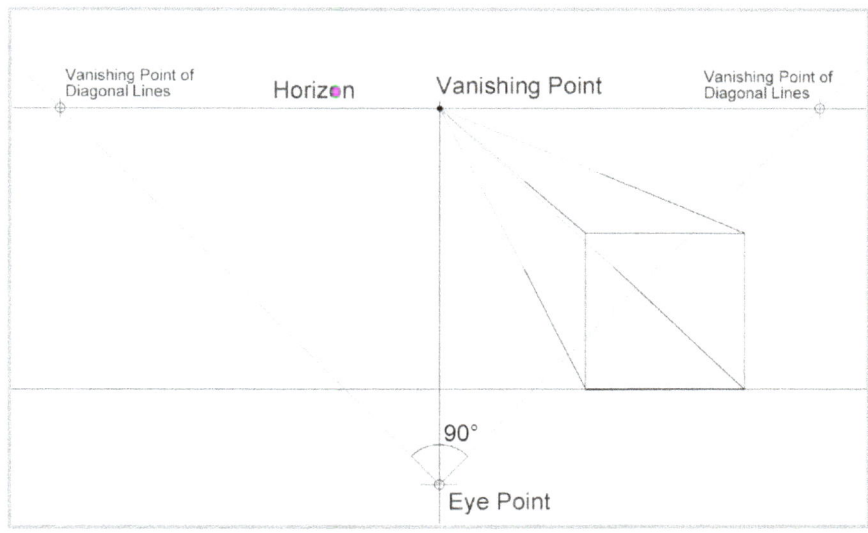

With the aid of these additional vanishing points, we can now draw in the diagonal lines on the upper face of the cube. At that point at which a diagonal intersects with the respective upper vanishing line of the cube, we can draw the rear horizontal edge of the cube. This sounds much more complicated in written form than it really is in practice. Just take a look at the following drawing.

The depth of the cube is thus defined. In principle, it would be sufficient here, of course, if we only drew one diagonal line.

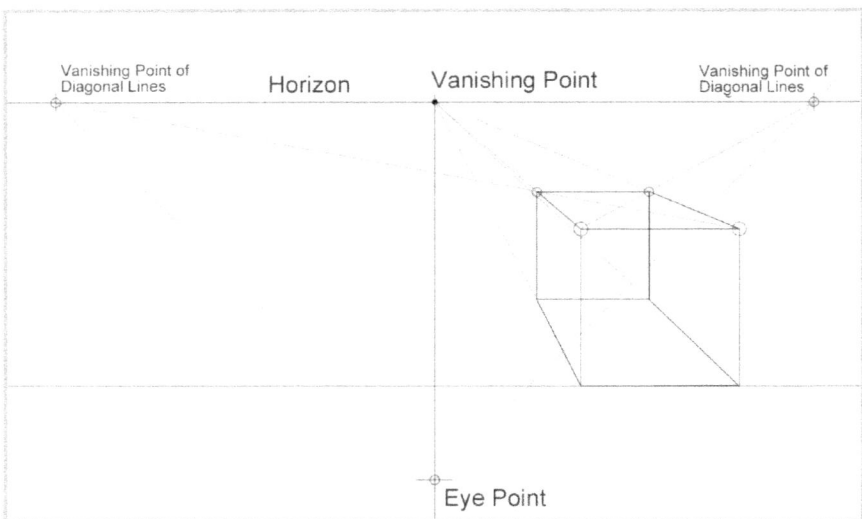

And here is how the cube looks without the aid of reference lines and construction lines:

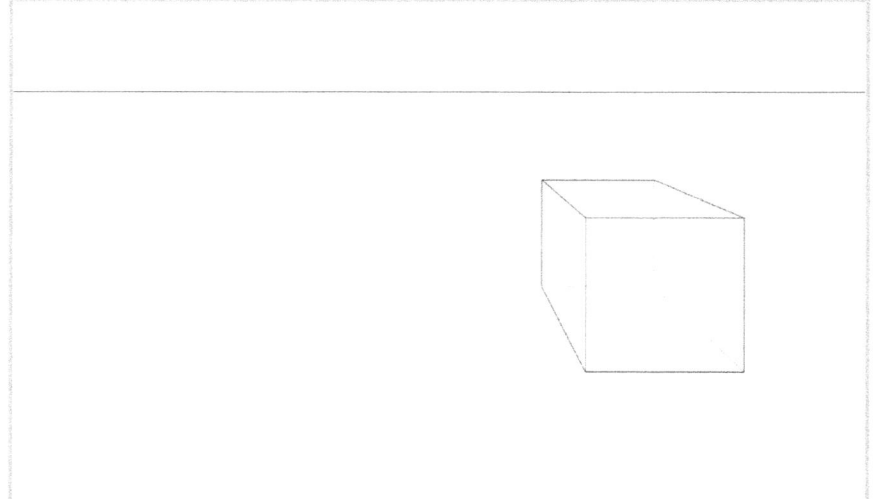

Representation of Space and Perspective

# How to draw an oblique Plane

You will quite often encounter oblique planes in perspective drawings. In the example shown here, we represent a body that resembles a house. That means we have two symmetrical inclined planes.

The basic object is a box:

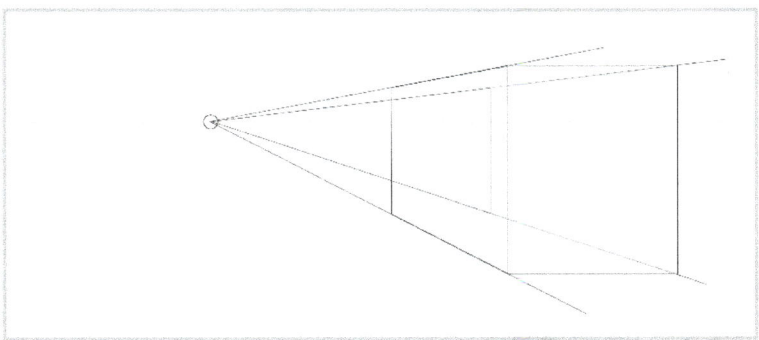

The thing that is however new here is the roof. A roof is an oblique plane that is, with a vanishing point in central perspective, still quite easy to depict.

Draw the diagonal lines of the end faces of the house, in order to determine the center point of these faces. Then a vertical line is drawn through each of the two center points.

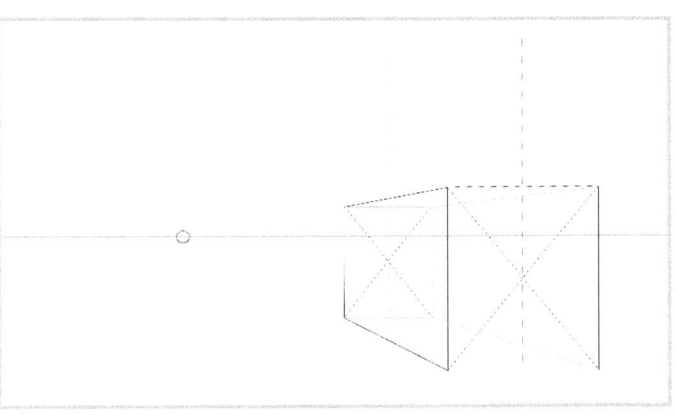

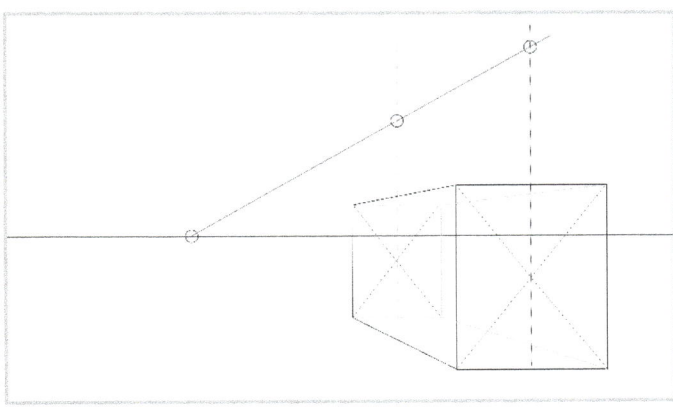

A vanishing line that intersects the two vertical lines forms the roof ridge (upper ridge of the roof).

And now you can draw the roof gable with the aid of the two intersection points. And now the house is finished.

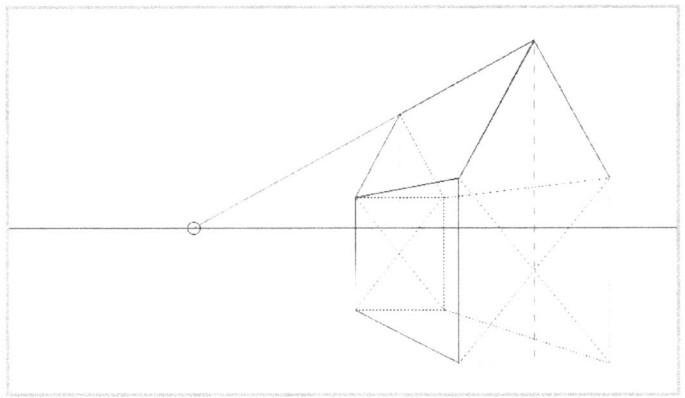

## Exercise – A house with Side View

Now try to draw, on your own, a house with a side view. You can see in the drawing below what the final result will look like.

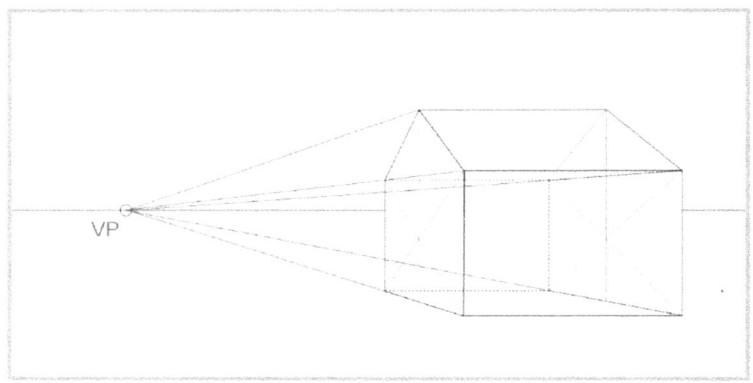

# Diagonal Perspective

In this chapter you will learn how you can draw objects in diagonal perspective (also called oblique perspective or two-point perspective). The central perspective covered in the previous chapter, included the limitation that one could only represent objects in perspective from the front.

Diagonal perspective, conversely, presents objects that are positioned at an angle (oblique) to the observer – as portrayed in the picture below. You will learn how to deploy this technique in the following exercise.

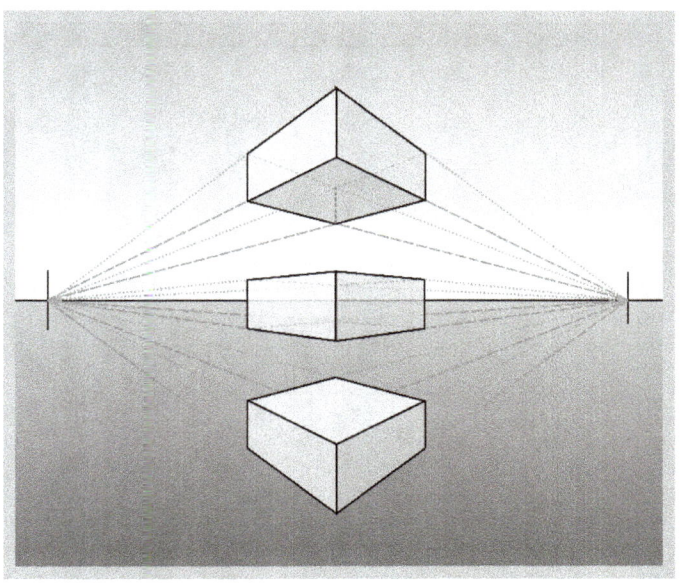

## Drawing a Box in Diagonal Perspective

In the following exercise, we would like to try to draw a simple box in diagonal perspective. This object represents one of the simplest motifs for this technique.
You can find the step-by-step development of the box on the following page.

1. For diagonal perspective we need two vanishing points (similar to the two vanishing points of the diagonals). Therefore, we first of all draw the horizon and mark two vanishing points – one left and one right.

2. Starting from the two vanishing points, we now extend two vanishing lines each which define the lower surface of the box.

3. The lower surface of the box can now be drawn in.

4. Next we come to the front edge of the box. The height of the box is then defined by this edge.

5. And now we extend two vanishing lines - respectively from the left and right vanishing point - to the upper point of the edge.

6. With the aid of these vanishing lines, we can now extend the two side edges up vertically. These two lines are automatically shorter than the front edge, as it is required according to the guidelines for perspective representation.

7. We can now draw two more vanishing lines up to the points at which these two side edges intersect the upper vanishing lines.

8. The two new vanishing lines define the height of the back vertical edge of the box.

9. Thus the form of the upper surface of the box is also defined.

10. If we remove all reference lines and the hidden edges, the drawing of a box in perspective is now complete.

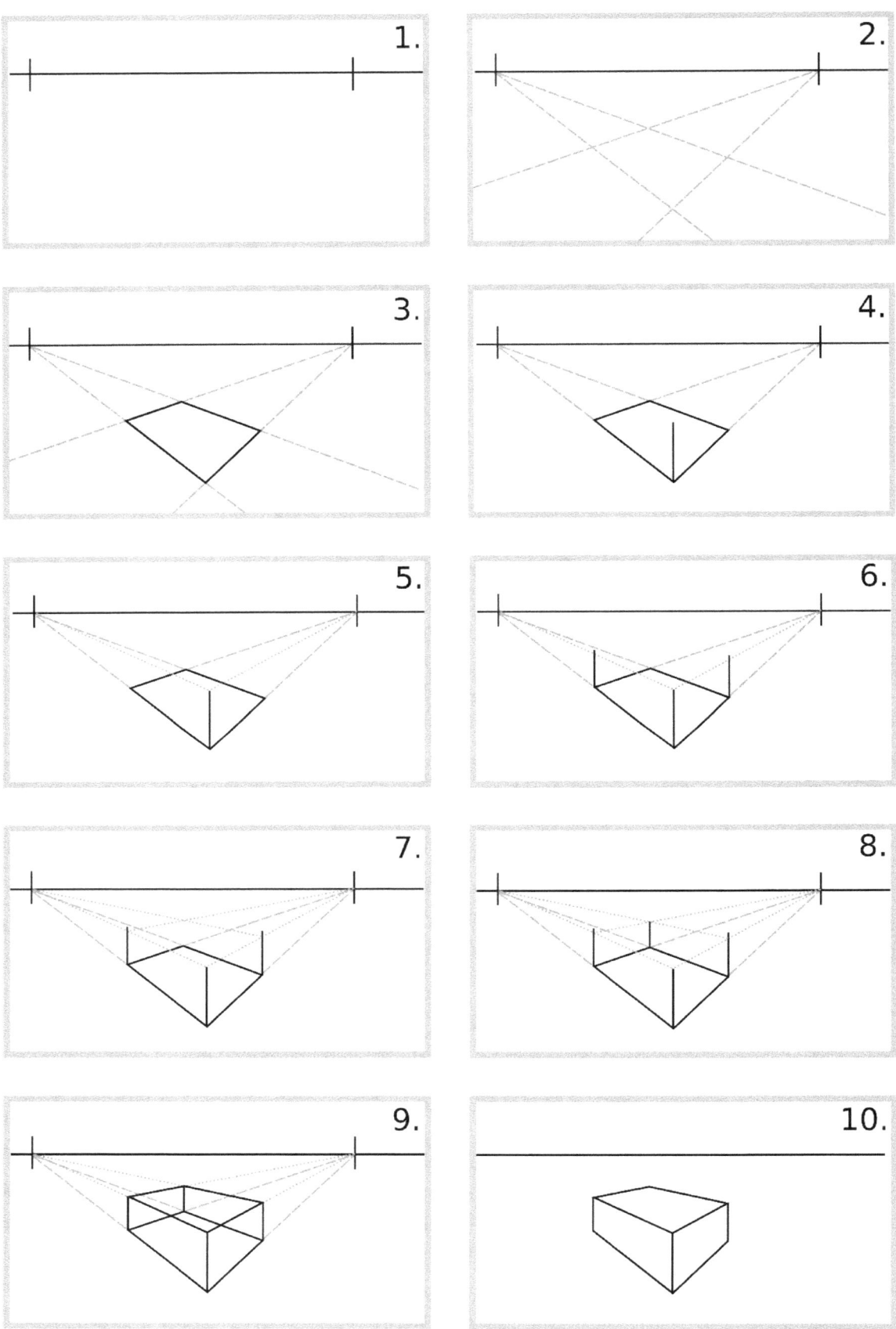

# Representation of Space and Perspective

## Drawing a Cube that has been shifted by 30°

In the previous exercise you learned how to draw a simple box in diagonal perspective. Now we are going to be a little more specific: We'll try to draw a box that is shifted by exactly 30°.

We'll begin the exercise with a representation of the most important construction elements. Important for a proper design is to draw the 90° triangle with an angle of 30°/60° to the horizon. This angle corresponds to the orientation of the motif related to the observer. The two vanishing points (VP-1, VP-2) are defined by the intersection points between horizon and 90° triangle.

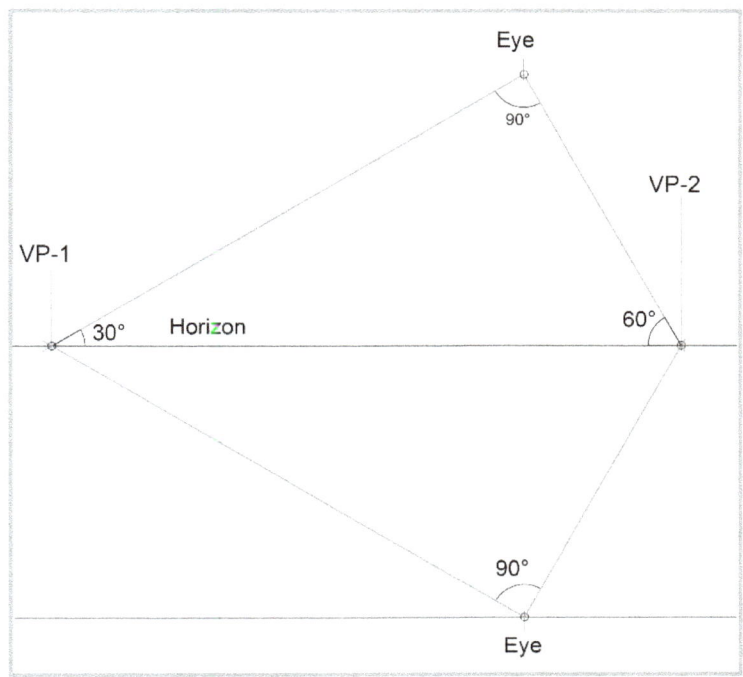

For the next step you'll need a compass.

Place the point of the compass precisely on the vanishing point 1 and draw an arc from the upper eye point down to the horizon. Repeat this for vanishing point 2. You will thus acquire the 30° and 60° reference points on the horizon line.

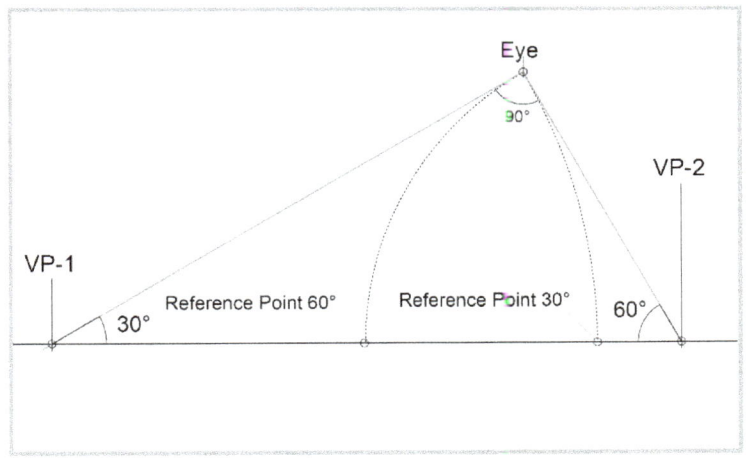

Now draw a base line, upon which the front corner point of the cube is to be located. And now you can represent the front edge and draw the vanishing lines for the upper and lower edges.

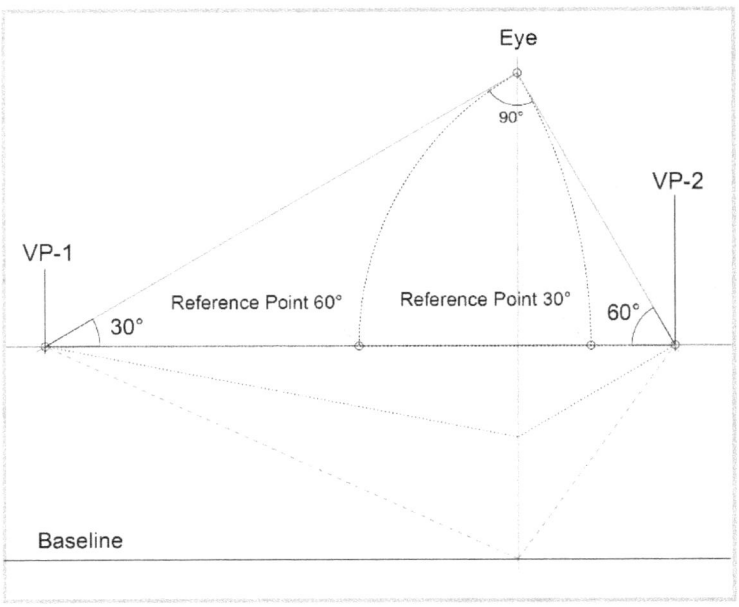

In this step you have to draw a semi-circle with the compass. The center of the circle is the point at which the cube touches the base line. The points at which the semi-circle touches the base line aid in the formation of two reference lines. These reference lines emerge – as in the previous example – through the connection of the semi-circle end-point with the 30° and 60° reference point.

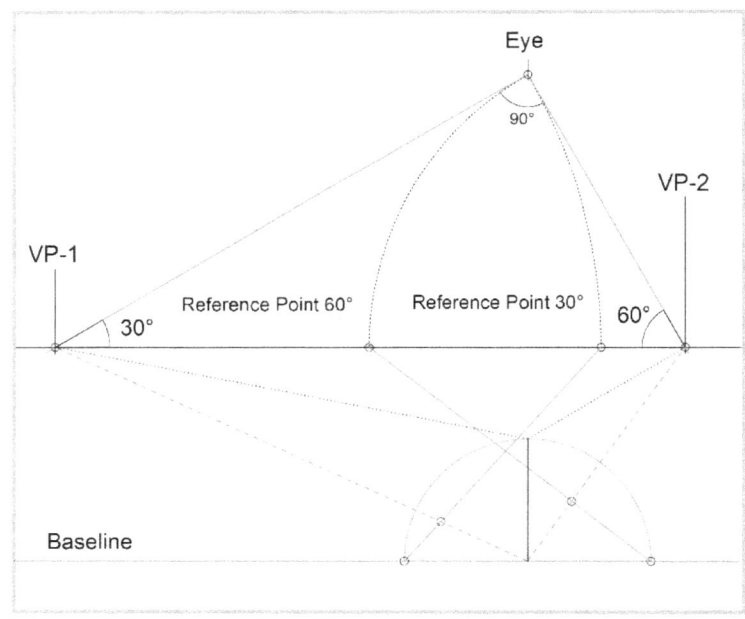

With the aid of these two new reference lines, two new points of intersection emerge on the lower vanishing lines, from which you can now extend upwards the two side edges of the cube.

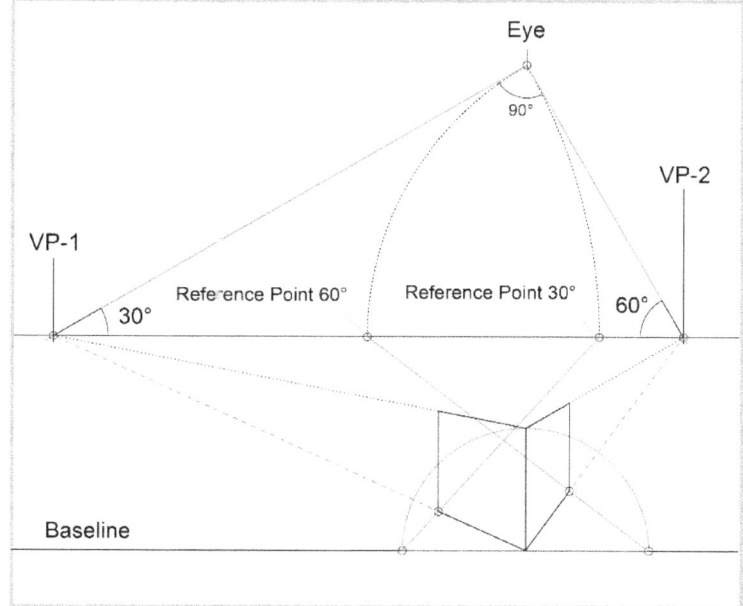

With the aid of the remaining vanishing lines, you can now complete the cube.

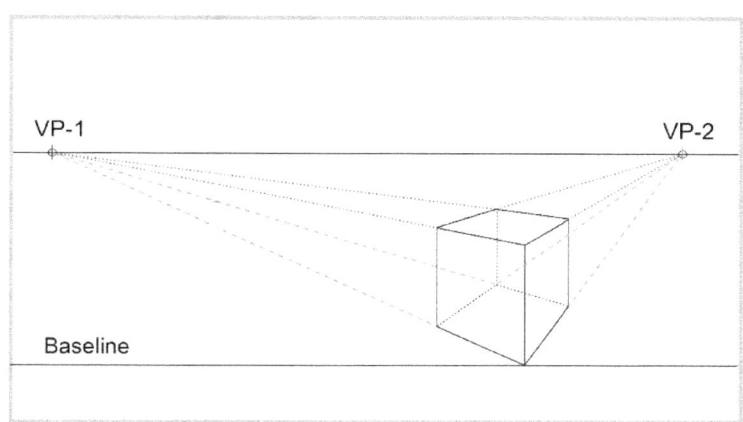

The final result is shown here without reference lines:

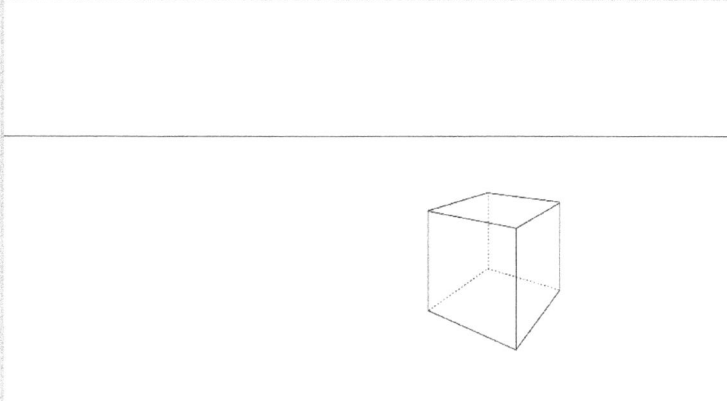

# Circles, Cylinders and Arcs

Circles, cylinders, arcs and other round elements are frequently found in drawings. It is unfortunately not so easy to draw these elements in a perspective representation. In the following exercises, you will find a few helpful techniques. Nevertheless, you will still need a bit of feeling in your drawing hand. For those of you who are still somewhat hesitant to try freehand drawing, you can make use of a French curve template as support.

## Drawing a Circle and/or Ellipse in Perspective

In this first exercise we would like to try to draw a very simple circle in central perspective. For this we need a bit of supportive geometry, in order to make life easier. We start out by drawing a square – as we learned to do early on. Take note here: a square, not a rectangle!

Also draw the surface diagonal lines of the square and its center lines. We will need both of them.

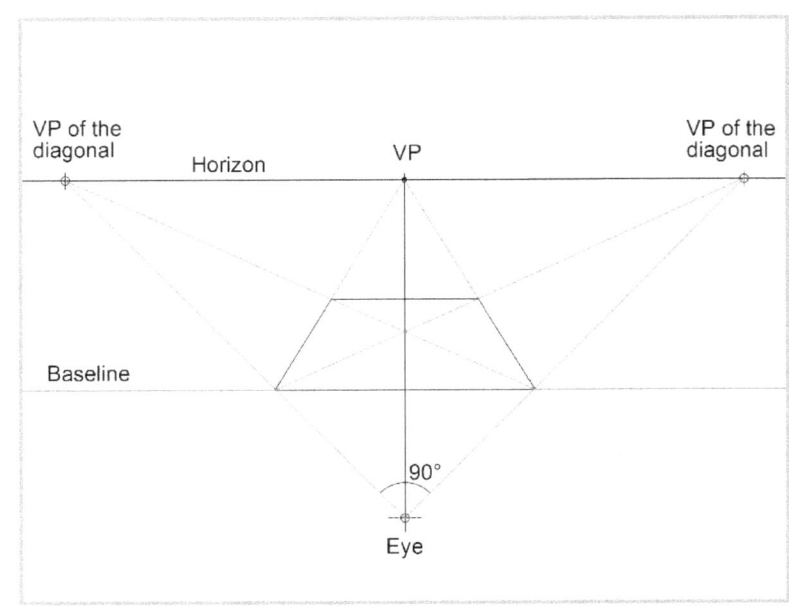

*A square as initial supportive geometry to draw the circle*

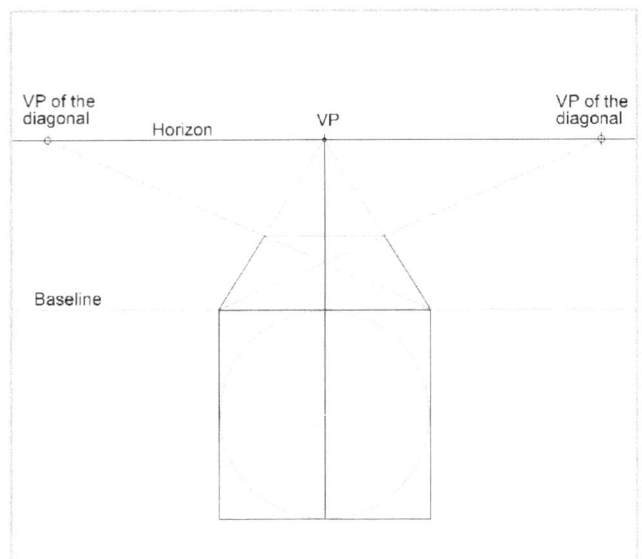

And now the second step – we draw directly under the perspective square another square that is not distorted by perspective. Here as well, we insert the face diagonals and center lines.

And now the important step – draw a circle within the confines of the non-perspective square. Mark the points where the circle intersects with the diagonal lines. Through these points of intersection, you can now extend two vertical lines that you transfer up to the square drawn in perspective. The two transferred lines extend back in the direction of the vanishing point VP, as illustrated in the picture.

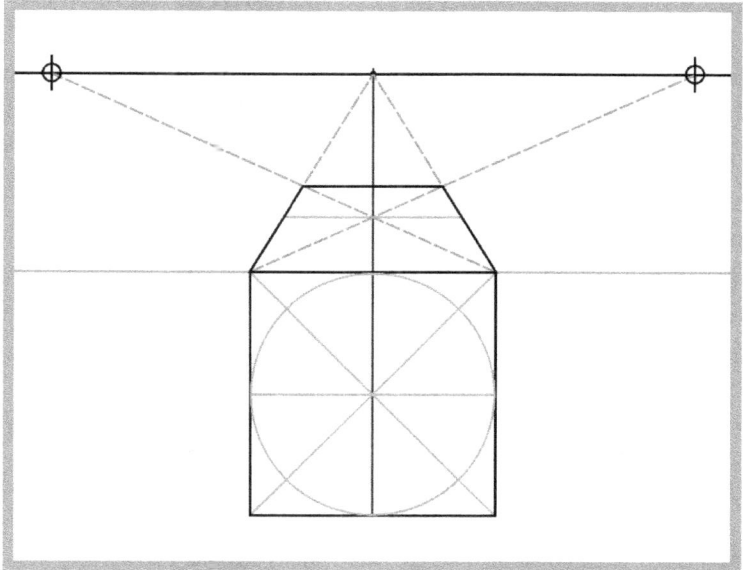

Now take a look at the circle that was represented without perspective. Look at the points of intersection that have arisen between circle, diagonals and the vertical reference lines. You have already transferred the reference lines onto the square in perspective. By using this trick you can now transfer the points of intersection in the circle as well. They are located at that point where the reference lines intersect the face diagonals. Four additional points of intersection in the circle are located where the center lines of the square intersect.

And now you have eight points that the circle should run through. With the aid of these points, you can now draw the circle within the square. In order to achieve this, you will need a bit of practice so that the circle ends up uniformly round.
Take also notice of the fact that die circle drawn in perspective becomes the shape of an ellipse.

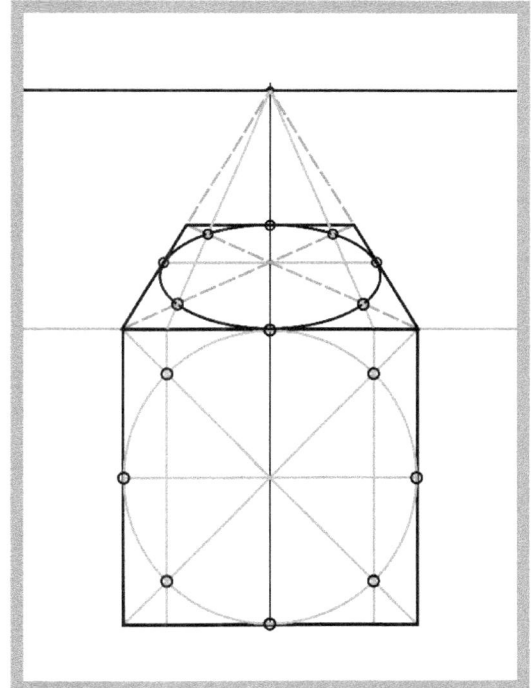

# Drawing a Cylinder

So now you have learned how to draw a simple circle in perspective. Now we will go one more step by trying to construct a cylinder. All that is needed for this is a second plane. Finally, we have already drawn the lower face of the cylinder, and now we just need to do the same thing for the upper face.

Draw another square in perspective directly above the existing one. Here as well we need to include the surface diagonals and center lines of the square.
By extending vertical reference lines from the square without perspective up to the upper face, you can now transfer the reference lines up to the new square.

You can now draw the circle just like you did for the lower face in the former example. The points of intersection for the upper circle should be located precisely above the lower circle.

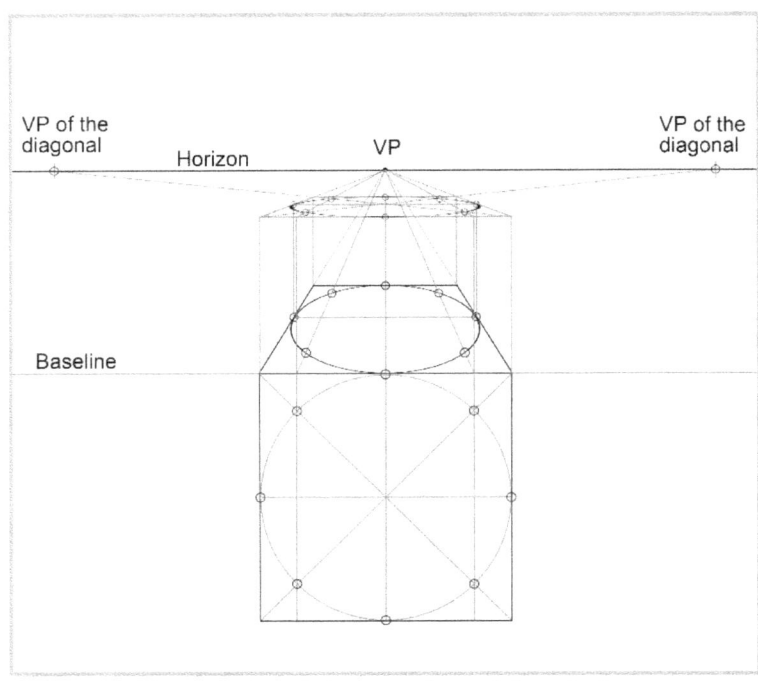

*Construction of the upper face of the cylinder*

Now connect the two outermost points of the circle with two lines in order to obtain the cylinder.

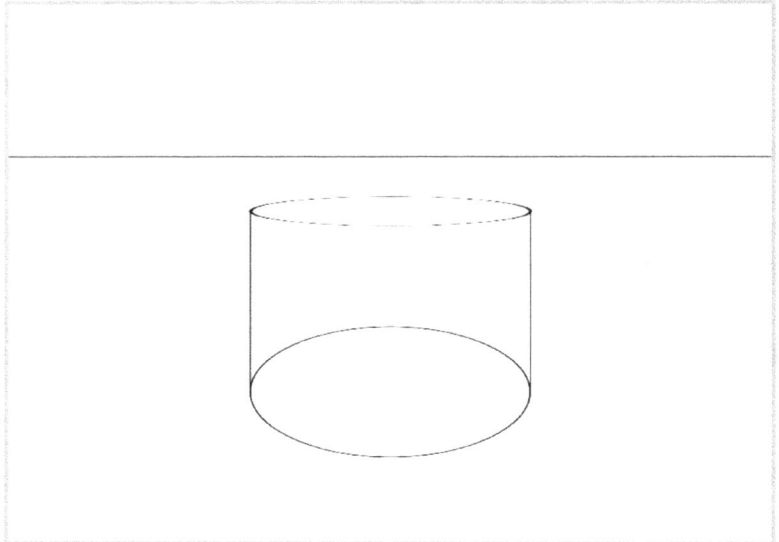

# Representation of Space and Perspective

# Shadows in Perspective Representation

And now that you have become acquainted with the most important fundamentals for drawing shadows, we can now tackle the issue of representing shadows in vanishing point perspective. We will begin with a simple exercise in which a rectangular solid is illuminated by a lamp.

## Light and Shadow from a Lamp

The starting point is a rectangular solid that is drawn in central perspective with one vanishing point. Moreover, this corresponds to the rectangular solid that was introduced in the first exercise of the book.

The second thing to be done is to determine the source of light. The source of light is shown as a gray point in the image below. The light source here could be, for instance, a street lamp, a floodlight or a ceiling lamp. By using a vertical line and a small black point, the position of the light source was also identified on the floor. This step is necessary so that the observer knows where the light source is located within the spatial depth.

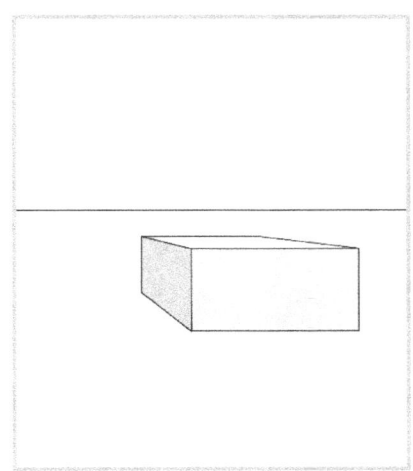
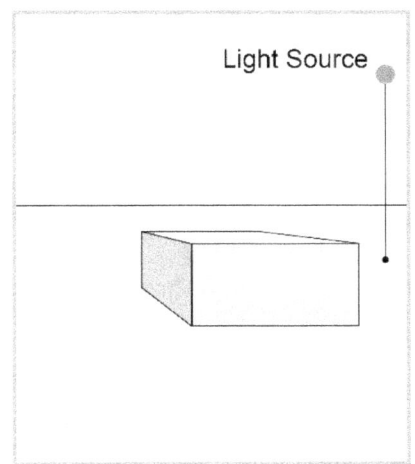

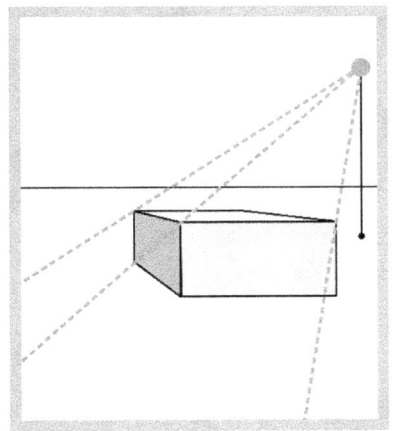
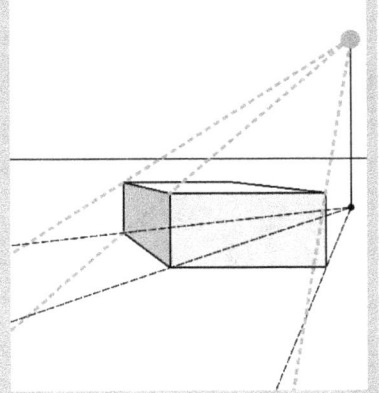

And now we draw rays of light that are emitted by the source of light. We first of all draw three rays of light to the three upper corner points that are positioned on the shadow side of the rectangular solid (drawing below left). These rays of light do not however end at the corner points; rather, they are extended out to the edge of the drawing.

Then three more (reference) lines are drawn which run from the floor point of the light source to the three lower corner points at the shadow side of the rectangular solid (drawing below right). These lines as well are to be extended out beyond the corner points.

After the previous steps have been taken, three intersection points have now emerged at that point where the rays of light intersect with the reference lines. These intersection points should now be connected together with two other reference lines, as shown in the image on the left below.

This step completes construction of the box's shadow. Extraneous reference lines are now erased, revealing the outline of the shadow (drawing on the right below).

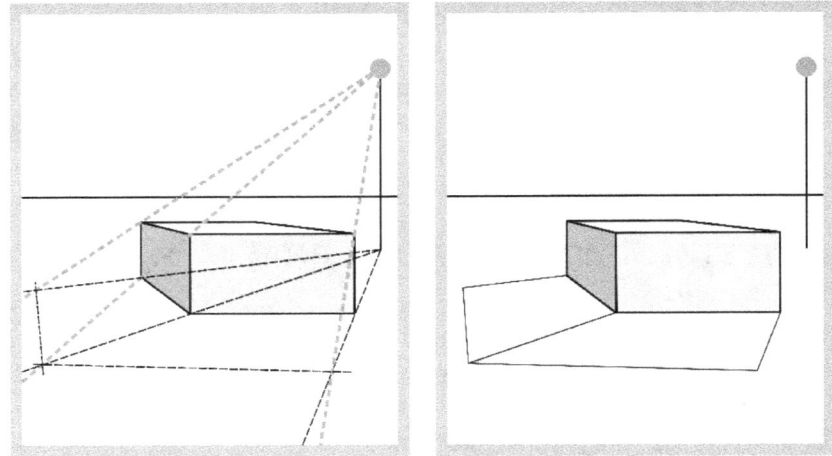

You can see in the next image on the left that the shadow just drawn is in accordance with the vanishing lines from our vanishing point. There is thus a logical correlation here.

In the drawing on the right, the shadow of the box has been shaded in with two different shades of gray – thus completing the drawing.

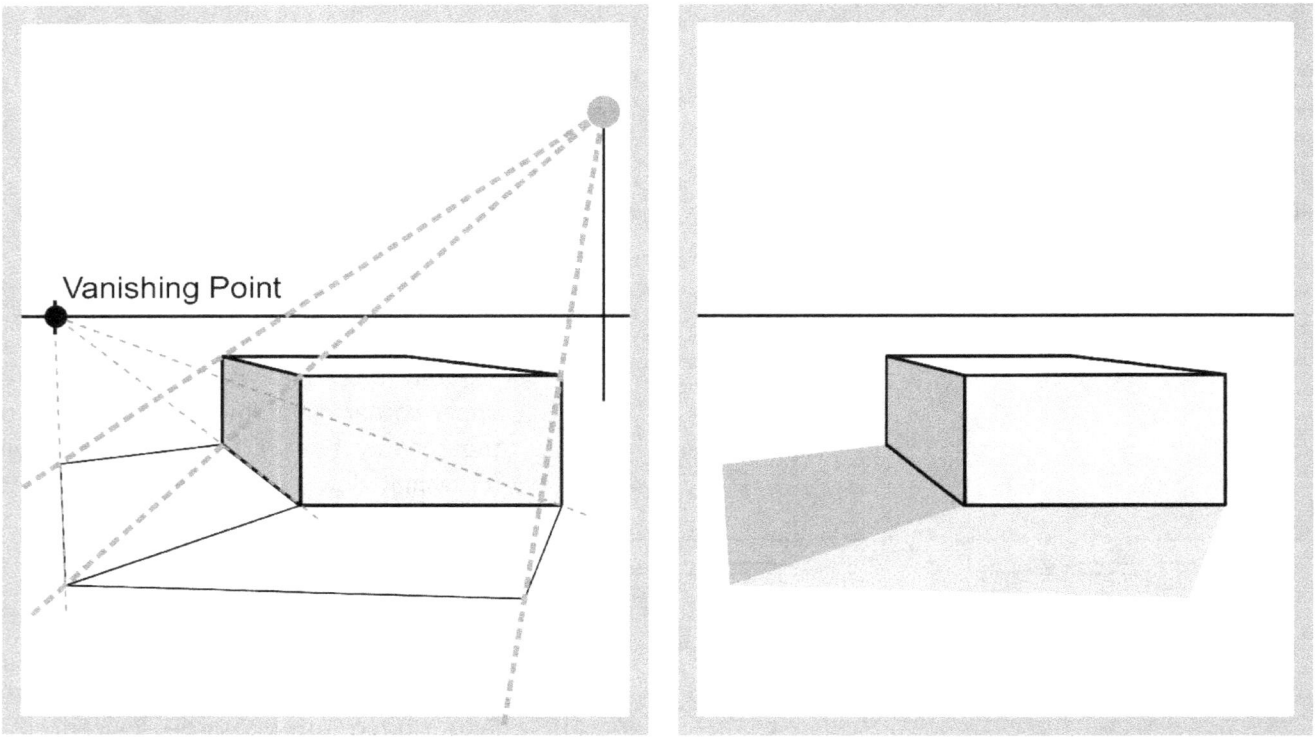

# The Sun as Light Source, and Shadows in Diagonal Perspective

In this example, we want to examine two different lessons: first of all, how to draw shadows when the sun functions as the source of light (as opposed to a lamp) and, secondly, we'll take a look at the construction of shadows in diagonal perspective.

## The sun as light source

In this example, the sun is in front of the observer. It would be a different case if the sun were shining on the observer's back. We'll take a look at this second situation later on.

If the sun, as in this example, is located in front of the observer, we can determine its position at any given point beyond the horizon. The critical difference in comparison to a lamp is its position within the depth of the room. We would still have to establish the depth position ourselves with the lamp example. The sun however is always located directly over the horizon line.
This means that the lower reference lines always extend from the horizon. Take a look at this in the following image.

## Shadows in diagonal perspective

As you can see from the image, construction of the shadow in diagonal perspective works the same way as central perspective. Here as well, we see the three rays of light and three reference lines on the ground. The points of intersection for these lines are connected by further lines and the hard shadow of the object emerges.

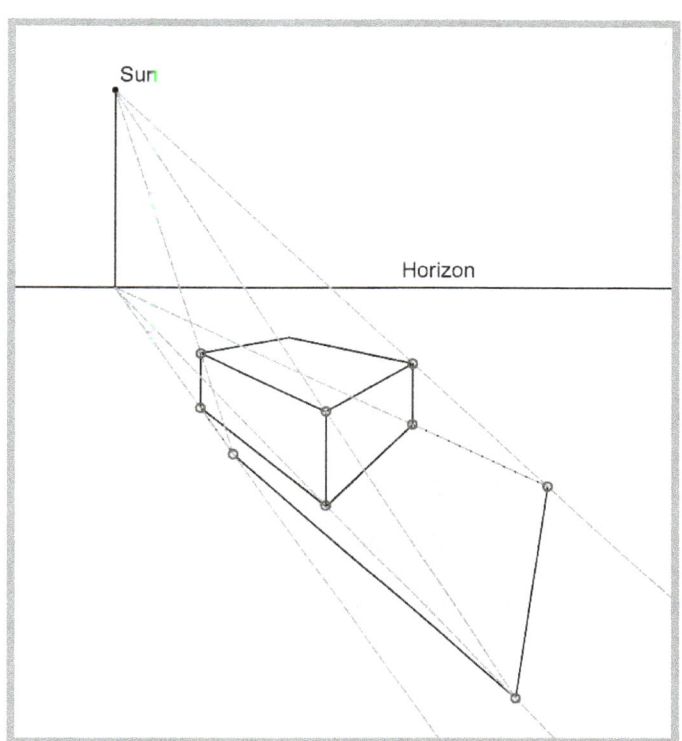

# Example 1 – Cartons and Boxes in Perspective

Now let's draw a still life in vanishing point perspective as an exercise. You can use the following drawings as a guide or you can draw your own still life. However, do not target objects that are too complex. It's best to start with a few simple boxes that have different orientations.

The following drawing shows an example in which some vanishing points are also a little further away. Note that each box has its own pair of vanishing points as the boxes are positioned with different orientations.

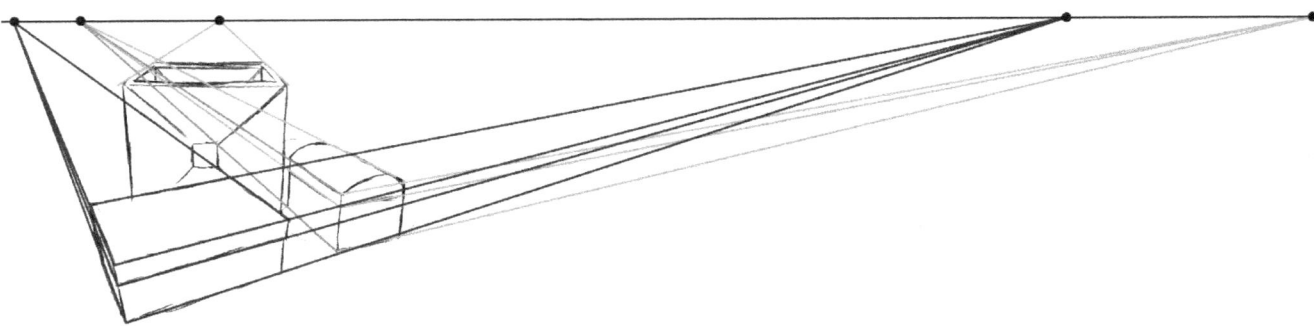

However, on the paper only a section of the image is shown in which the vanishing points are not visible. This makes drawing a little more difficult, because you have to mark the points on the drawing board or something similar. The picture on the right shows the drawing after all vanishing lines have been erased.

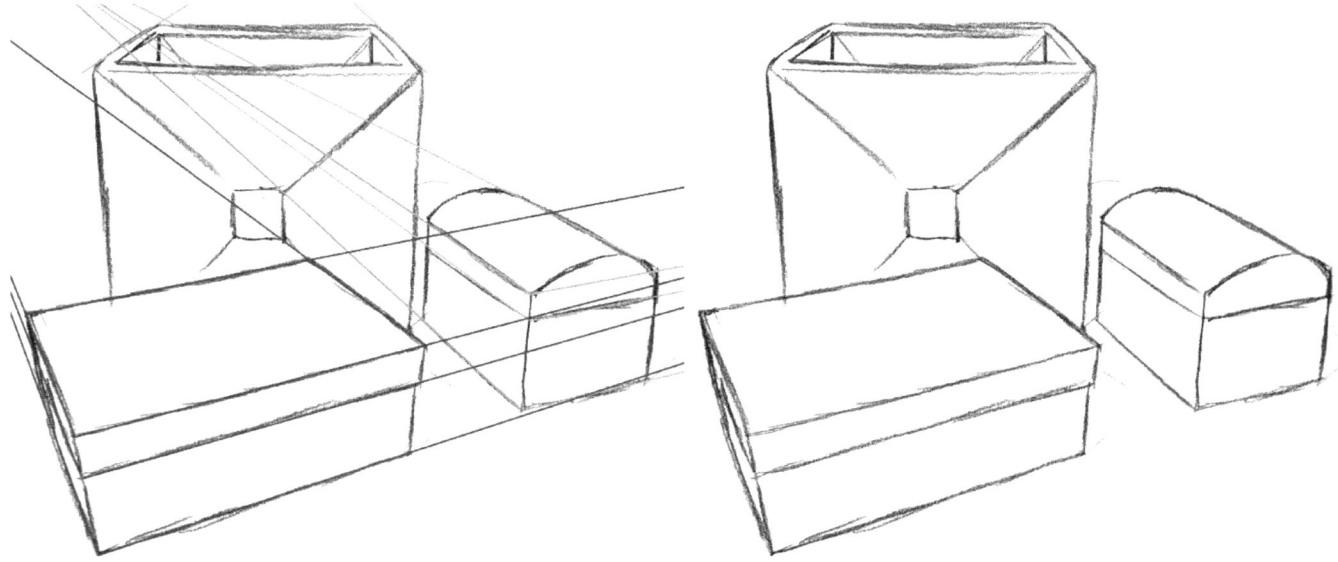

# Representation of Space and Perspective

After a little work with hatching and structuring, we created a nice still life on the paper.
The use of the vanishing point perspective makes the drawing look very realistic.

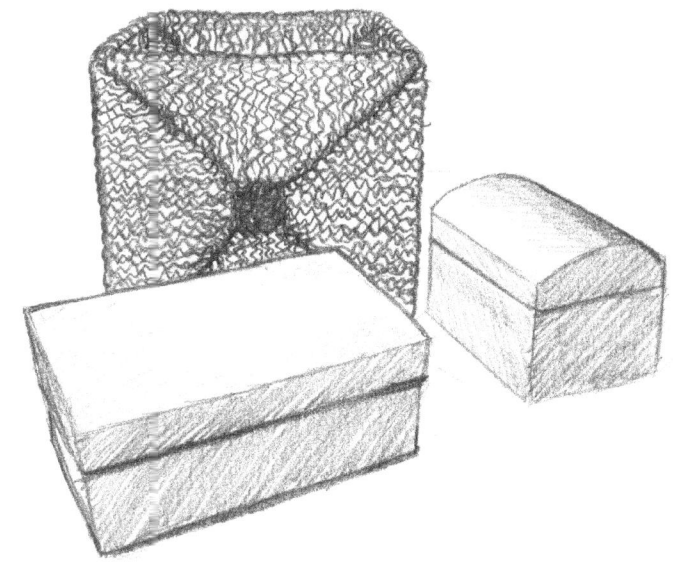

# Example 2 – Still Life in Perspective

An even more complex example is shown in the next still life with cartons and boxes. The bodies shown are still kept very simple, but the construction of this arrangement with vanishing points is already much more complex.

The fact that the still life was drawn in a vanishing point perspective is not visible at first glance. But it is exactly through the use of this method that the drawing appears extremely authentic. In addition, the entire drawing is completely imaginary and the arrangement never existed in reality. As you can see, creating your own still lifes with the help of the construction method with vanishing points is very accurate.

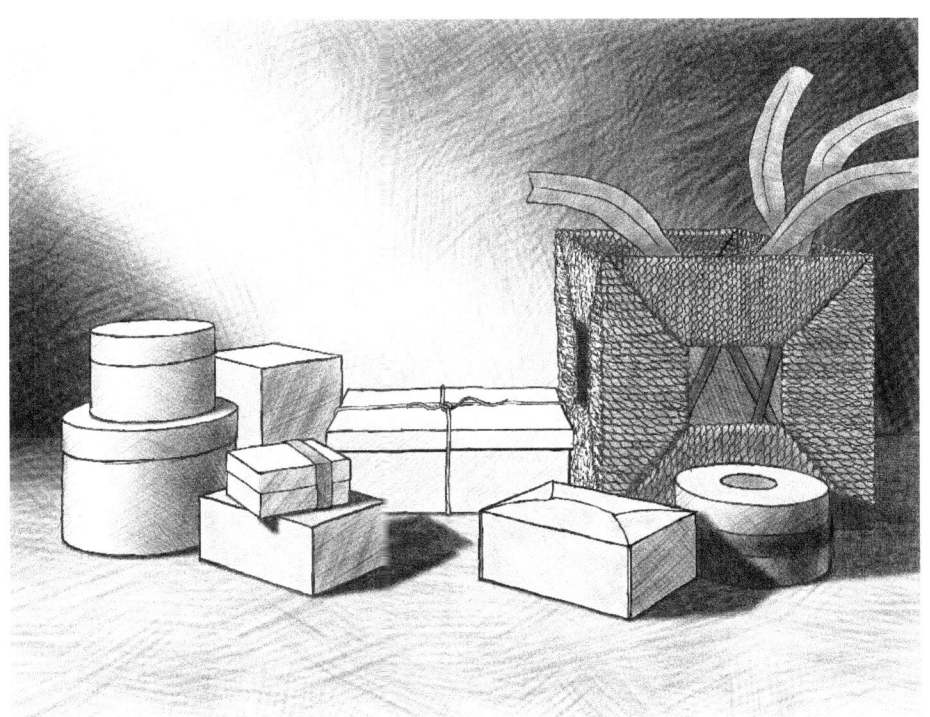

# Picture Design and Composition

*» In the design – talent emerges, but in the execution – art. «*

- Marie Freifrau von Ebner-Eschenbach -

# Picture Design and Composition

The success of a painting does not only depend on artistic and craft skills. From the very beginning, a lot of attention should be paid to the harmonious design of the picture. The more thought the artist invests prior to the first stroke on the paper or canvas, the more beautiful the picture can become. The depiction of a natural scene on flat paper is subject to its own laws of drawing and painting. Therefore, after the selection of the motif, it is worthwhile to think carefully about how it will be implemented on the canvas or drawing surface.

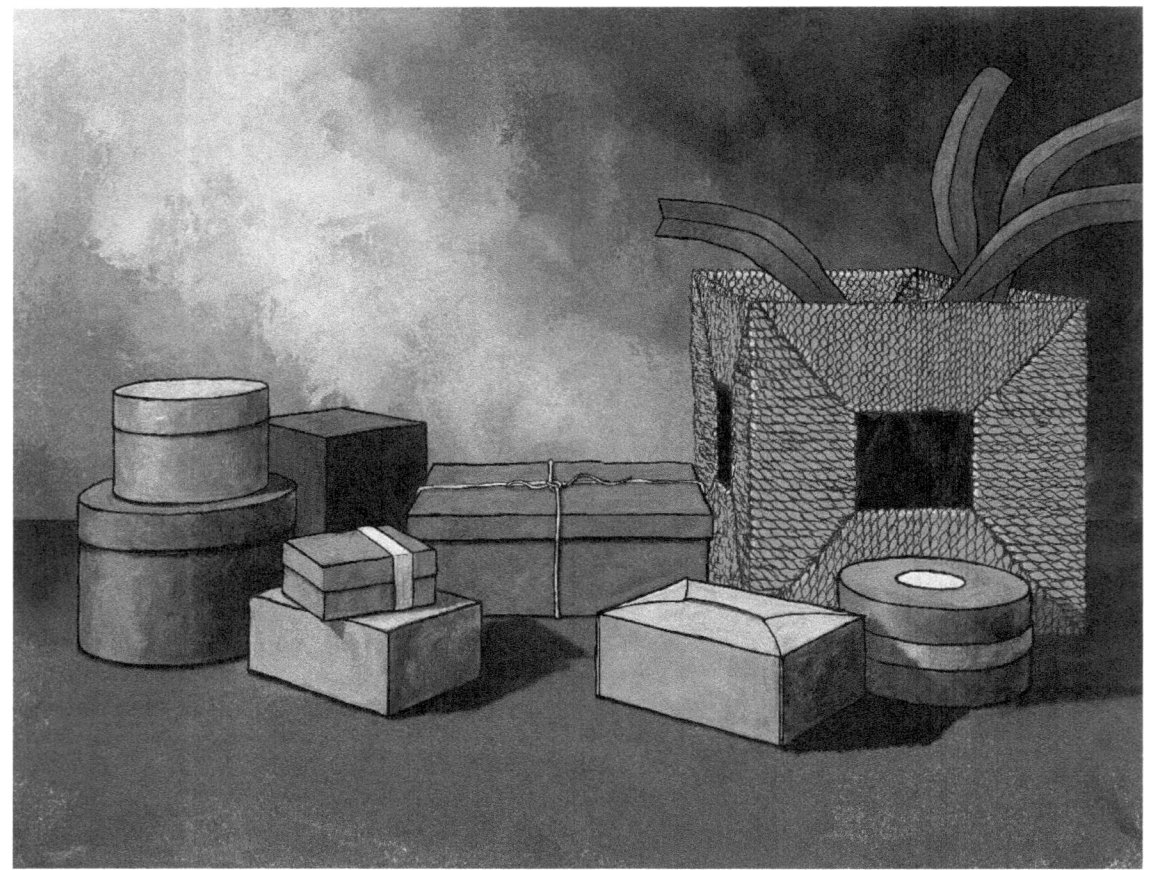
*Still life with boxes*

From my own experience I can confirm that one can improve a picture considerably with a certain amount of planning. From a relatively static and unexciting presentation you can develop your own picture into an interesting and dynamic work of art. In retrospect, I was always glad that I didn't spontaneously start the final picture with the first idea, but rather gave the composition the opportunity to really develop itself. By means of small tricks and improvements the picture effect can already be increased quite a bit. Sketches always help me a lot.

# Methods for Subdividing an Image

In this chapter we deal with methods of image subdivision. This is one of the most important composition techniques, because subdividing a picture is an enormous help for us in the creative process. With the subdivision of the basis for the image, one determines in principle the basic structure of the work. The methods presented here help the artist to create a successful composition that can appear balanced or even exciting. However, one should always be aware that the described techniques are only orientation aids. It is neither a panacea nor a guarantee that a good picture will be created in the end.

## Symmetry – Center Lines and Diagonals

In image composition using central axes, the image is divided into two halves of equal size. The center axes can be used individually or together. The diagonals extend from one corner of the image to the other. This method can be used again and again with landscape pictures.

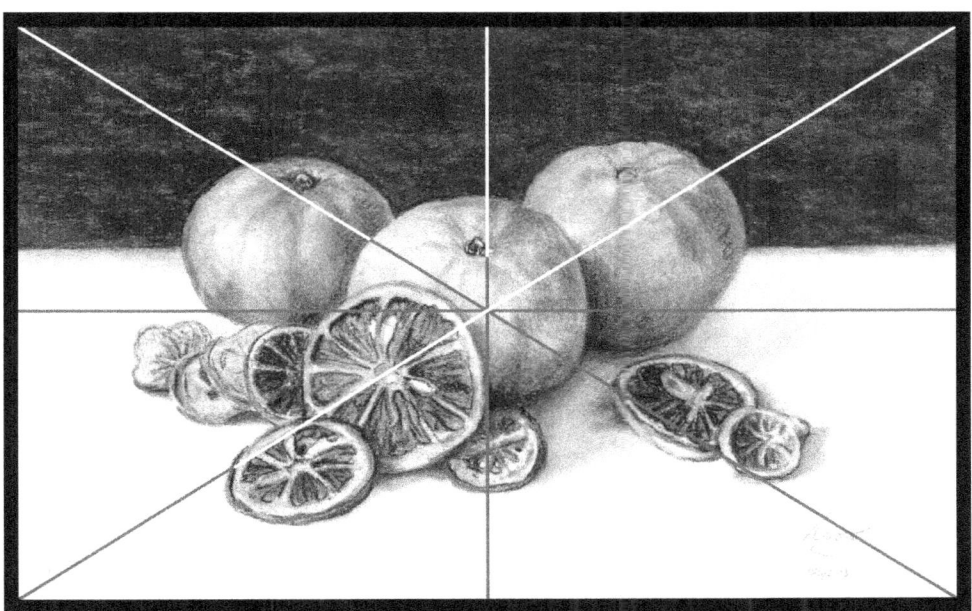

*Symmetrical structures in a still life with tangerines*

Composition of pictures by means of central axes and diagonals was often used in the Renaissance, since paintings in this period were often constructed symmetrically. Nowadays, this method is rarely used, as the opinion that the main motif should not be placed in the middle has prevailed.

# The Golden Ratio

The golden ratio is an aid for subdividing images according to a defined ratio. The resulting lines can be used to align image objects. The subdivision can be used both vertically and horizontally. In addition, the subdivision can be made in such a way that the entire image is subdivided into nine rectangles. The intersection points that result can also be used to align image objects. The golden ratio is one of the best known design techniques and is very often used for landscape motifs.

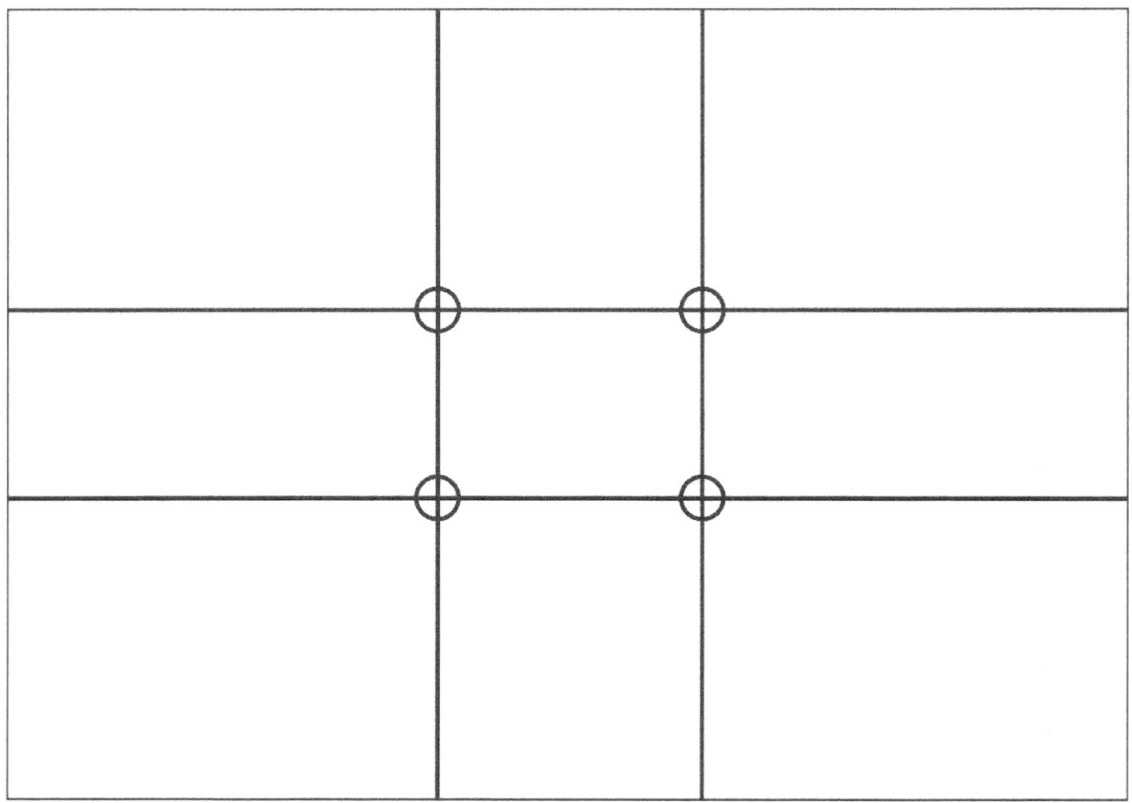

*Golden ratio with intersections*

Orientation according to these lines and intersections can help to create a harmonious image composition. However, the golden ratio is never a guarantee for the creation of a good image. It is - among many other design techniques – purely an aid, the use of which also requires experience.

# Applying the Golden Ratio

Subdivision according to the principle of the golden ratio ensues by means of the following formula:

$$\frac{a+b}{a} = \frac{a}{b} \quad \text{or} \quad \frac{a}{a+b} = \frac{b}{a}$$

If we consider the overall length of a side to be 100%, then the individual lengths of a=61.8% and b=38.2% are what emerge.

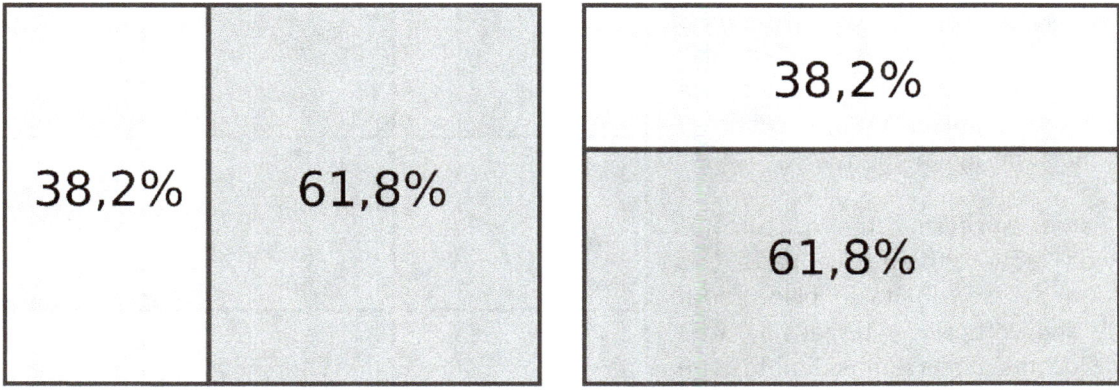

*Segmentation according to the golden ratio*

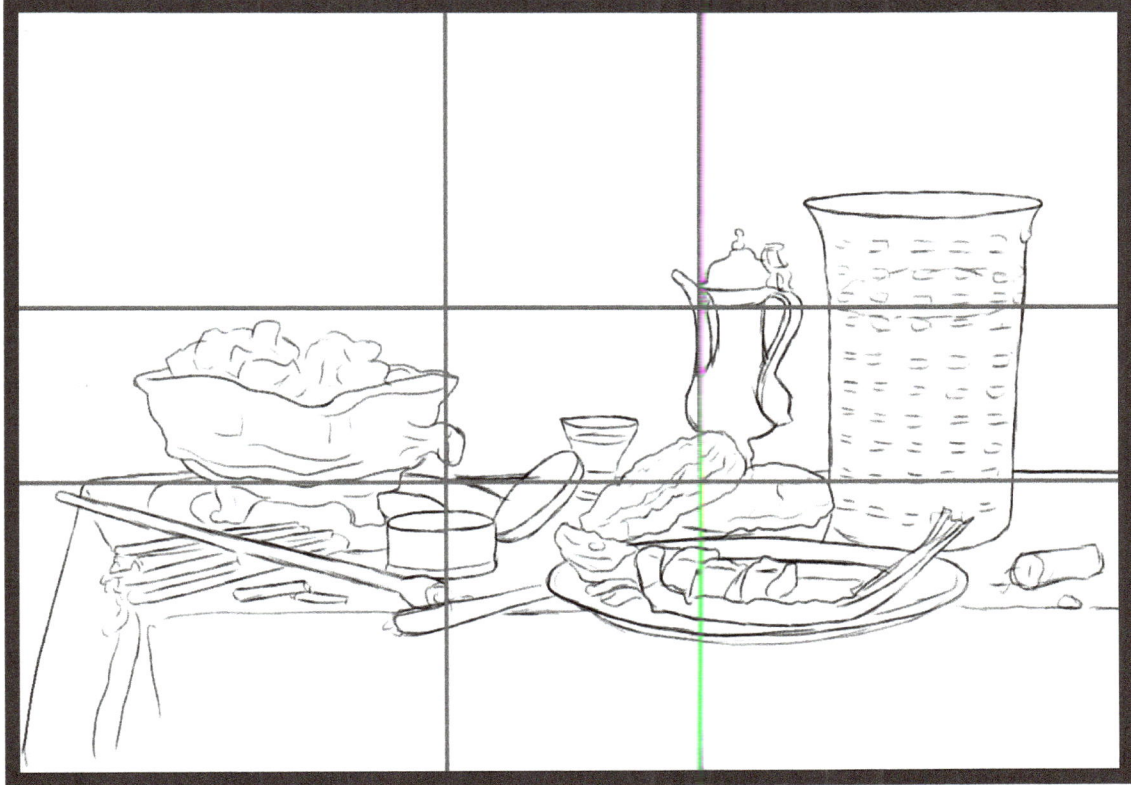

*Still life drawing with the golden ratio as orientation*

It is noteworthy that the orientation according to the relationship of the golden ratio comes from nature and can be found again and again in natural forms. This is probably the reason why division according to the golden ratio is perceived as particularly harmonious by humans.

Examples of the occurrence of the golden ratio in nature are the dimensions of an ivy leaf or the arrangement of leaves in various plants. This is also referred to as the golden angle, which is about 137.5°.

# The Rule of Thirds

The "rule of thirds" is a composition aid based on the subdivision of pictures according to the rules of the golden ratio. The rule of thirds is mainly known from photography, but also plays an important role in other areas of the visual arts. Like the golden ratio, it is one of the most popular design methods.

As the name suggests, the picture is imaginarily divided into three equal parts. This division into thirds can take place both horizontally and vertically. Alternatively, it is usual to divide the picture directly into nine equal fields, which are very helpful for the design.

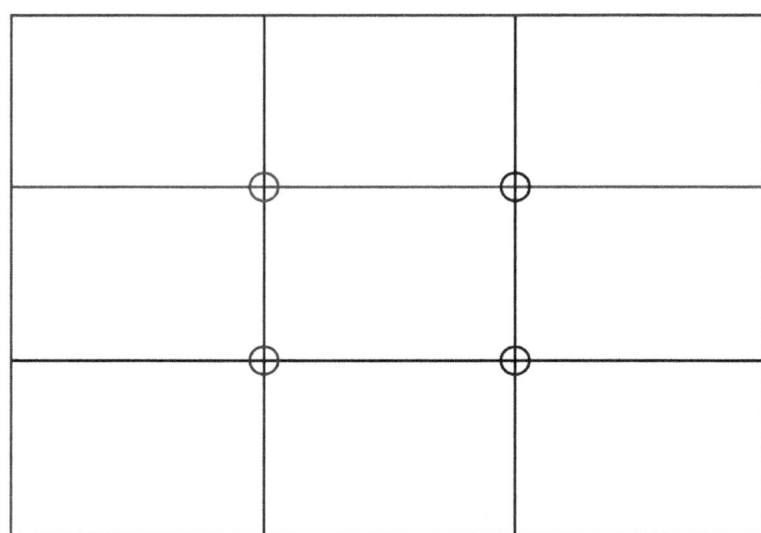

*Subdividing into thirds with intersections*

There are intersections between the subdivision lines which can also be used as composition aids. Often good images are created by placing the main motif on one of these intersections. With these aids it is possible to create harmonious compositions and to bind the viewer to the optical design.

When applying the rule of thirds, however, be aware that the rule of thirds - contrary to what the name may promise - is not a fixed rule, but rather a design aid. The use of this method does not guarantee an appealing composition. The aim of the rule of thirds is above all to prevent the main motif from being placed in the center of the image, as this is usually boring and static.

You can use the rule of thirds without any further aids. If you like, you can also sketch the subdivision lines on paper beforehand. However, the image is usually divided into nine parts rather than three. With this help you will orient yourself to the subdivision lines when positioning your motif. You can skip the center, or place elements there that do not flow, or only subordinately flow, into the picture design.

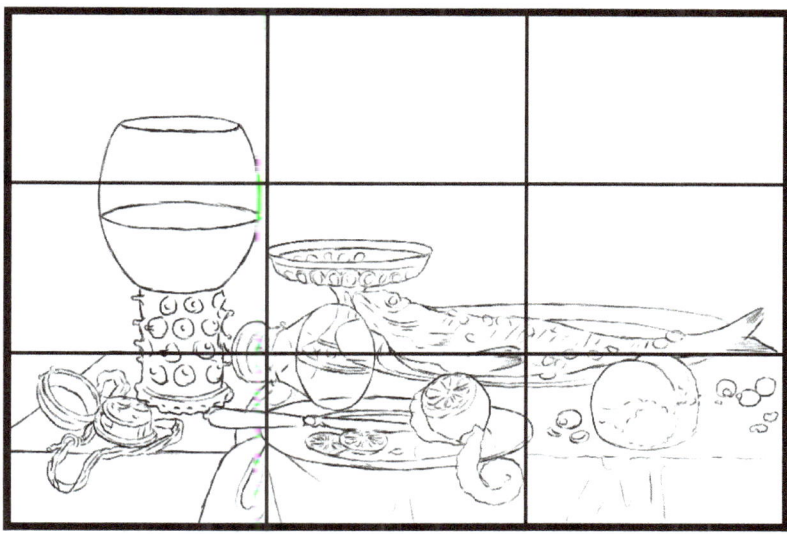

*Rule of thirds recognizable on a still life (sketch of a painting made by Willem Claesz Heda)*

Make sure that you move the most important design elements to the side. However, it is important not to push them too far to the edge. As already mentioned, you can also use the four intersection points to create the picture. Often it is very appealing if striking elements of the picture composition are positioned at these points.

# Lines as an Element of Design

When we speak of lines as a design element, we mean visible lines in an image. So here we are not talking about lines that serve to align objects, such as the golden ratio. Rather, it is about lines created by the objects themselves and the effect these lines have on the viewer. On the one hand, this effect can be emotional, for example by conveying feelings such as stability, narrowness or dynamism. Dynamic features, such as movement in a certain direction, can also be visualized by lines. On the other hand, lines often guide the viewer's gaze through the picture, which is of great importance for a successful picture composition.

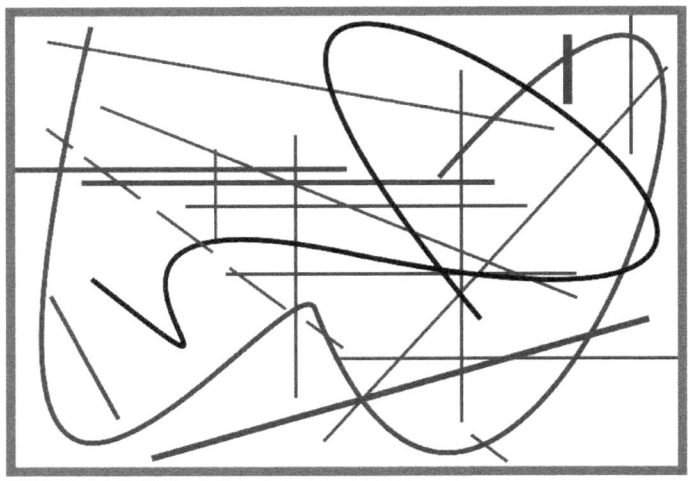

*Lines in different directions*

Lines can be created by copying a concrete line. This technique is often used in drawings and illustrations. On the other hand, lines can also be created by boundaries, for example in places where light and shadow separate, where surfaces with different tonal values adjoin each other, or where different patterns or structures meet. In this way, lines emerge, especially in paintings and photographs.

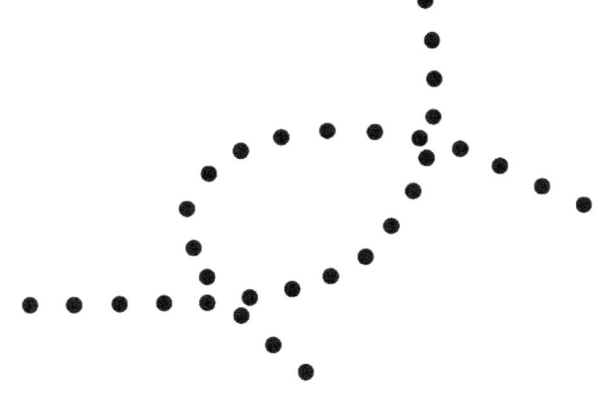

*Dots become two lines*

A series of dots can also be mentally completed to form a line by the viewer if the dots are close enough to each other and describe a continuous line. One thinks here of the Gestalt (form) law of proximity or also the law of good continuation.

## Horizontal Lines

A picture inevitably contains at least two horizontal lines: The upper and lower sides of the frame. The third horizontal line in many pictures is the horizon. Especially in landscape paintings the horizon is the basis for the composition. It represents the reference lines for all contained objects and conveys the feeling of gravity in the pictorial world.

What the viewer associates with horizontal lines are properties such as stability and tranquillity. Our field of vision is aligned horizontally, so horizontal lines can be used to create the effect of space and depth. However, these lines are not very dynamic and bring little movement into the composition.

## Vertical Lines

As with horizontal lines, there are automatically at least two vertical lines in an image that are created by the image frame. If you allow more vertical lines to appear in the image, they can create a certain visual balance together with horizontal lines.

Vertical lines are more likely to represent speed and motion than horizontal lines. However, if used awkwardly, they can act as a barrier or grid. In addition, vertical lines can quickly lead the viewer's gaze out of the image if the gaze is not recaptured by other design elements. At the edge of the picture, on the other hand, they can serve as blockades that keep the gaze in the picture. Portrait is the best format for displaying a single vertical line in an image. The landscape format is ideal for compositions in which several vertical lines are represented that form a horizontal structure.

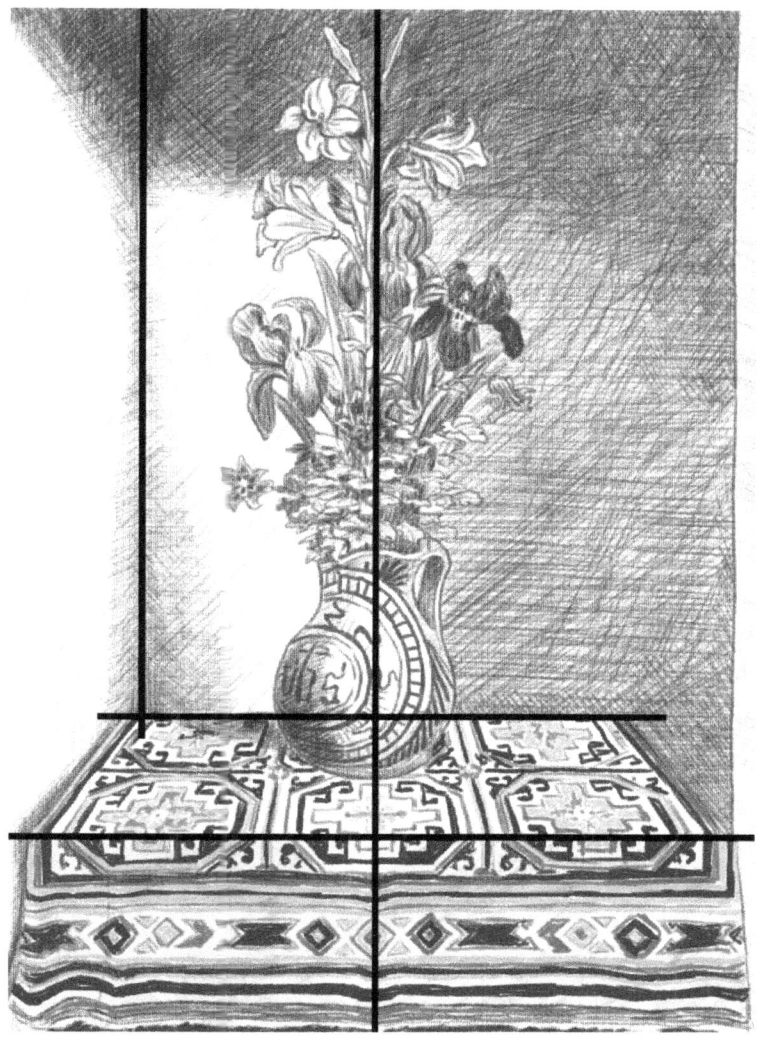

*Horizontal and vertical lines in a still life*
*Drawing after a painting made by Hans Memling „Vase with Flowers"*

# Diagonal Lines

The image design can be made more dynamic with diagonal lines, which are more interesting and effective. While horizontal and vertical lines appear rather static, diagonal lines create a high degree of dynamics. With diagonal lines the viewer suggests movement and speed. Additional tension can be created by displaying diagonals at different angles. The higher the difference in the angle of the various lines the greater the resulting contrast. A single diagonal is sufficient, since each diagonal line creates a contrast with the vertical and horizontal lines of the picture frame. The maximum contrast is created by diagonals at a 45° angle.

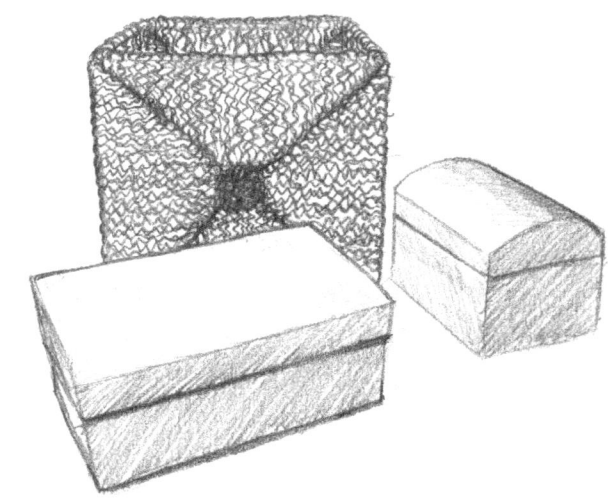

*Diagonal lines in different directions creating tension in a simple still life*

Another special feature of diagonal lines is that they can convey an impression of space and depth. This makes them perfect for landscape drawings. Only diagonal lines can make the perspective effect visible. The depth effect can unfold particularly intensively when an oblique point of view is displayed on picture objects. In general, diagonals are often a product of the viewing angle, since most scenes and objects actually consist primarily of horizontal and vertical lines. From a drawing point of view, the objects are then depicted in so-called two-point perspective.

## Curves

Curves are lines that represent a particularly robust but also more difficult-to-master design element. Curves appear elegant and at the same time dynamic to the observer. They convey an extremely bold feeling of movement and speed, which is a much stronger effect than diagonals are capable of creating. This is because curves are created by a continuous change of direction, which is typical of motion sequences.

As is the case with diagonal lines, the eye of the observer effortlessly follows a curve that can be seen in a picture. In this way, the eye can be guided through the picture.

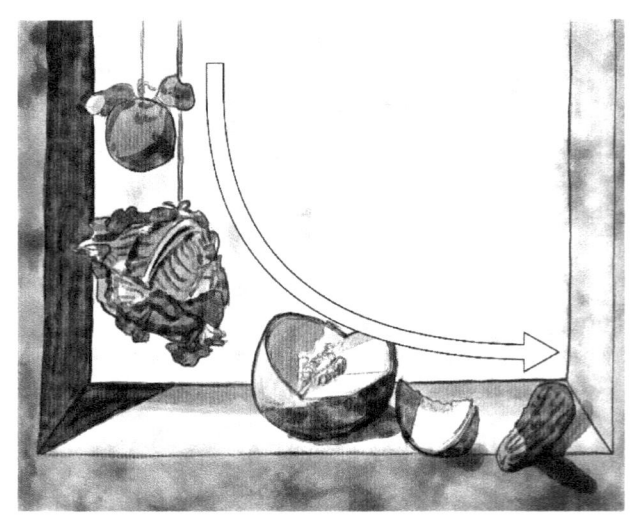

*Arrangement of the objects allows a curve to emerge. Drawing after a painting by J. S. Cotán*

# Contours

The contour refers to the outline (also silhouette) of a figurative element. Contours are an important design element in painting and drawing. In painting, contours are created by clear color transitions in a very small space. For example, a transition from blue to yellow produces a visible contour. Even strong differences in tonal value in a small space make a contour visible.

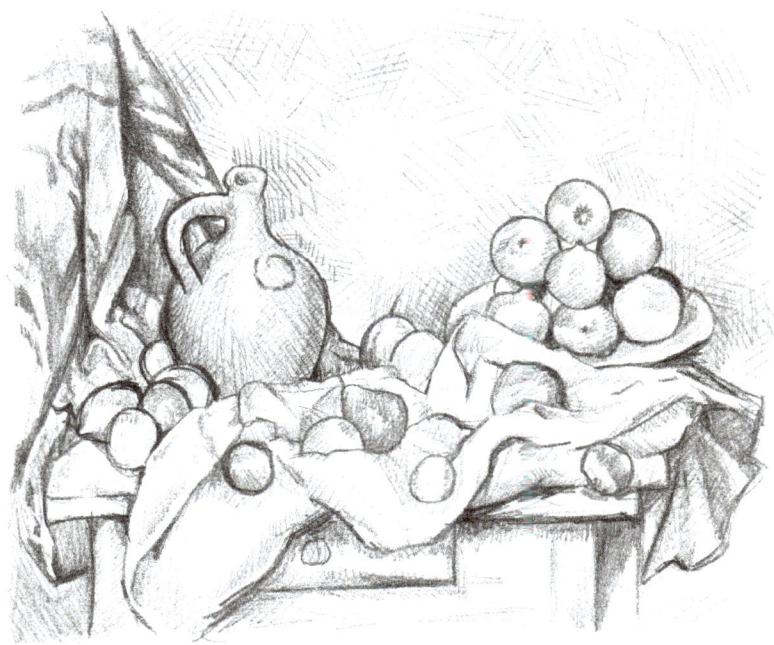

*Drawing with clearly defined contours*
*Sketch after a still life by Paul Cézanne "Still Life with Curtain, Jug and Bowl of Fruit"*

Depending on how pronounced the contours are, you can develop a very dominant characteristic in the picture and significantly shape the overall impression of a picture. As mentioned previously, you can also use them to give a painting an aesthetic and graphic impression. Image design with contours is also successful through the rhythm of the contours. They can be round and curved but also angular and dramatic.

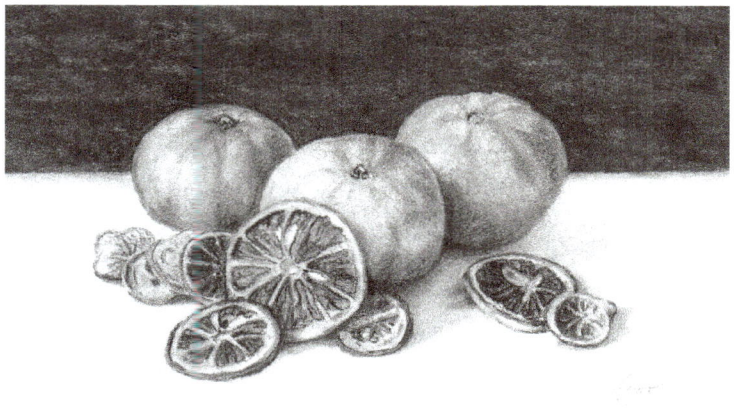

*Illustration without explicitly-drawn countours*

# Form

Every surface that is limited in a work of art (even if it is simply the edge of the picture) indicates a form. Fundamental to the perception of forms are the simplest basic forms. These basic forms are the triangle, the circle, the oval, the square and the rectangle. Geometric shapes stand for certain characteristics. They can simply be present due to the outline of the motif, but can also be created by several objects that together form a certain shape. Thus geometrical forms are also very suitable as design elements to arrange objects in a picture.

## Triangular Composition

One of the most frequently used stylistic devices, which we can discover again and again in still lifes, is the triangular composition. The triangle as a principle of arrangement of pictorial objects embodies clarity, calm and harmony. The form appears solid like a mountain and thus automatically gives the viewer a feeling of stability.

In many still lifes one can differentiate between two types of triangular composition: The right-angle triangle and the pyramid form.

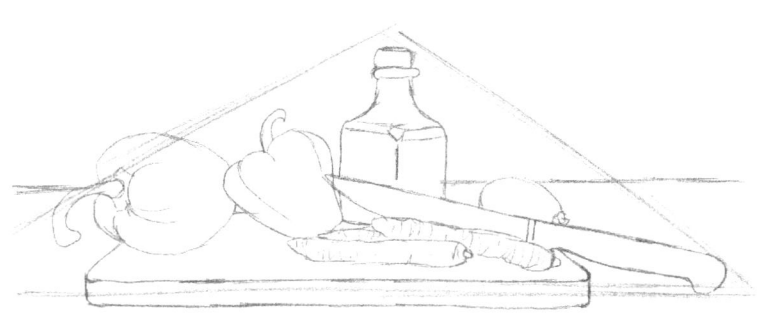

*Draft of a still life in a triangular composition*

### Right-angled triangle composition

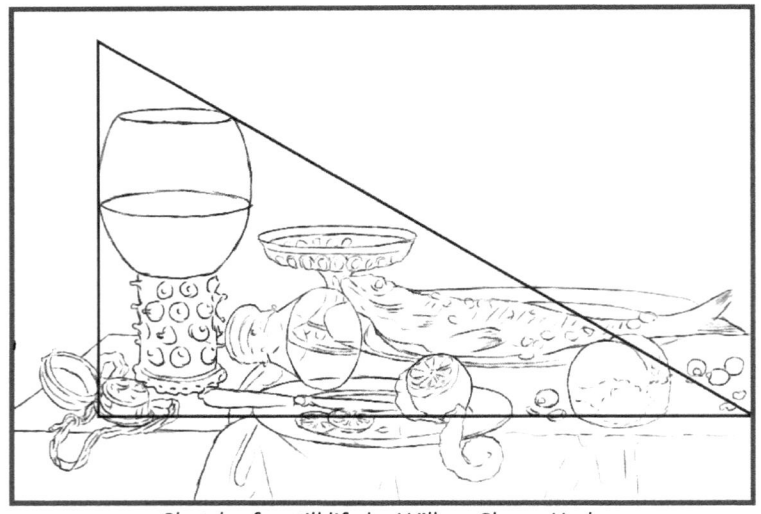

*Sketch of a still life by Willem Claesz Heda "Still Life with Roman-Style Wine Glass and Watch", 1629*

The right-angled triangular composition is an arrangement on the table that starts from one of the two vertical sides of the picture. The vertical side of the triangle is located far to the right or left of the image and forms a right angle with the horizontal lower side of the triangle.

With this example of arrangement there is only one compositional support. The mid-section of the picture usually leads the eye automatically out of the centre of the picture.

# Picture Design and Composition

## Pyramids

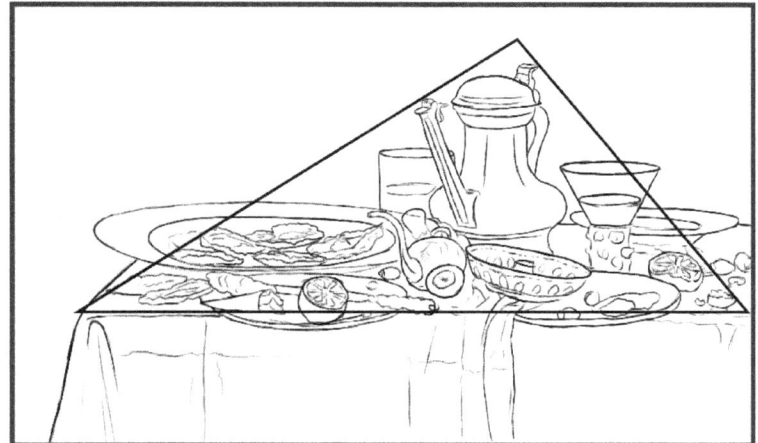

*Sketch of a Still Life after Willem Claesz Heda*
*"Still Life with Pewterware"*

The pyramid shape can correspond to an isosceles triangle - but it does not have to. The diagonal pyramid is more popular, as here the centre of gravity of the composition comes out of the middle of the image. This makes pictures look less static - think also of the compositional techniques of the golden section and the rule of thirds. This scheme as well is arranged with only one compositional support.

## Double triangle

A variation of this is the double triangle, in which two triangles are arranged into an overall composition.

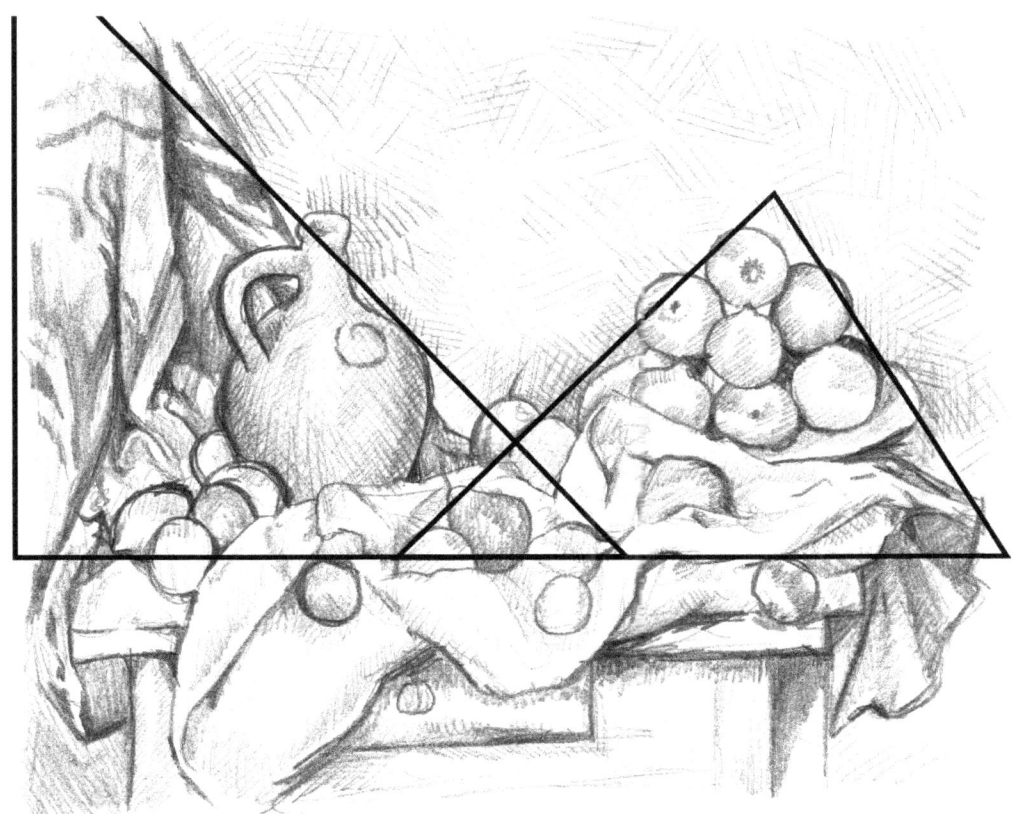

*Sketch after a still life by Paul Cezanne*
*„Still Life with Curtain, Jug and Bowl of Fruit", ca. 1894*

# Circles and Ovals

Circles and oval shapes in the composition of the picture create the effect of unity. Everything that is within this geometric form is bound within it. In addition, round forms create a certain feeling of movement – i.e. rotation.

In order for the shape of a circle or oval in a picture to be recognized as such, it must be very clearly outlined and easily recognizable. The difficulty in achieving this is due to the fact that circles and ovals are often difficult to find or create. A popular example can be found in still lifes. Here, fruits, vegetables or other compositional objects can be placed in a round bowl, which is then viewed from one angle, typically from above.

However, when using this composition aid, the illustrator should always bear in mind that circles and ovals capture the attention of the observer very strongly. For this reason, these forms should be deployed with care and very specifically.

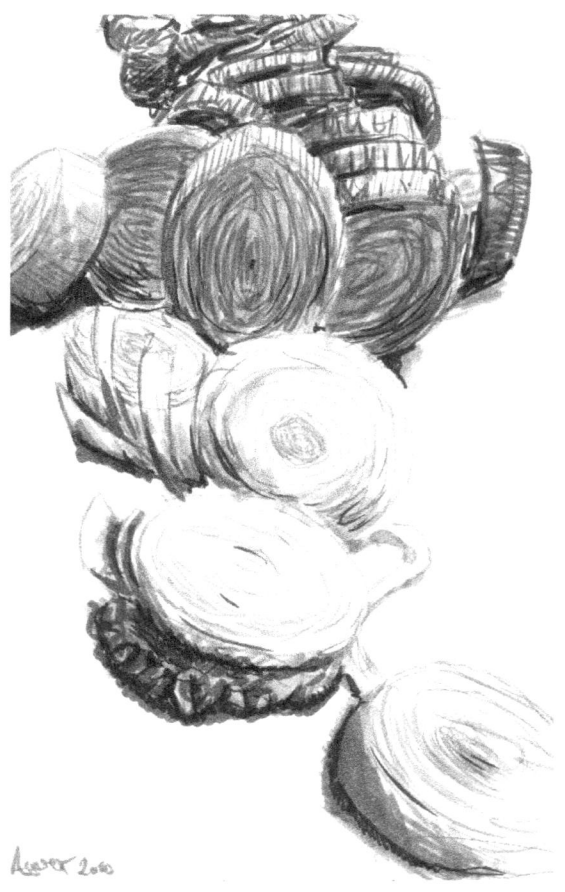

*Still life with sliced leeks*

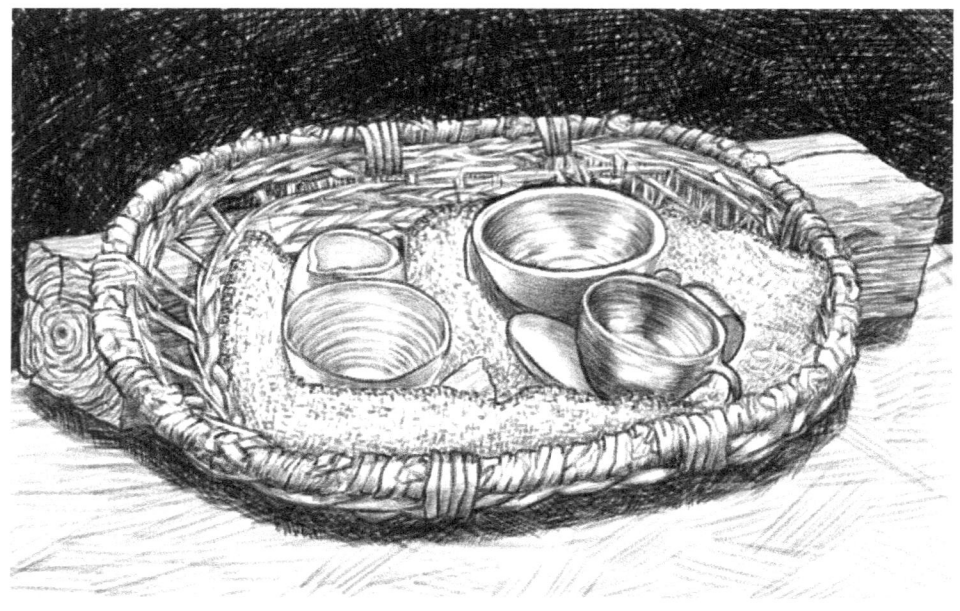

*Still lifes with cups in an oval basket*

Picture Design and Composition

## Squares and Rectangles

The rectangle as a geometrical composition aid is rarely used. The shape does not correspond to typical natural forms and occurs primarily in man-made objects. In still lifes, rectangular objects are often arranged in combination with round objects to create a contrast. Also the application in the form of a frame within a picture can be seen again and again.

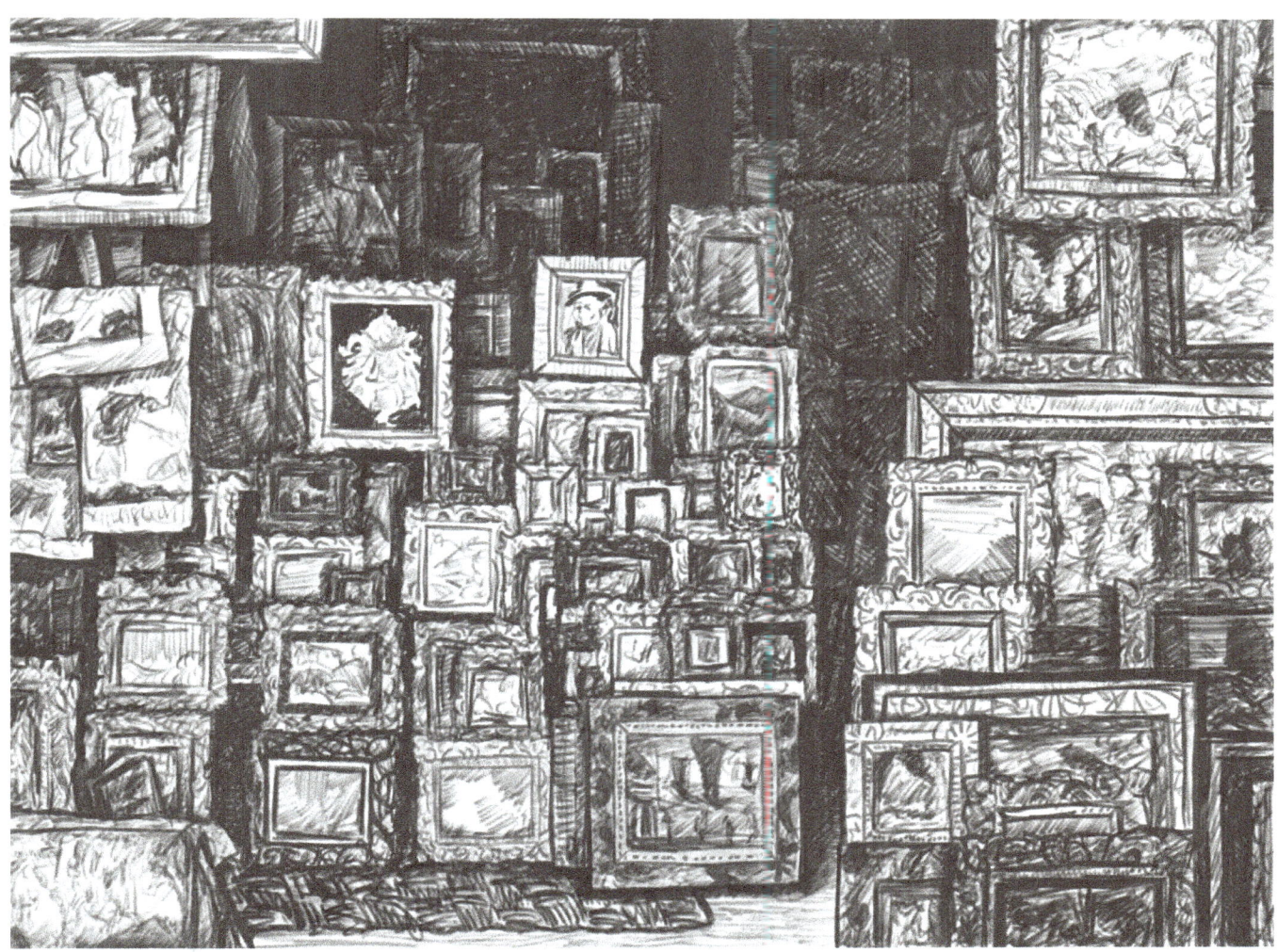

*Still life with pictures and frames*

When using rectangles in the composition, however, it must be borne in mind that these strictly geometric forms appear static and motionless. As a rule, they do not create any dynamics or movement in the picture. Rather, one associates rectangles - above all the square - with gravity, solidity, precision and the sharp demarcation from their environment. These are various aspects that should be taken into account when creating a picture, but can also be used in a targeted manner.

# Further Design Elements

In addition to the methods for arranging the picture plane and the graphic design elements, there are other possibilities for design techniques which, although they are of equal significance for the composition of the picture, function in a different manner.

## Light-Dark Contrast

The light-dark contrast results from the different brightness of elements. This tonal value contrast can occur with the uncolored colors black, white and gray, but is also found with the primary and secondary colors to the same extent. In the case of chromatic colors, one speaks of the color brightness.

Light-dark contrast is used very frequently and very specifically in image design. It can be used to add depth to an image or to draw attention to certain elements. For example, surfaces with the same brightness appear to be on the same plane. Strong tonal contrast, on the other hand, creates plasticity. Bright elements appear as if they are further in the foreground, while dark elements recede into the background. Painters and draughtsmen consciously use the light-dark contrast to clearly separate light and shadow. In the motif depicted, the contours become more recognizable, which leads to an impression of corporeality and three-dimensionality.

Strong contrasts are also a tool for directing the viewer's gaze to the most important areas of the picture. Display the elements of your drawing that you want to focus on with the strongest contrast. Dragging the less important areas with low contrast will take away the attraction.

The other effect of light-dark contrast is the weighting of picture elements or picture areas. Because bright elements attract the viewer's attention, they appear more important than things that lie in the dark. This method can be found in countless pictures of different artists from different epochs in art history. Again and again it can be seen that the significant elements are depicted in a bright light, while things that the viewer is not supposed to deal with any further are obscured in the darkness and disappear.

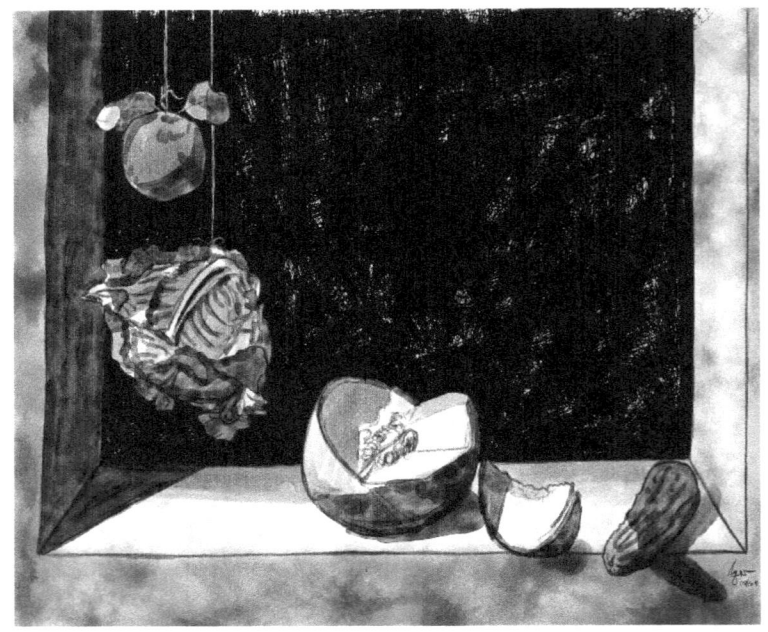

*Still life with strong light-dark contrast*
*Drawing after a painting by J. S. Cotán*

Picture Design and Composition

# Perspective and Space

The term perspective refers to the angle from which the artist depicts the motif. Conversely, it is also the point of view from which the viewer sees the scene. The perspective changes automatically when the artist moves - be it up, down, left, right, forwards or backwards. Every inclination or new orientation of the vista also changes the perspective.

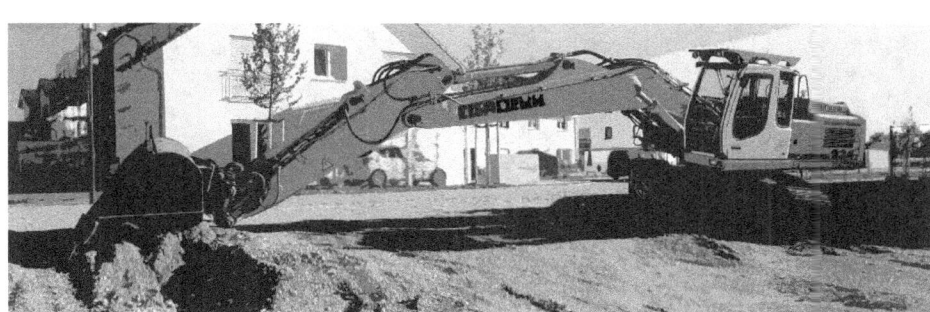
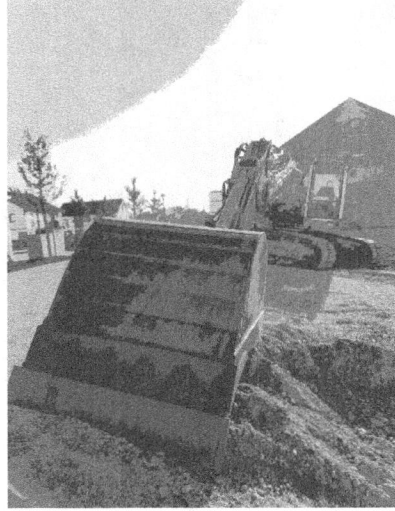
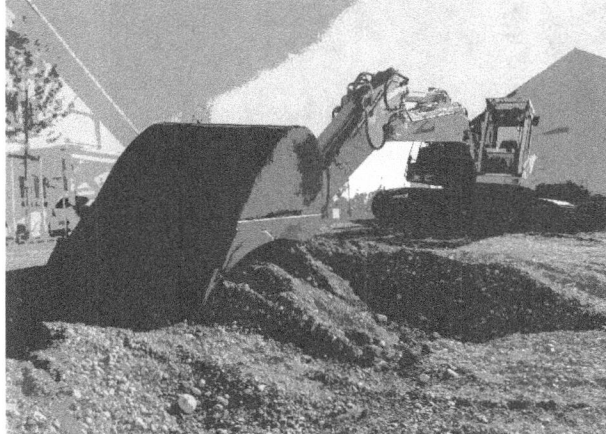
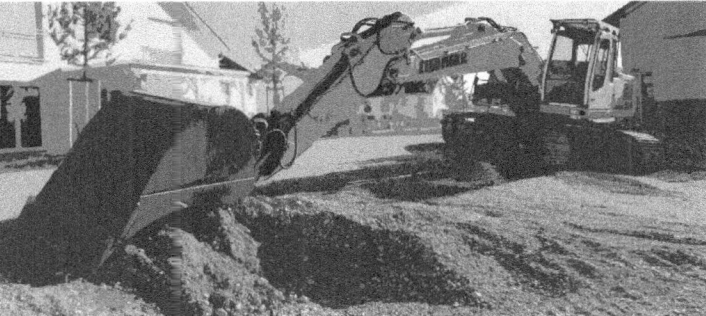

*The same excavator from different viewpoints*

Perspective is a particularly powerful instrument of image design, as it can be used to directly influence the effect of the image and to create targeted effects. The view from above (bird's eye view), for example, creates a completely different impression than the view from a low point of view - even if nothing else changes in the motif.

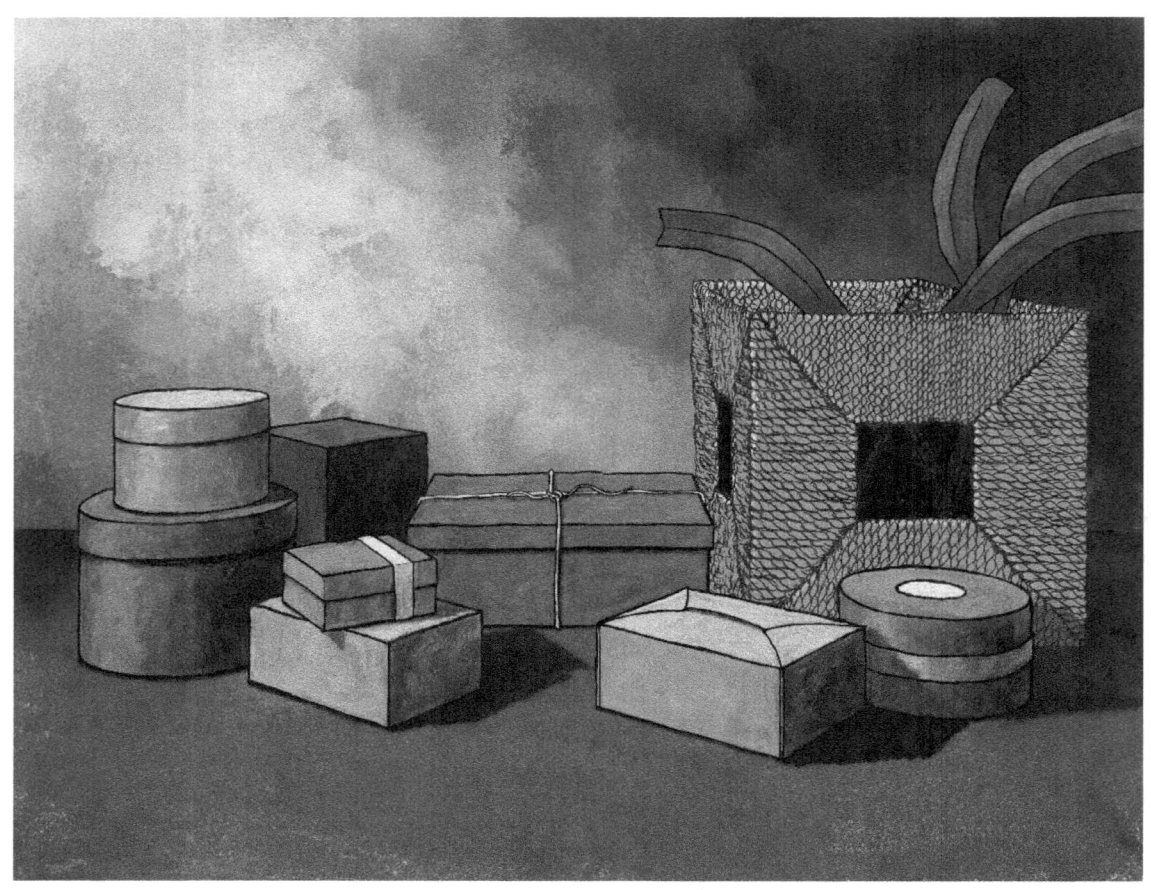

*Example of a still life drawn in vanishing point perspective*

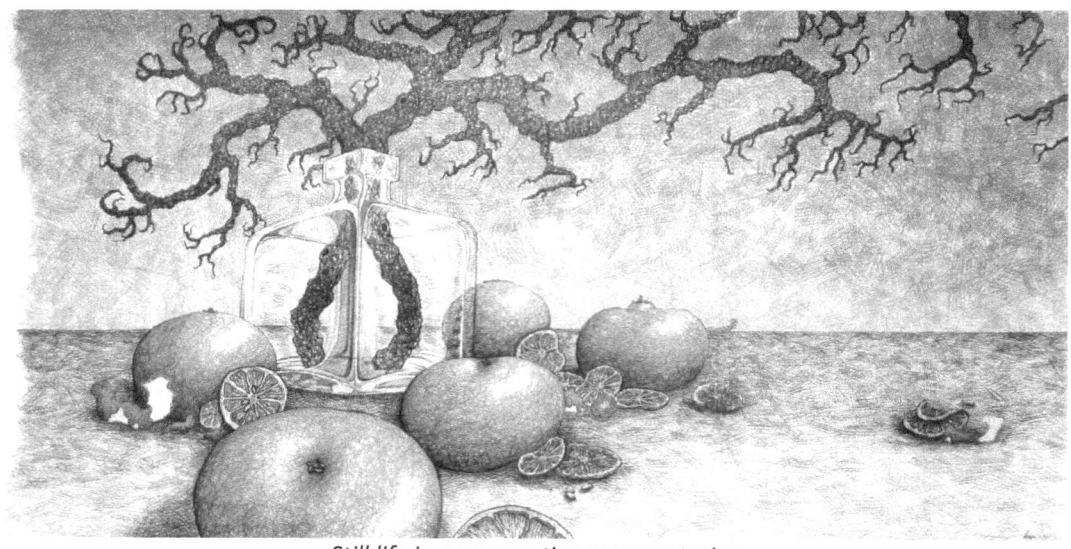

*Still life in a perspective representation*

# Picture Design and Composition

## Conveying Spatiality through Light and Shadow

Through the targeted use of light and shadow, the spatial effect of objects can be increased. Light and shadow describe the shape of both small and large bodies, which also works at a greater distance. The vanishing point perspective is also a suitable instrument for perfecting the representation. The vanishing point perspective can thus be used to construct shadows correctly.

# Light and Shadow

Light and shadow are among the most important - perhaps even THE most important - means of creating image design. This is because everything we see only becomes visible through light. And it also determines decisively how we see things. Light can be hard or soft, the amount of light can be high or low, light can come from different directions and light can also have a certain color. The factors that you can influence here are important image properties such as plasticity, spatiality and, last but not least, the atmosphere. By positioning the light source accordingly, you can create a dramatic shadow or create a contemplative mood with soft light.

## Direction of Light

As previously explained, it is very important for the image effect to clearly depict from which direction the light hits the motif in relation to the position of the observer. A distinction is made between the lighting situations: Incident light, frontal light, front light, side light, grazing light and back light.

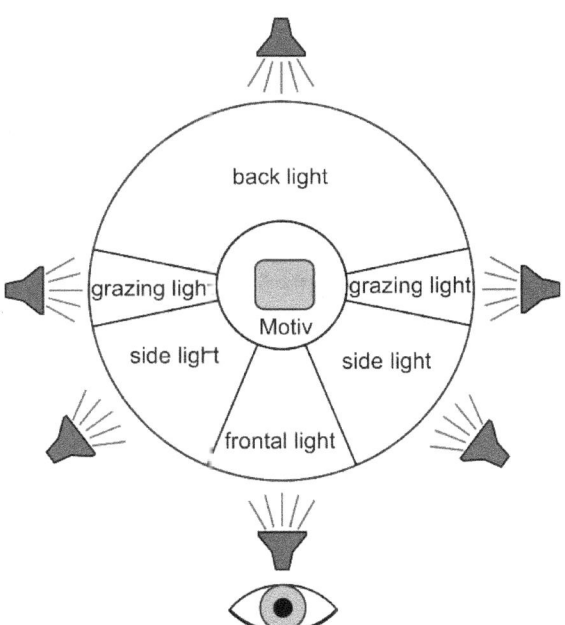

## Frontal Light

In the case of the frontal light, the light shines frontally on the motif, which means that the light source must be located in the artist's back. The result is that hardly any shadows are visible on the motif, as they are located behind the motif. Especially with monochrome drawings this light situation often seems unspectacular. In the case of colored paintings, however, the effect may be desirable, since this makes the colored areas the main focus of attention and three-dimensional forms fade into the background.

## Incident Light

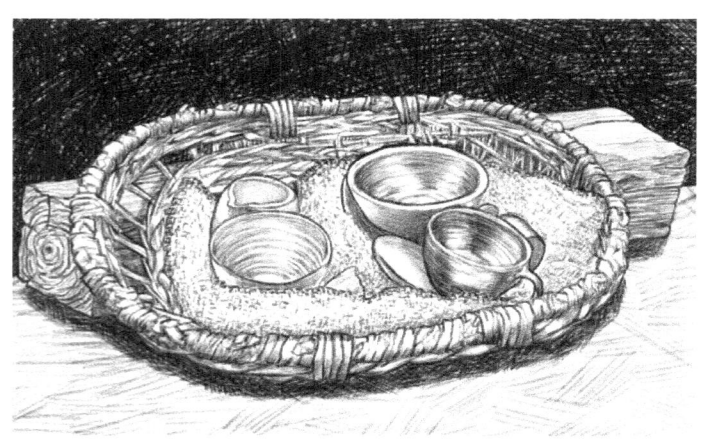

Incident light is the lighting in which the light source shines mainly from above on the subject, as is the case with landscape pictures around midday. Incident light ensures good illumination and short shadows are cast. Depending on what one wants to achieve, the incident light is advantageous or should rather be avoided. Especially if you want to play with light and shadow during the creation of your pictures, you should choose a more suitable lighting situation.

## Side Light

When the light falls on the subject at an angle to the side, this is called sidelight. This category includes lighting at an angle of approximately 30 to 60 degrees to the viewing direction. Side light is ideal for describing the three-dimensional shape of the motif by means of striking shadows. Effective shadows are also created in landscape pictures, which can bring tension and atmosphere into the composition. The side light is therefore the most popular lighting situation for drawings and paintings.l

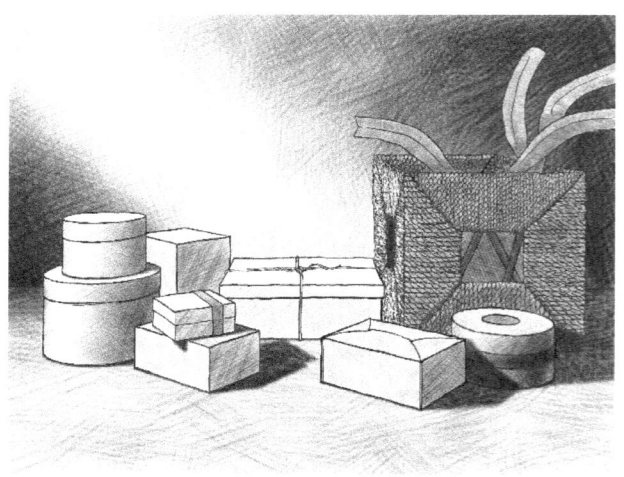

## Grazing Light

If the angle between the lines of sight and the lighting exceeds 60 degrees and thus hits the motif extremely sideways, this is referred to as grazing light. The light therefore grazes the motif from the right or left side. The result is that surface structures are very clearly visible and appear particularly three-dimensional. For this purpose, grazing light is usually used very specifically.

However, the characteristic of this lighting is often undesirable, because a motif can quickly appear inappropriate. Depending on the desired result, the cast shadows often appear exaggerated and create a drama that is not desired.

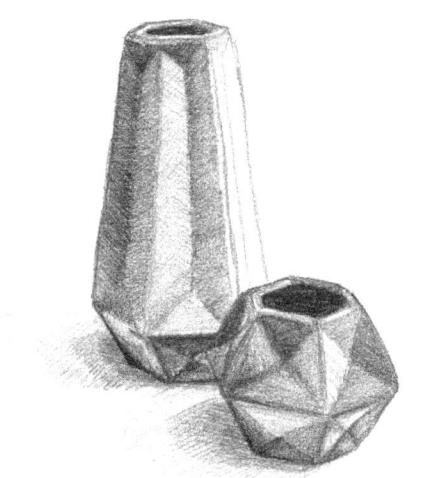

## Back Light

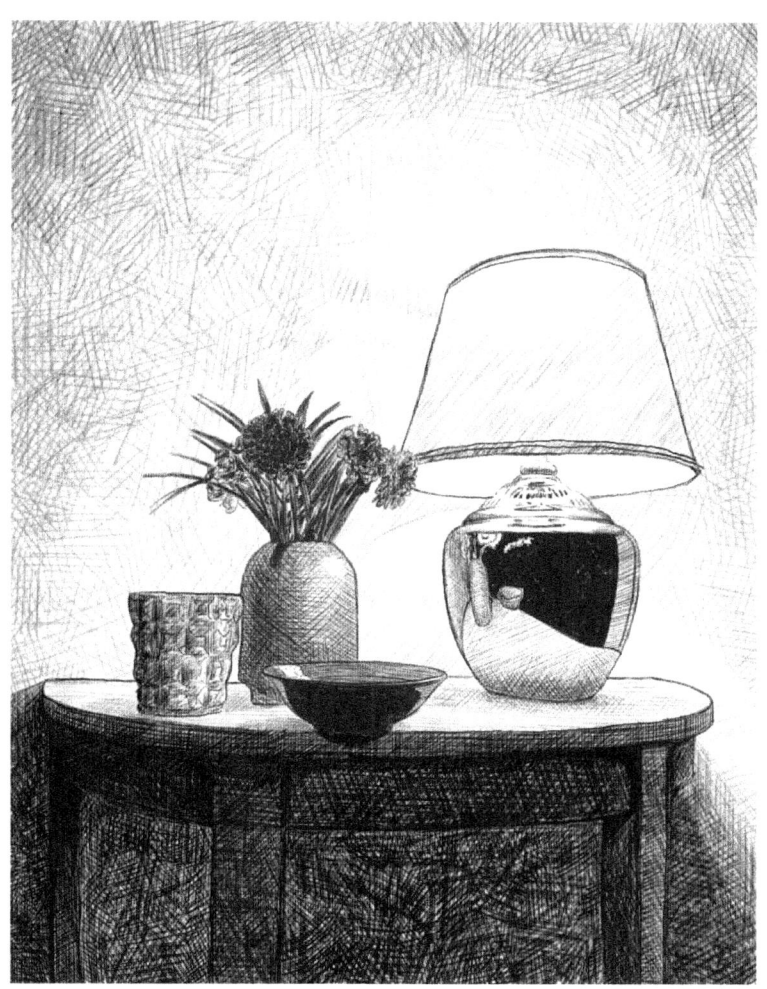

Backlighting means that the light comes from the direction of the subject and shines towards the artist. Objects are usually only silhouette-like in backlight and become very dark. The background is cross-faded by the light source and often no longer visible. These effects offer interesting design possibilities, but also represent a certain challenge for the artist.

In the drawing shown with The Lamp, a kind of backlight scene is found. The light source itself is a central component of the still life, which gives the drawing its special charm.

# Direct und diffuse Light

The quality of the light also has a great influence on the visual effect. The light can be direct or diffuse. For example, if strong light hits an object directly, it is highly illuminated at the side facing the light. The opposite side almost disappears in the shadow and is even slightly brightened by the small amount of light scattered in the surroundings. Through this hard light, extreme tonal contrasts are created. This kind of light quality is called directed light.

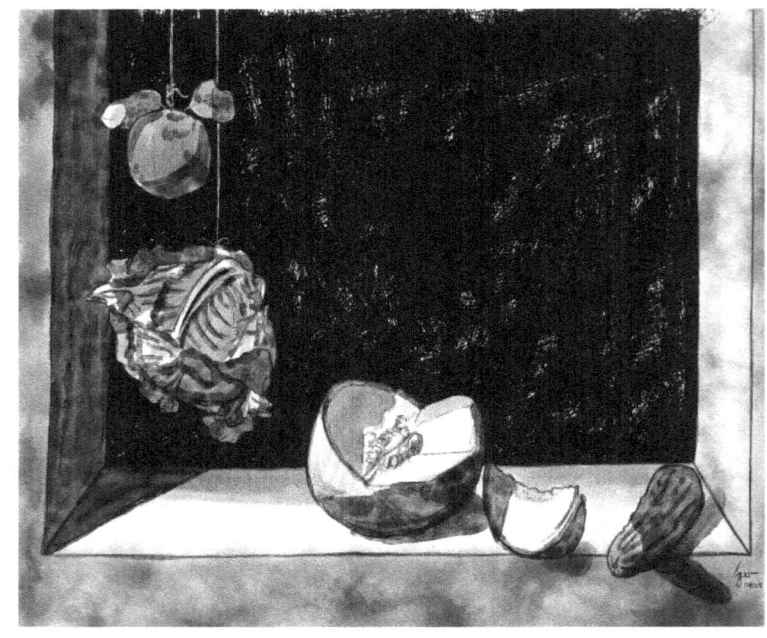

*Still life with direct, extreme light*
*Drawing after a painting by J. S. Cotán*

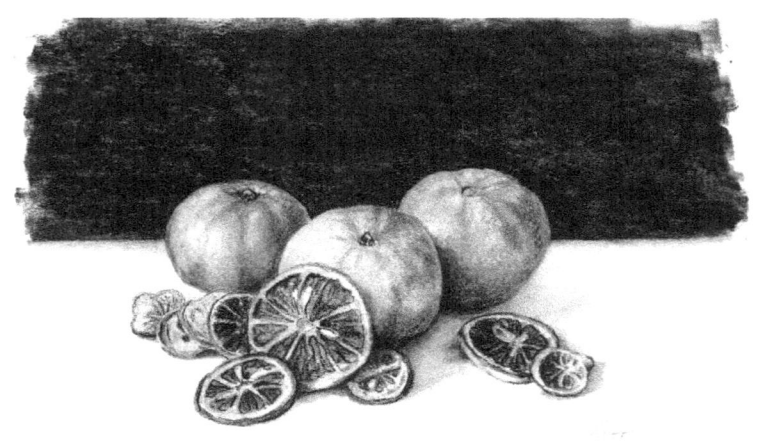

*Still life with more diffuse light*

Diffuse, soft light occurs, for example, when the light is rather soft and the surroundings scatter or reflect the light strongly. As a result, the sunny side of the object experiences less light intensity, while the shady side is brightened by an increased amount of light. In extreme cases, there will be little or no visible shadows. The tonal value contrast in this lighting situation is accordingly low.

You can observe and analyse the graphic design use of light yourself in most of the pictures shown in this book.

# Exercises – Still Lifes with Complex Image Composition

*» The artist is nothing without talent,
but talent is nothing without work. «*

- Émile Zola -

# Exercises – Complex Still Lifes

In the following exercises we will draw more complex still lifes. You can draw these exercises yourself and improve your own drawing skills. At the same time, you will learn more about the composition of pictures and also learn more about artists and art history.

## Still life with Vase, Paprika and Chili

This arrangement is to be made up of a vase, a plant, two paprikas and two chili peppers. In order to find an appealing picture composition, I reassembled the different objects again and again. From time to time I took some photos to be able to choose the arrangement I like best. The triangular arrangement and the rule of thirds were deployed to compose the pictures.

### Step 1 - Sketch

In the initial step we sketch a relatively vague drawing.

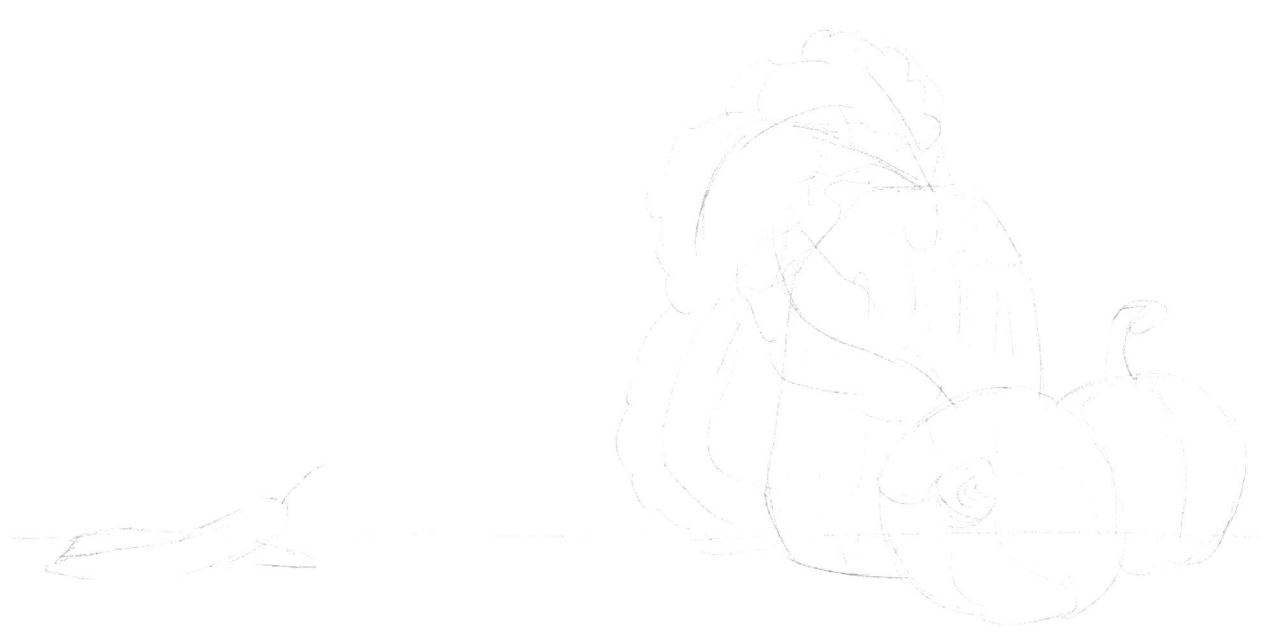

## Step 2 – Detailing the Sketch

In this second step we draw the lines more clearly, thus defining the final contours.

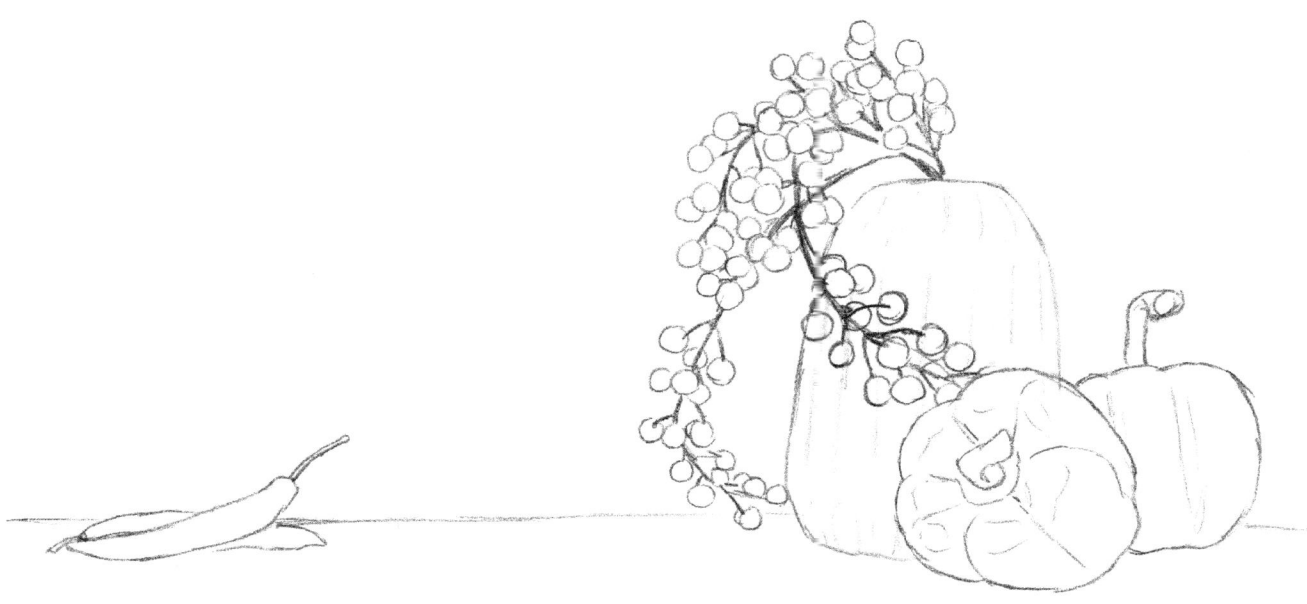

## Step 3 – Shading the darkest Areas

In this exercise we first of all shade the darkest areas – not the lightest. This approach has the advantage thereby that you can easily place orientation markers. You must however take care to avoid shading too much too dark.

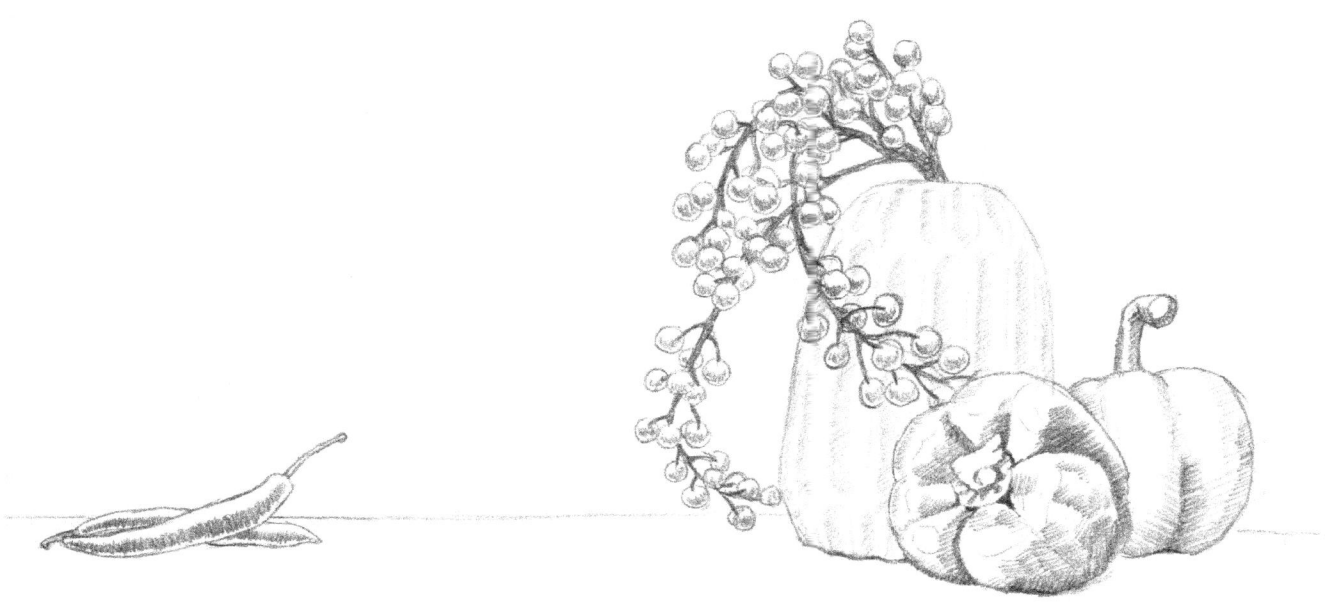

## Step 4 – Shading the lighter Areas

And now we come to the lighter areas. It is good to try out both approaches in order to find out which one is your personal preference.

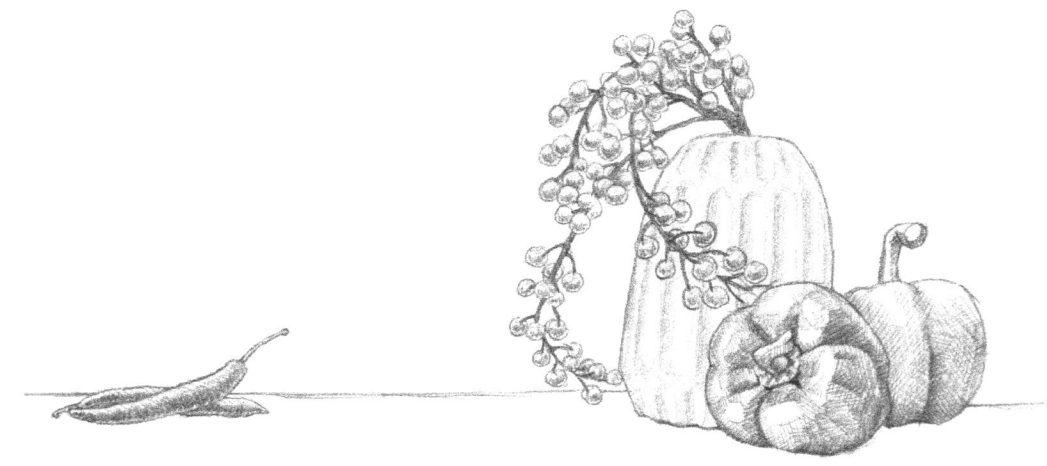

## Step 5 – Representing the Cast Shadows

Finally, draw the cast shadows and the surrounding area. When you draw a still life on your own, you must always remember from which side the light comes and at what angle. I also explain how to construct shadows in my book "Drawing Basics: The Basic Knowledge of Drawing Techniques".

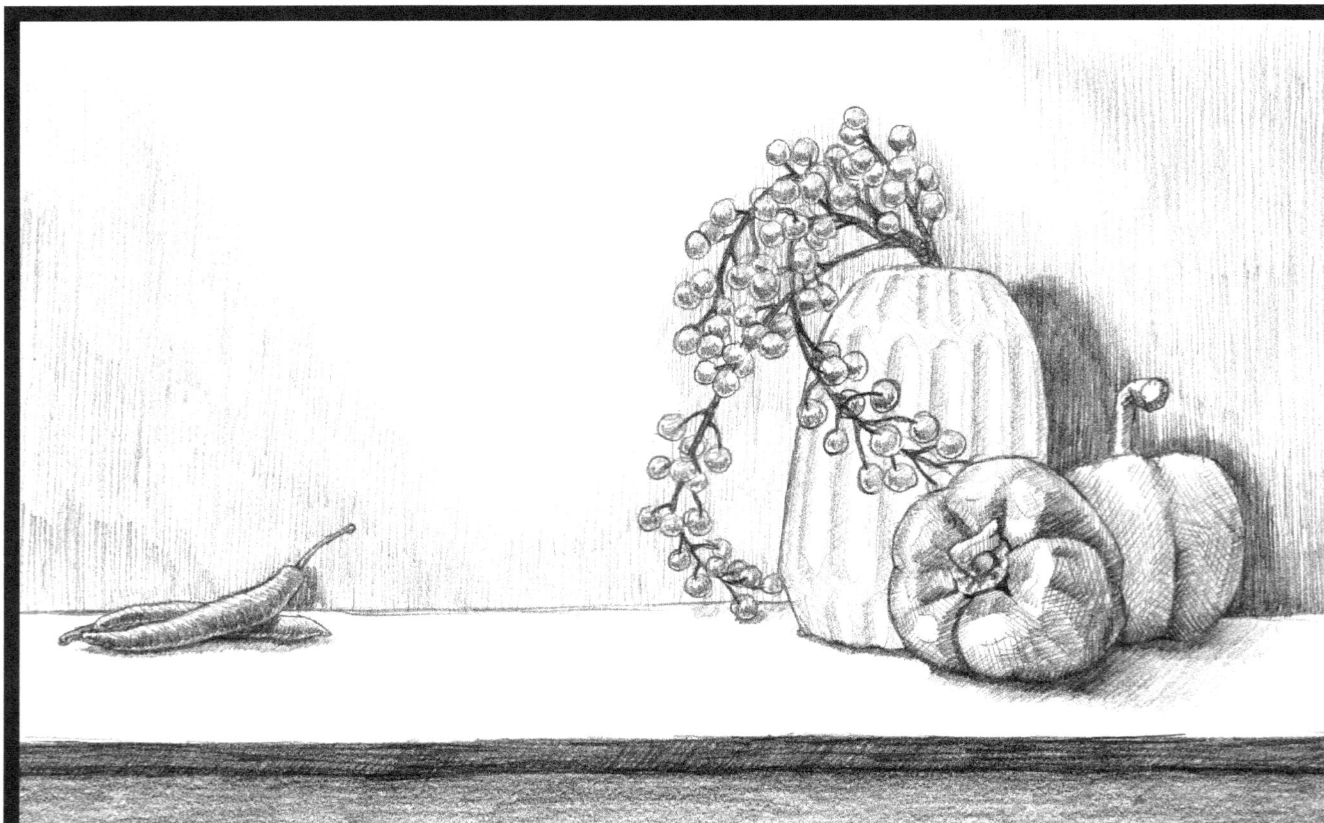

# Couch with Books

Since a still life in a broader sense is simply the representation of motionless objects, it does not matter how large these objects are. The couch that we will draw in this example represents such a slightly larger object.
But before we start, we will do a short analysis of the composition of the picture, so that you know what you should pay attention to in this exercise.

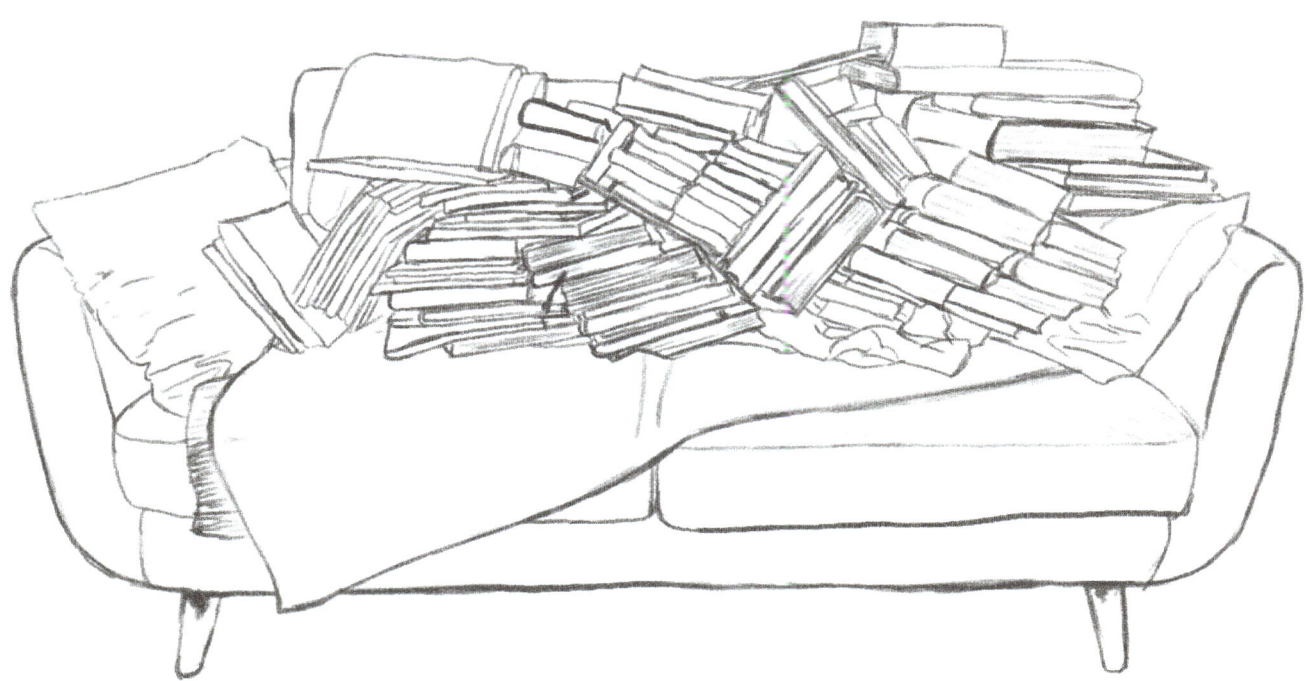

## Regarding the Image Composition of this Drawing:

The composition of the still life with the couch is more multifaceted than one might initially think. At first glance, one recognizes the couch with the books lying on it as a rectangle. The motif seems heavy, block-like and solid. The depth effect is very slight. Moreover, the image is relatively symmetrical and one can see horizontal as well as vertical lines. Due to these characteristics, there is little dynamic in the drawing at first glance.

If you take a closer look at the still life, you notice that there are also many diagonal lines. These are caused by the books which are not all lying orderly on top of each other. Even the cloth that lies on the seat of the couch hangs down at an angle and thus contributes considerably to the lively effect of the picture.

The books also create a kind of structure, which becomes a main element of the picture design of this still life. The structure of the books stands in a certain contrast to the structure of the blanket on the seat, the blanket hanging over the backrest, but also to the hatching in the background.

The interplay between these design elements creates an appealing pictorial composition that is not necessarily recognizable at first glance

## Drawing a Still Life with Couch and Books

The preliminary drawing has already been shown. As always, it is the first step when creating a drawing. Then you can start to shade the picture objects, which gives life to the sketch. Between the stacks and books there is often a dark shadow. You can also depict single pages of a book using thin lines. For the overall impression to be effective, a minimum of strokes within a few books will suffice.

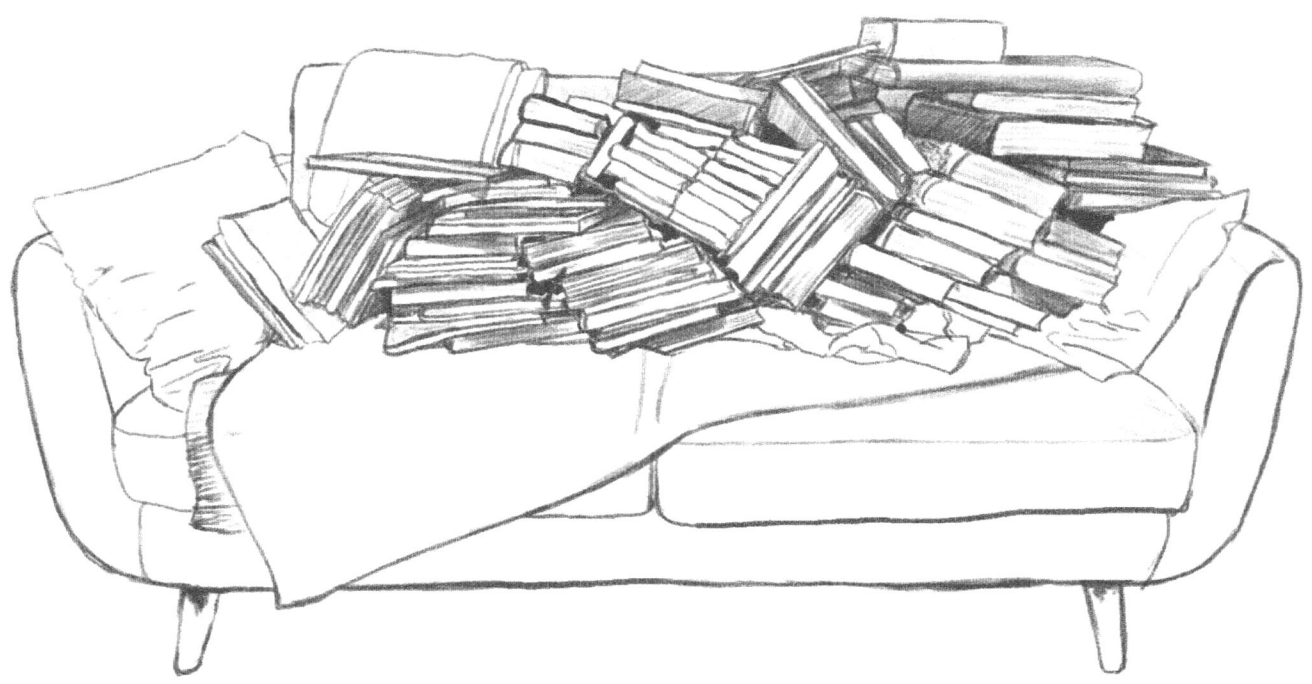

The blanket, which is laid over the seat of the couch, has its own light structure. Gentle shadows also stand out on the blanket. The seat cushions of the couch can also be separated from the blanket with a few stronger shadows.

Exercises – Still Lifes with Complex Image Composition

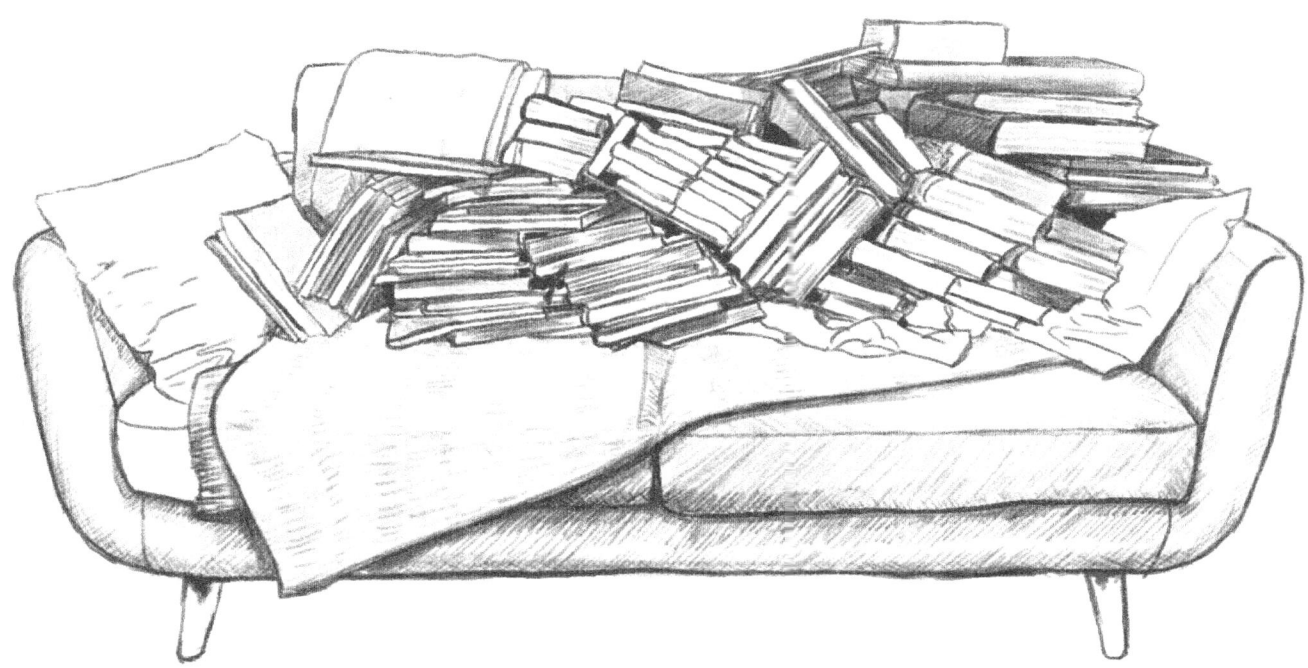

Now you can also draw the second blanket that is laid over the backrest. It is a knitted blanket, which accordingly has a different structure. In the following drawing you can see that the cushions are shaded. Here great attention is paid to the folds, which also appear where the books lie on them.

In this step you can also draw the shadows of the feet and the cast shadow that the couch throws on the floor.

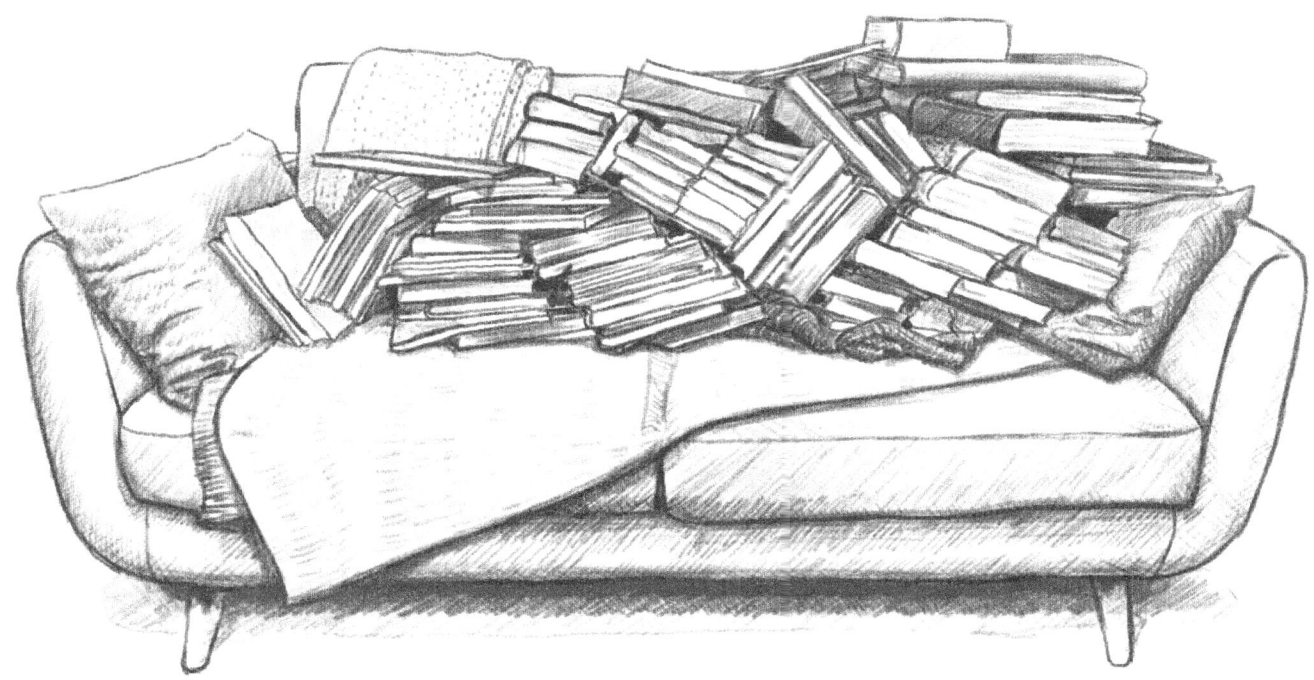

In the last step you can give the still life a finishing touch. Some shadows have been darkened, so that the form of the motifs is more prominent.

The background has been darkened by hatching, so as not to distract further from the actual motif and not to bring any unnecessary restlessness into the composition. Now the still life is finished.

## Light Composition

As an example of a picture composition with special lighting conditions, in this exercise we will draw a still life that is illuminated only by a lamp. Especially with such difficult light compositions it is advantageous to be able to see and understand the scene in real life.

The following picture shows the preliminary drawing of the still life as I arranged it myself.

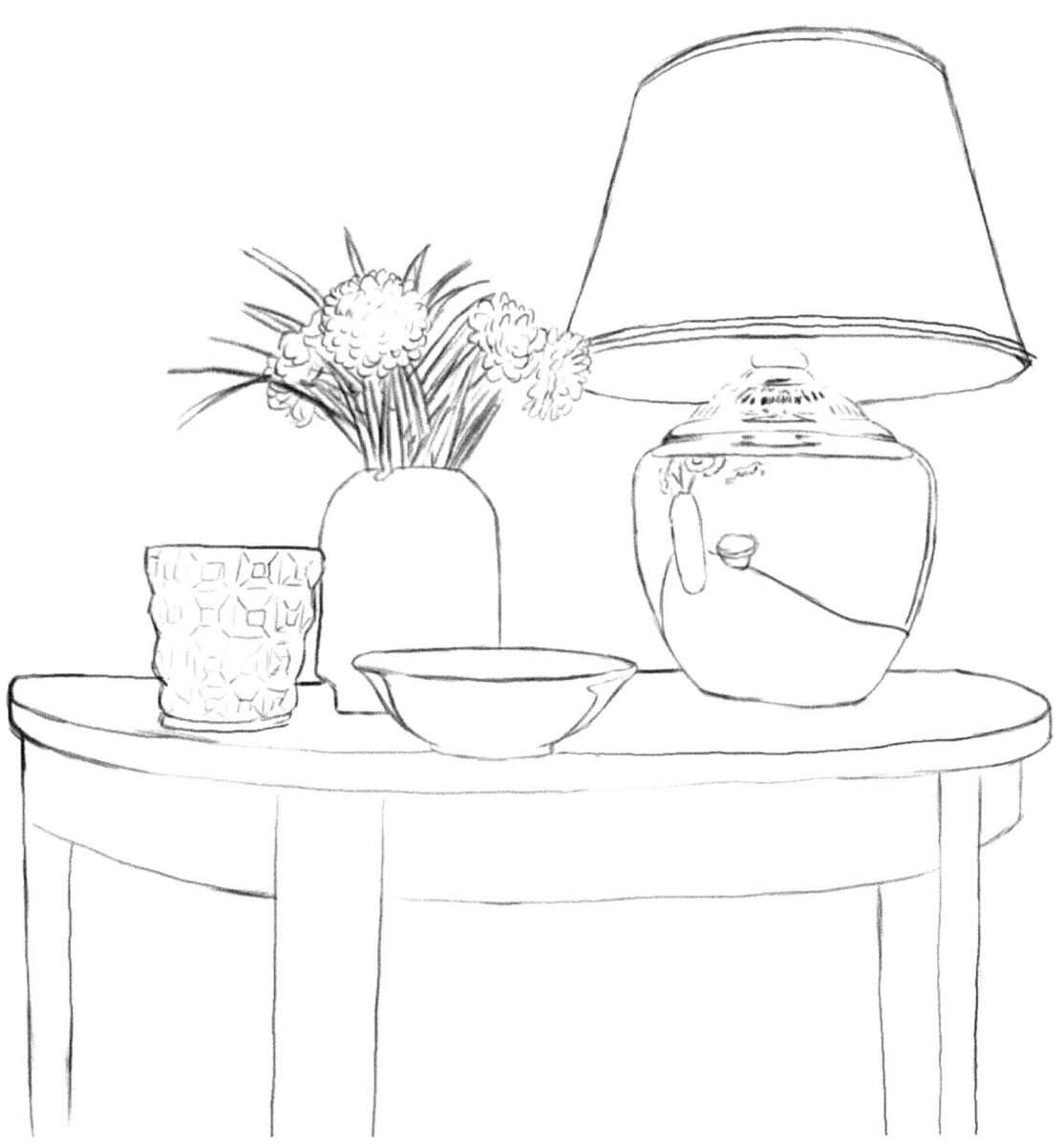

In this still life, I worked out each object one after the other. I started with the lamp. Especially remarkable is the silver body of the lamp, in which the surroundings are reflected in a distorted manner.

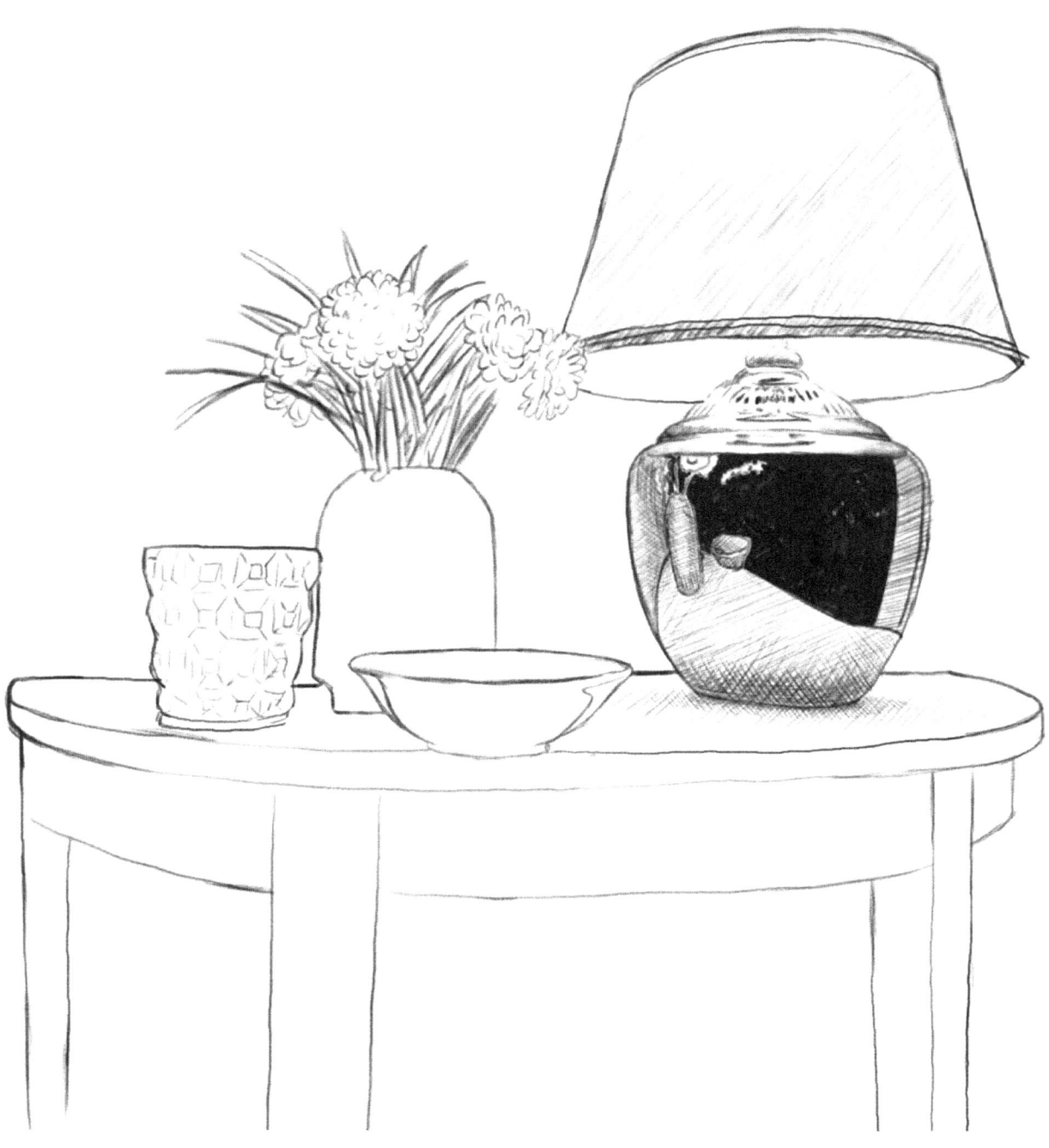

Exercises – Still Lifes with Complex Image Composition

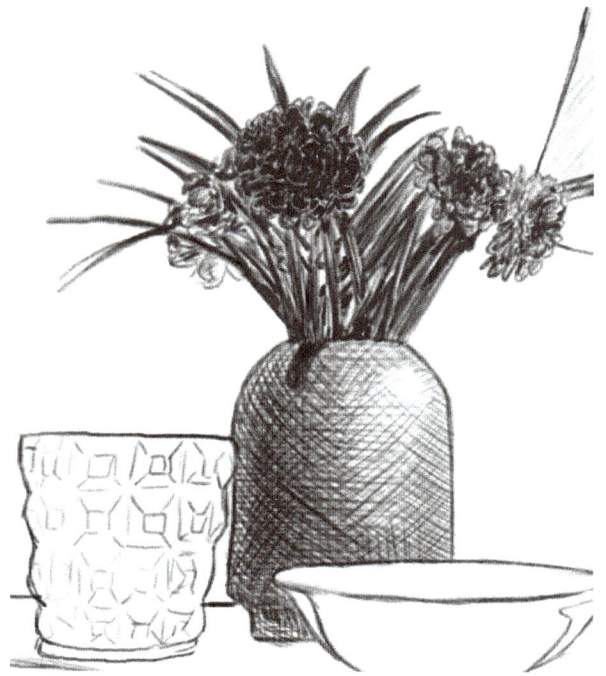

Then follows the vase with the bouquet of flowers. The bouquet creates a contrast in form and provides a more open and lively look.

The bowl exhibits a rather intense reflection on the inner surface, which can be left entirely white. In contrast, a rather dark shadow is extended across the outer surface of the bowl.

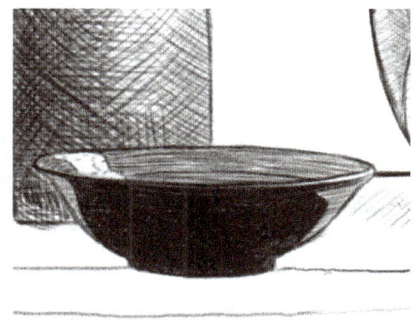

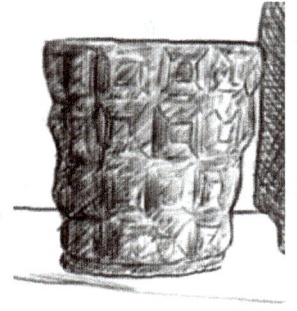

The glass has a surface with small truncated pyramids. Each of these bodies has its own shading with lighter and darker areas. Parallel to this, the glass has its own light-dark gradient that covers the shading of the pyramid protrusions.

After all objects have been shaded, you can display their cast shadows. The semicircular table itself is shaded very darkly, since - with the exception of its top - hardly any light falls on it.

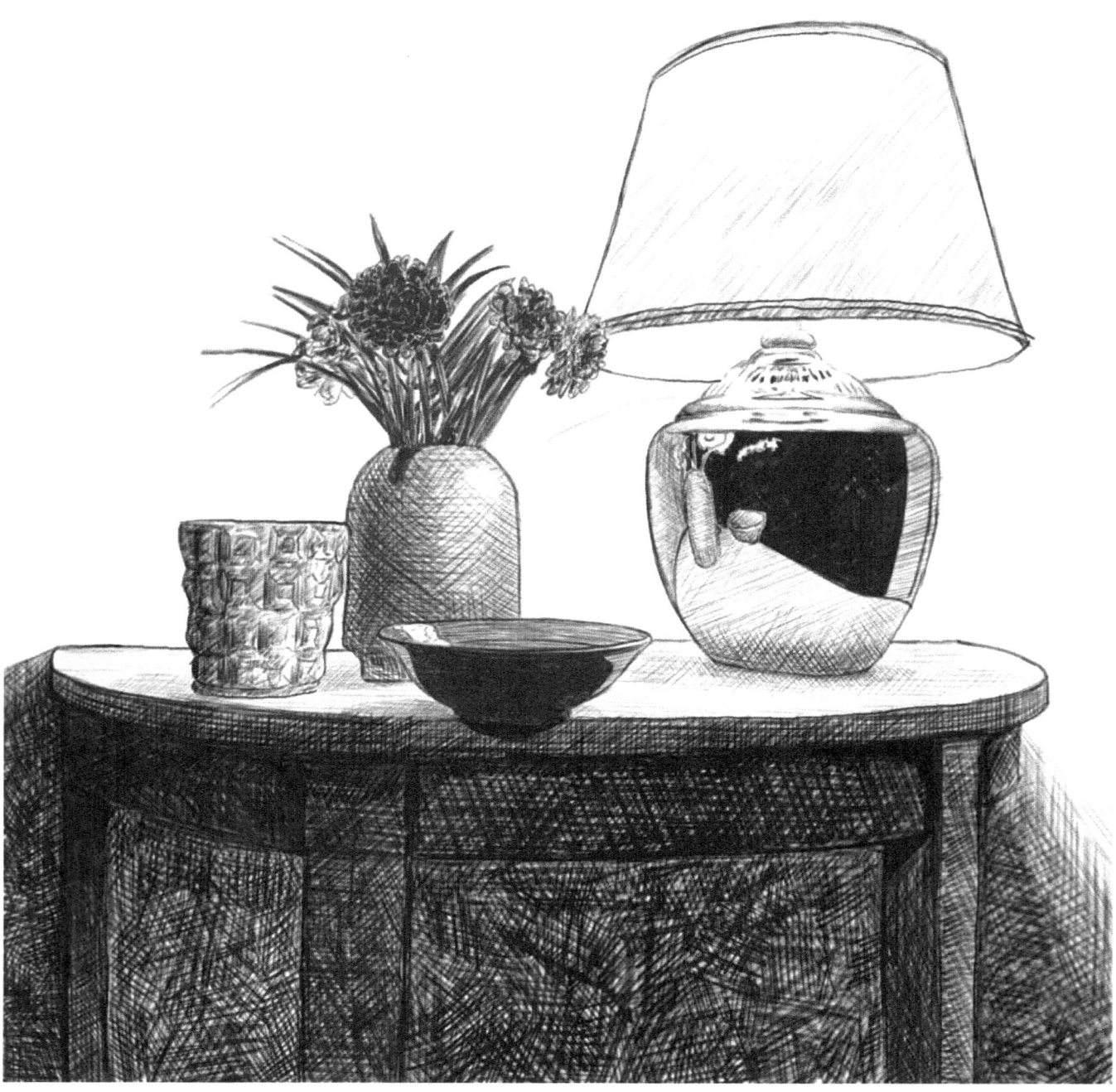

Exercises – Still Lifes with Complex Image Composition

What is still missing is the background. The table stands directly against a wall, which is illuminated by the lamp. It is important to note that part of the light is subdued by the lampshade. On the other hand, at the openings of the lampshade at the top and bottom the wall is visibly brighter.

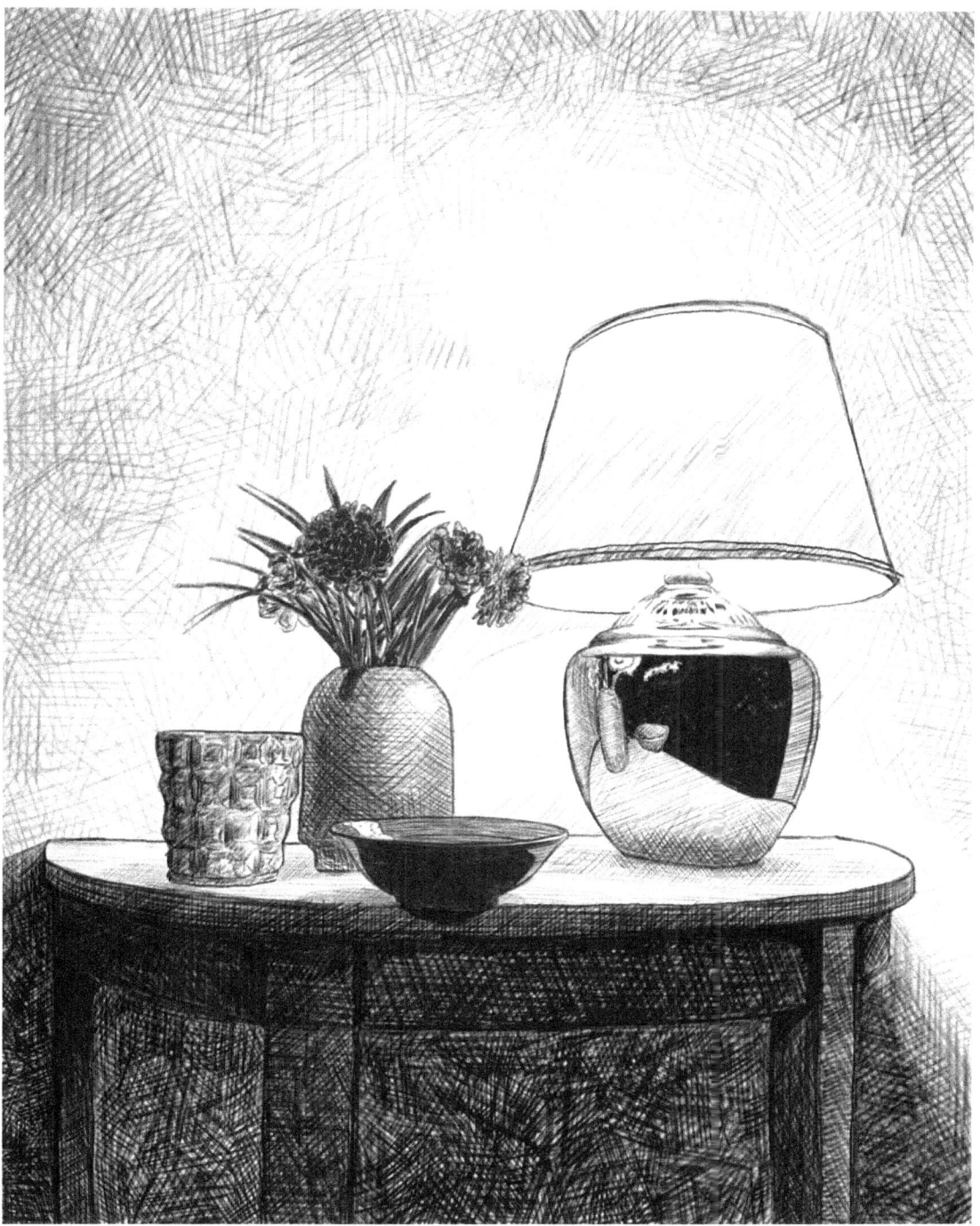

# Still Life with Cheese

We can now attempt a more elaborate still life. It is a mealtime still life with cheese and other side dishes. Cheese still lifes of this kind were very popular in the 17th century and they are available in many different variations.

The original painting, which serves as a model in this exercise, was originally by Clara Peeters, a Flemish painter born in Antwerp in 1594. The painting was painted around 1625 and is fully entitled "Still Life with Cheese, Artichoke and Cherries".

## Step 1 – Preliminary Sketch

The preliminary drawing is a little more elaborate in this relatively complex still life. You can calmly use a method like the raster method or a light table to draw the contours.

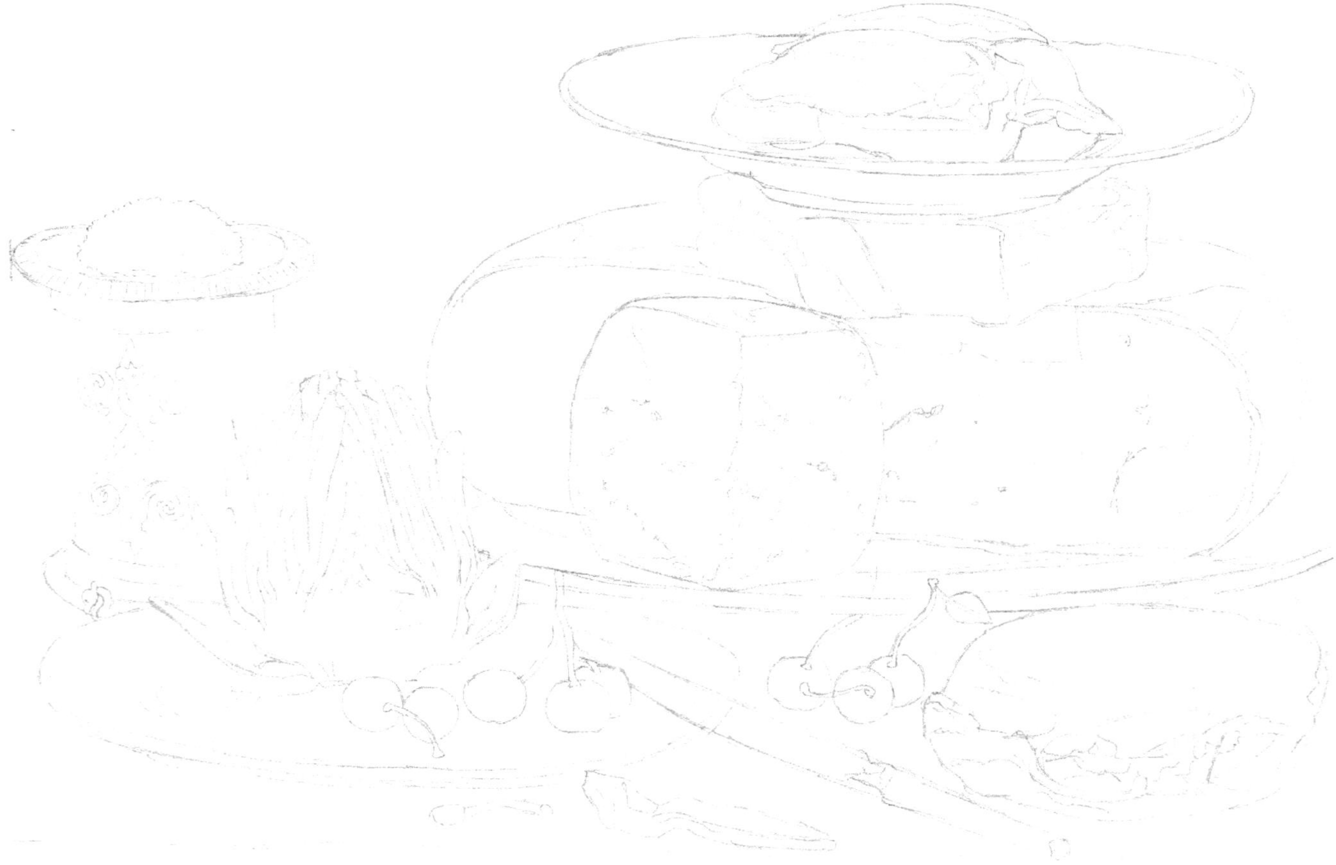

A picture of the original oil painting by Clara Peeters can be found through the following link (QR-Code) at the site *Google Arts & Culture*:

## Step 2 – Drawing the darkest Areas

In this still life we want to proceed in such a way that we start with the darkest areas first. You can also draw the cast shadows - the shadows that the objects cast on the ground or other objects.

Pay special attention to the metallic objects such as the bowl, plate and knife already at this stage. The dark accents on these objects are very important for their realistic effect of the whole motif.

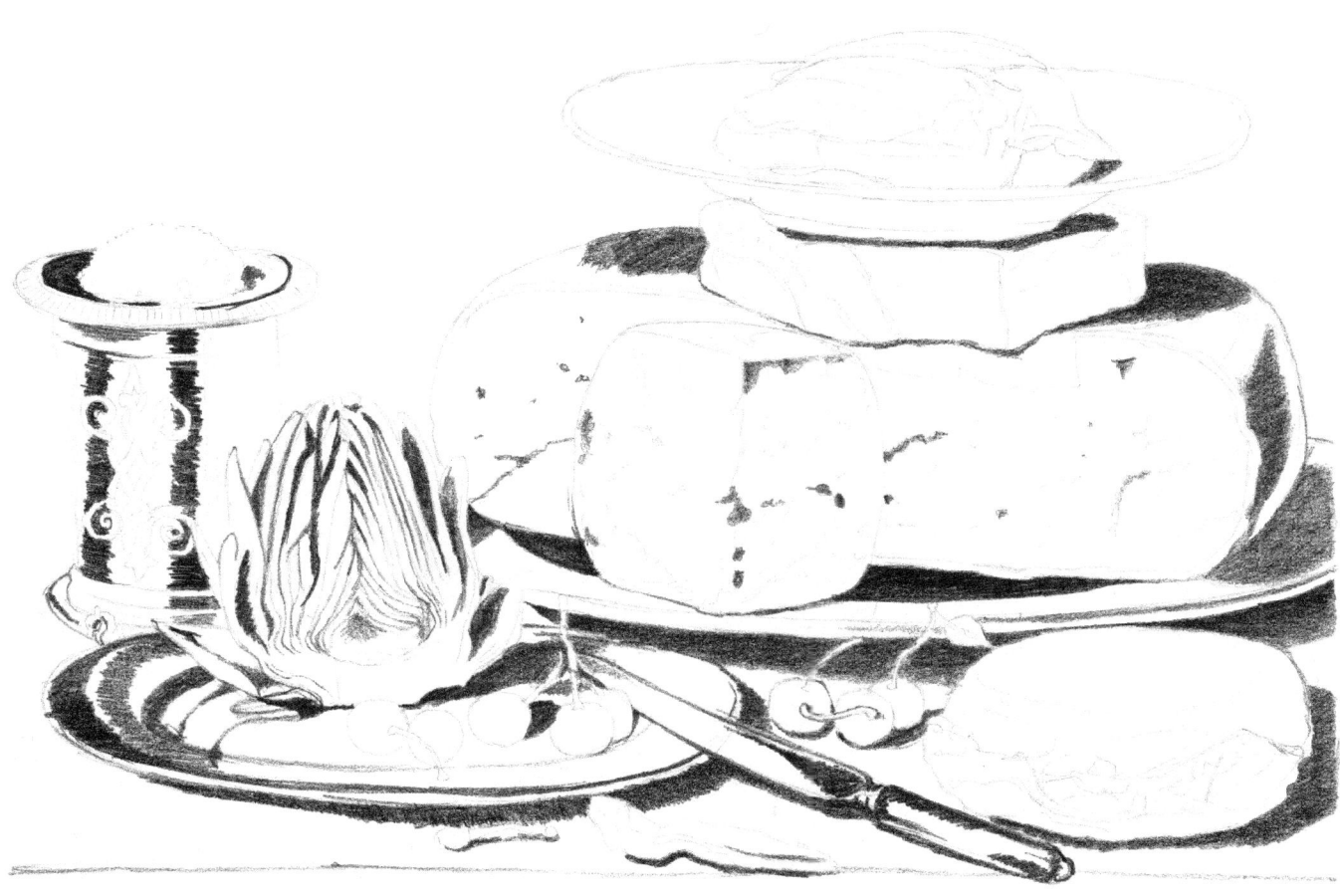

## Step 3 – Drawing the lighter Areas

Now we start to display the brighter areas bit by bit. As in many other still lifes, the different materials of the depicted objects play an important role.

In addition to the metallic objects already mentioned, one can also find, for example, cherries with a smooth surface or cheese with a matted surface and characteristic structure.

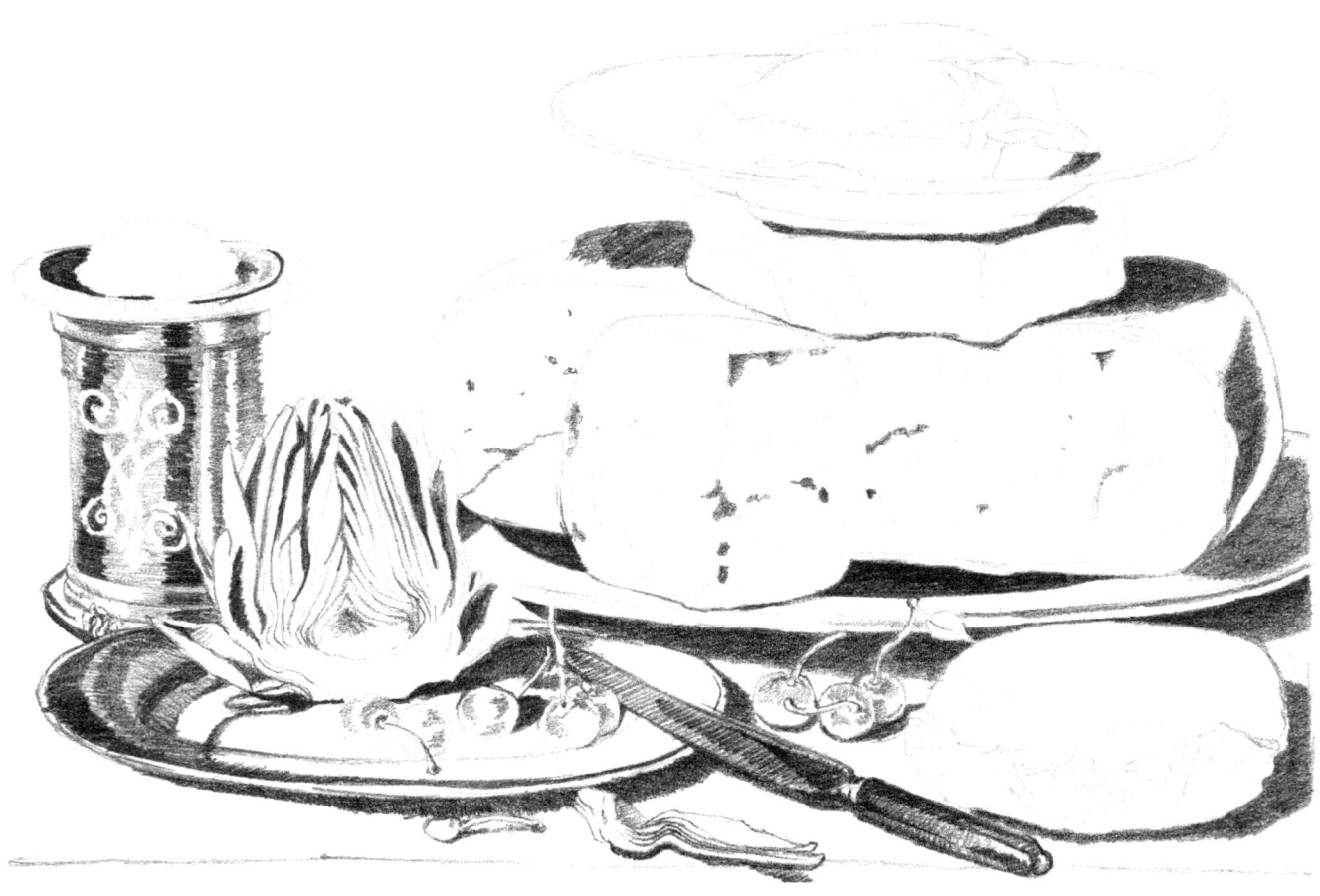

# Step 4 – Completing the Still Life

The final step is to give the still life the final touch.

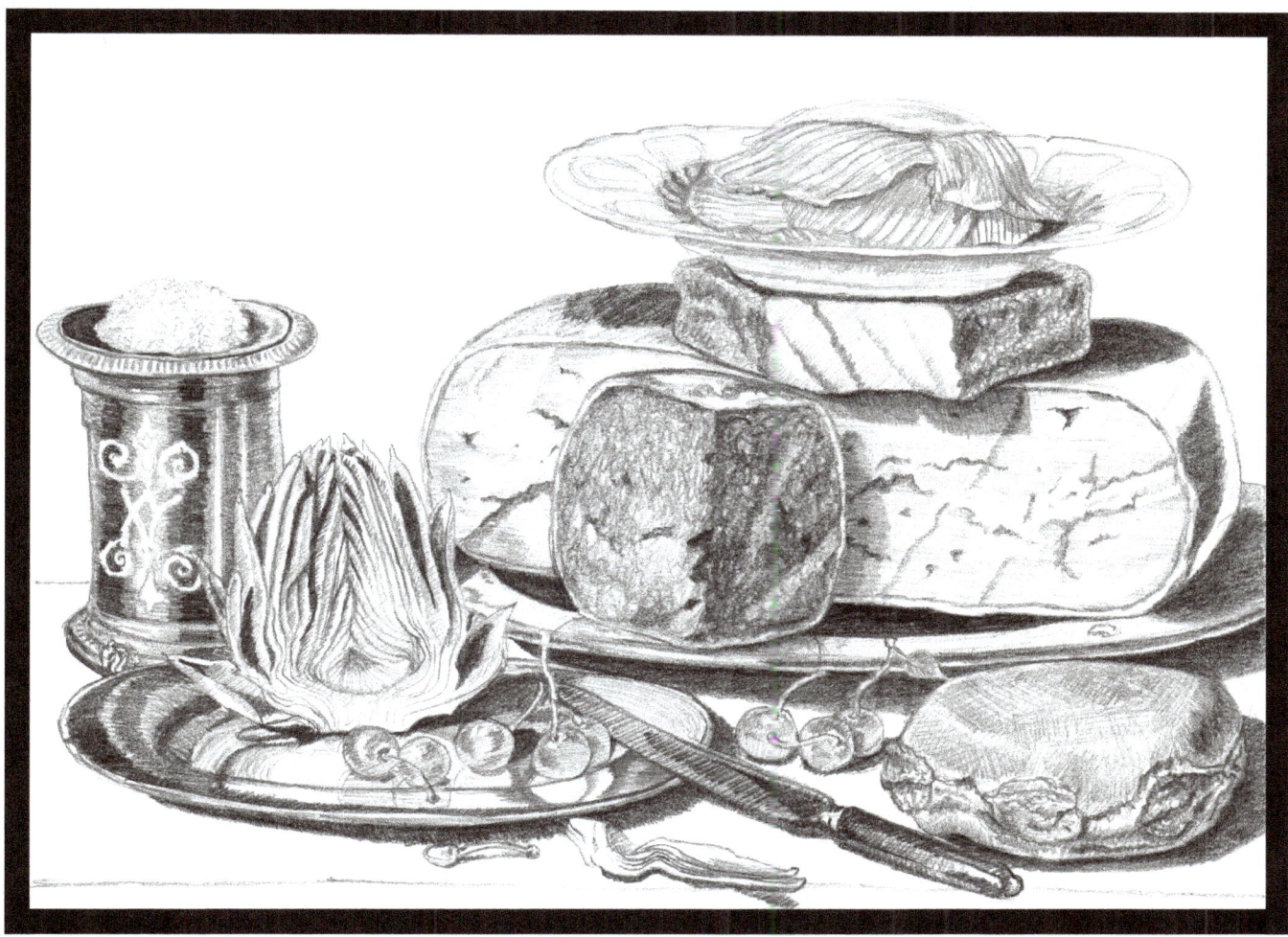

In addition, I would like to draw your attention to a creative trick that you very often encounter in still lifes: You can see that the knife and a piece of the artichoke protrude over the edge of the table. Through this optical trick, the objects visually penetrate the space of the viewer and expand the space of the still life.

If all objects remained behind the edge of the table, this would be recognized as a clear dividing line between the picture and the viewer. The composition of the picture would become flatter and would therefore have less depth effect.

# Smoker's Still Life with Indian Ink

For the smoker's still life, which we will look at in this exercise, we will use a new drawing medium: India ink.

Ink is one of the classic drawing media that was used hundreds of years ago. Compared to pencil, ink cannot be used to vary the tonal value by changing the contact pressure. The stroke is always black. This characteristic poses a certain challenge, but wonderful pictures can be created with ink.

## Step 1 – Preliminary Sketch

As always, we start with a preliminary drawing, for which we still use a pencil.

The smoker's still life is also a painting by Jan Fris, who lived in Amsterdam in the 17th century. On display are a clay jug, a deck of cards and smoking paraphernalia such as a pipe, tobacco and a small clay barrel with glowing coals.

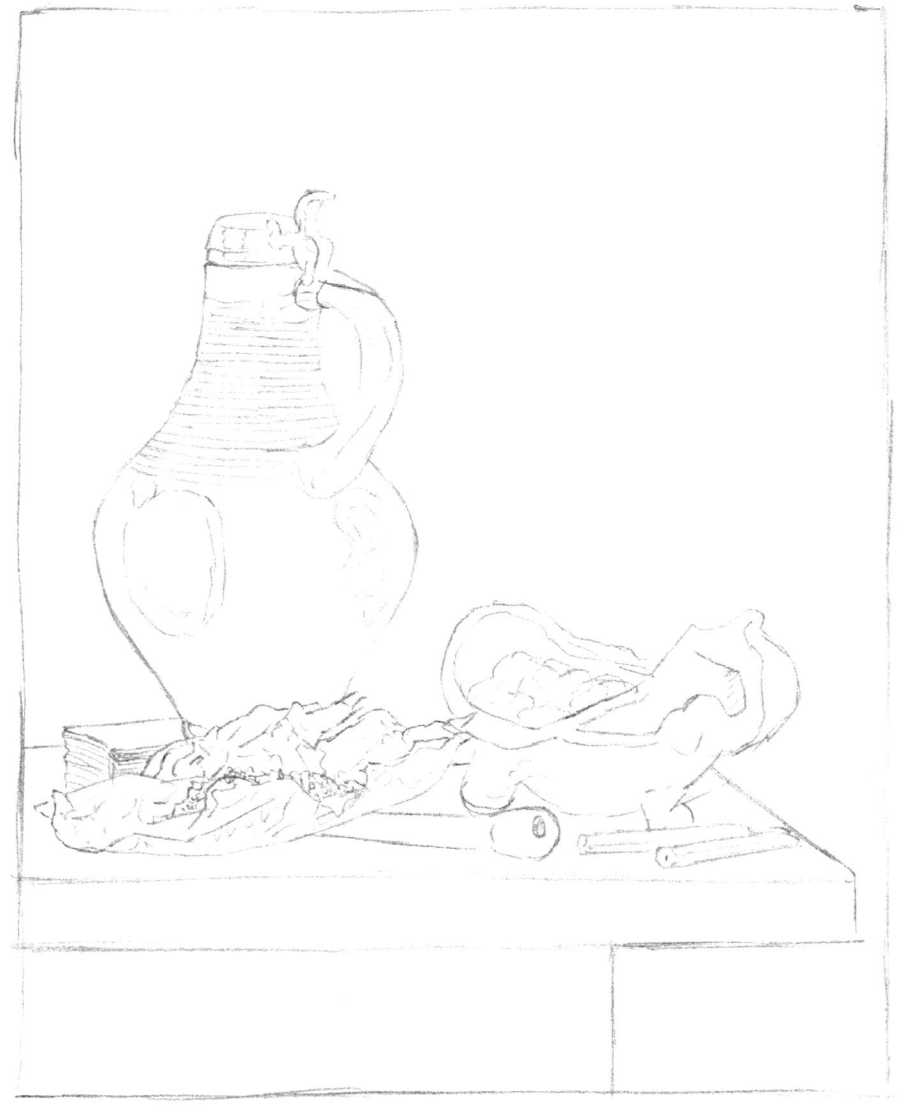

*Preliminary sketch of the still life drawn with pencil*

## Step 2 – Shading the dark Areas

You can also proceed with ink in such a way that you first show the darkest areas. So we draw the darkest shadows and areas that are almost completely black first. As a drawing technique we can use the different variations of hatching.

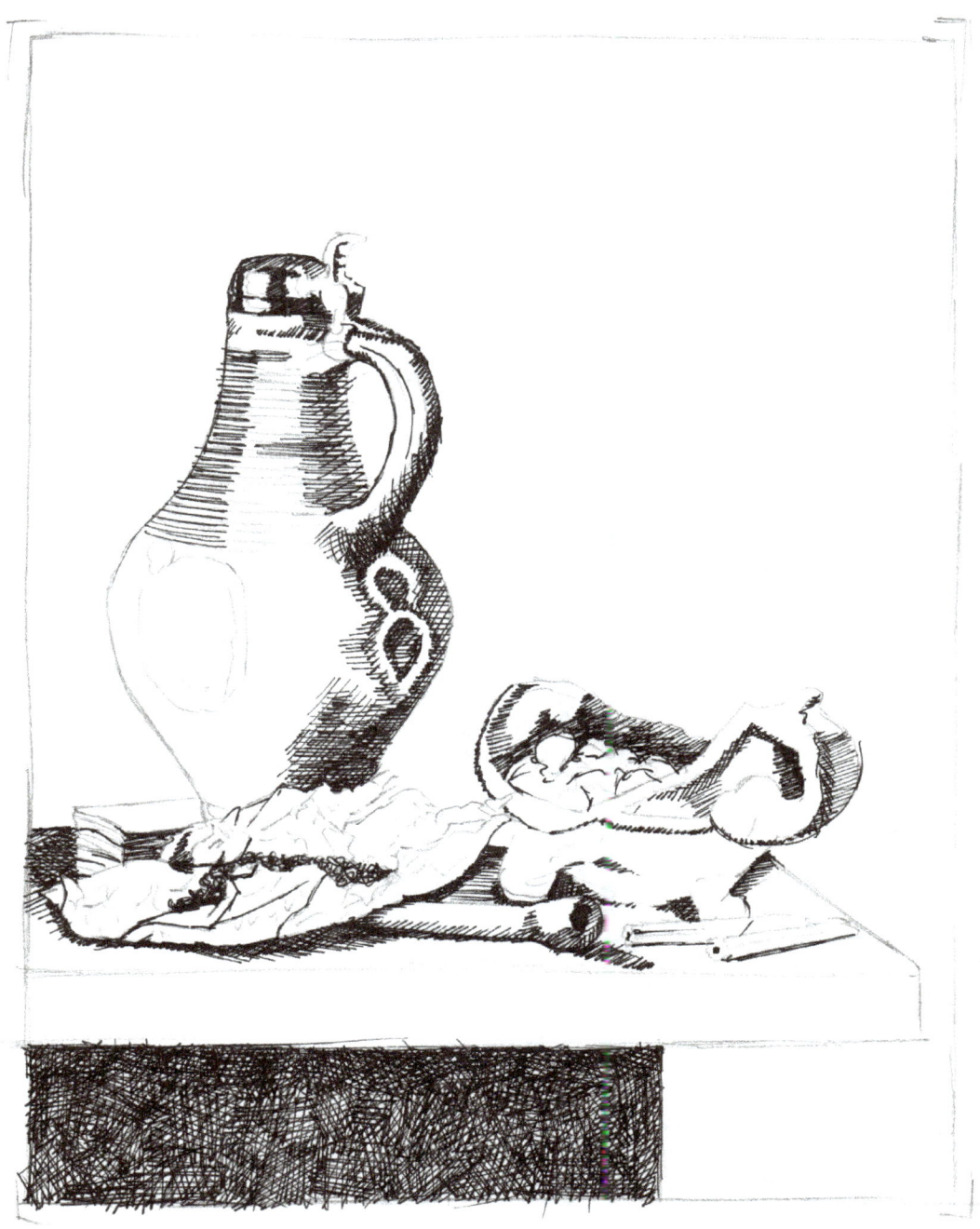

*Depiction of the dark areas first*

Step 3 – Working out further Shadows

Now lighter shadows can also be drawn. The dark areas that we have shown before give us a good orientation.

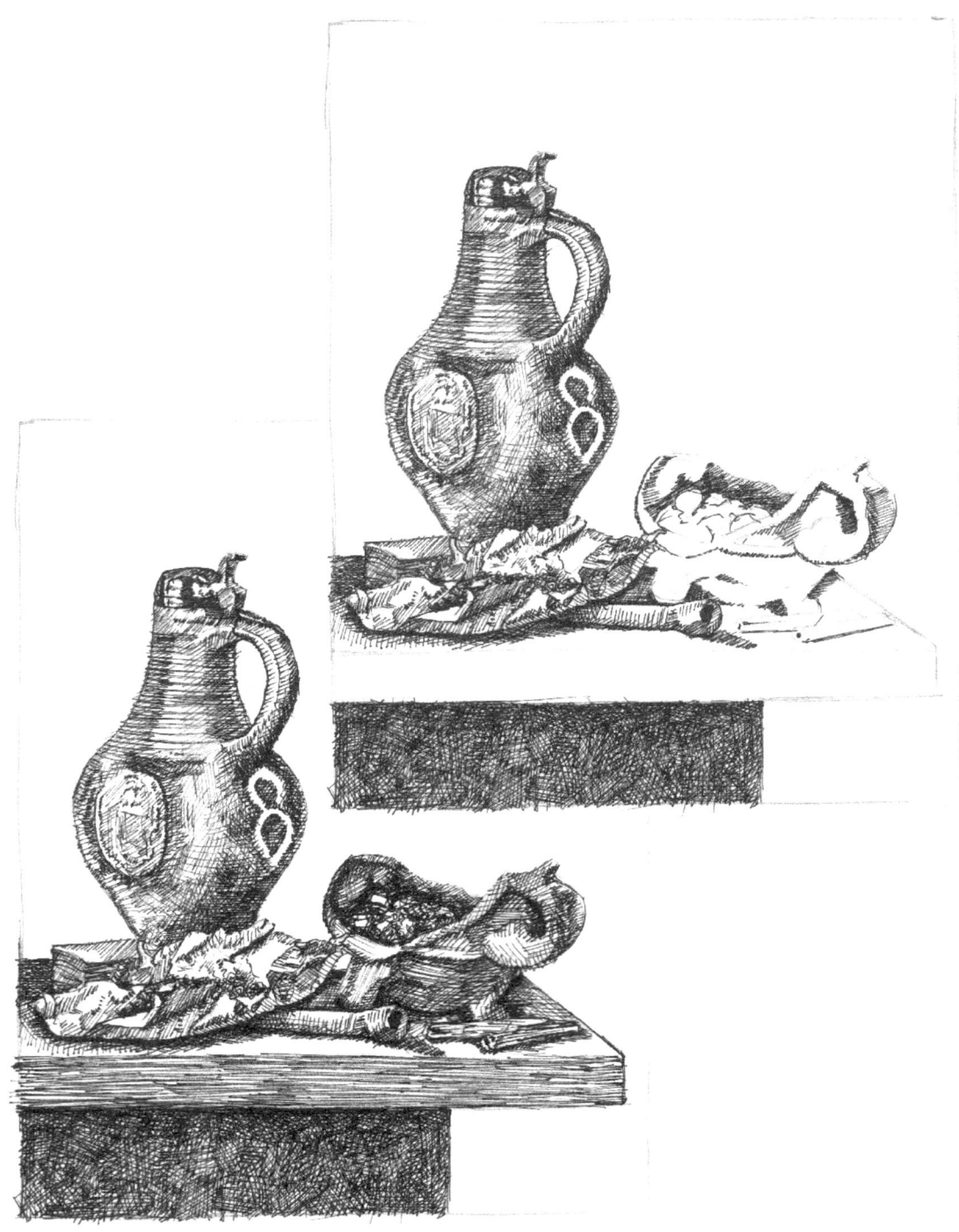

## Step 4- The Background

The last thing that follows is the background. What you should pay attention to here is that the background clearly differs in tonal value from the objects in the picture. This means that the background should be hatched either much lighter or darker. Otherwise, the motifs are optically too similar with gray on gray.

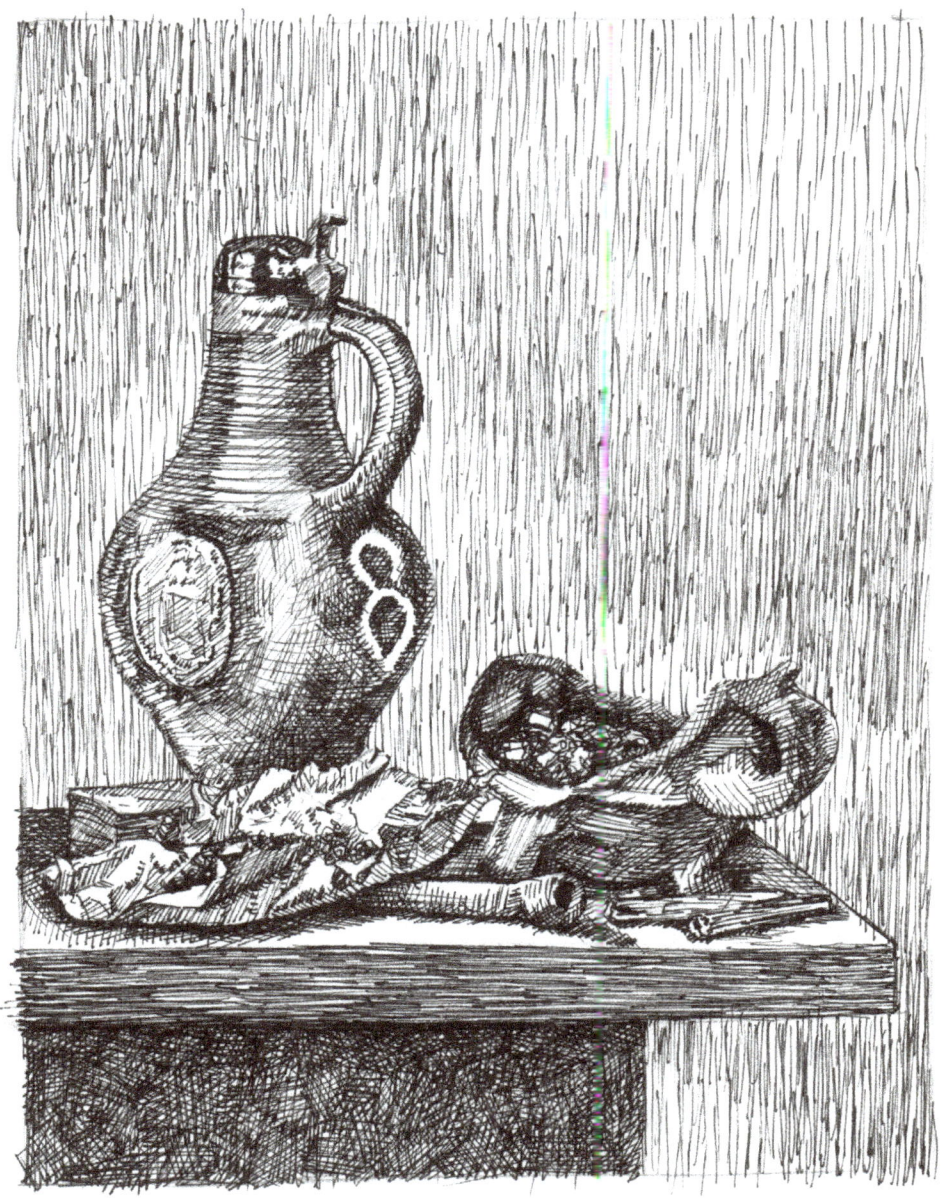

# Still life according to Cézanne

Finally, we can try our hand at a wonderful work by the artist Cézanne. In his still lifes he did without linear perspective. He preferred to depict the motifs in the dimensions that were appropriate for his composition. Thus he made some objects larger and others smaller than they were in reality, in order to create the inner pictorial balance and a composition full of tension.

In Cézanne's still life, it is not the objects themselves that should attract attention, but the arrangement of forms and colors. Since color was an important part of the composition, it is much more difficult to reproduce the effect of the picture when drawing with a pencil. But even despite this disadvantage, one can create wonderful still lifes in the style of Cézanne with a monochrome drawing.

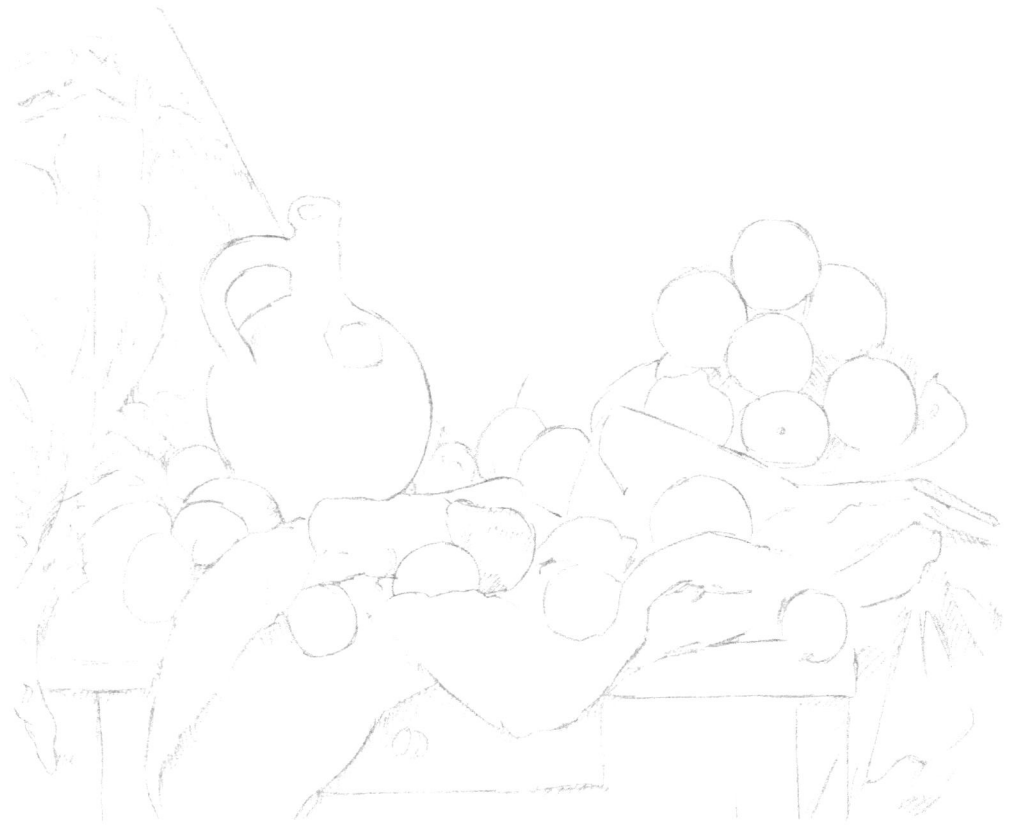

In the drawing shown you can see the preliminary sketch of the still life of this exercise. The sketch is based on the still life "Draperie, Jug and Fruit Bowl" by Paul Cézanne.

When drawing, you should not try to reproduce the motives realistically. Rather draw powerfully and accentuated. By using strong countour lines you can emphasize the shape of the objects, just like Cézanne's picture composition.
Even with the representation of the crumpled cloths you do not have to lose yourself in details.

Draw only the most important, shape-describing folds, so that the geometry is clearly highlighted. The shading can be done with loose hatchings. Individual lines may remain visible, as this only makes the drawing more characteristic. Then the drawing is finished.

Exercises – Still Lifes with Complex Image Composition

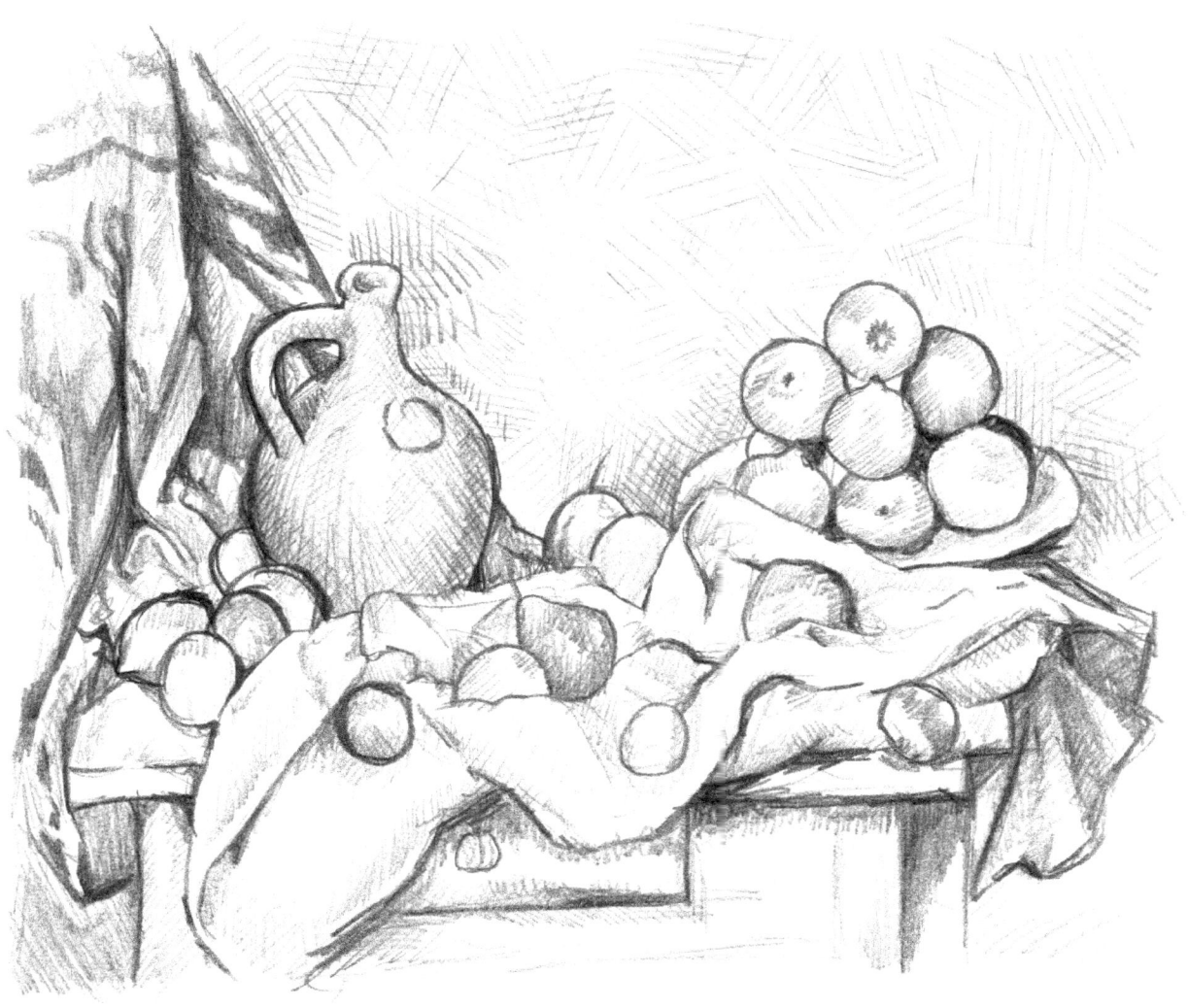

# Closing Remarks

*» The old saying "The first step is always the hardest." is only valid for skills. In art, nothing is more difficult than ending – which at the same time means perfecting. «*

- Marie Freifrau von Ebner-Eschenbach -

# Closing Remarks

With the concluding chapter of exercises we have reached the end of this book. I hope that you have enjoyed it and, above all, that it has helped you. Certainly, reading and working through the book does not make you an ingenious artist in the field of still life representation, but the book should convey the most important basic knowledge. Through the exercises, I have tried to convey many more tips and to increase the level of difficulty without overwhelming beginners from the beginning.

In order to further improve one's own drawing skills, a lot of practice is required. Let yourself be inspired by your surroundings to create your own still life drawings. You can also practice your composition skills and gain experience in creating appealing picture compositions.

As you have seen, still life paintings are very versatile and include several visual arts themes. They already belong to the more complex subjects in the world of drawing, but offer almost infinite possibilities. In addition, still lifes can also be used as a part for a portrait, an animal motif or other subjects of art. So it can happen that sooner or later you can fall back on the knowledge of still life representation, if you also enter into other subjects of the visual arts.

And if you have enjoyed this book, I would also be very happy if you would recommend it to friends, acquaintances or on the net.

You can also visit me on my website! There you will find more instructions on how to learn to paint and draw and many of my own pictures:

    www.art-class.net

Thanks and greetings to all readers and all who have supported me in creating my book!

Markus S. Agerer

# Book Recommendation

## Start Drawing Landscapes
Basic Principles, Composition and Exercises

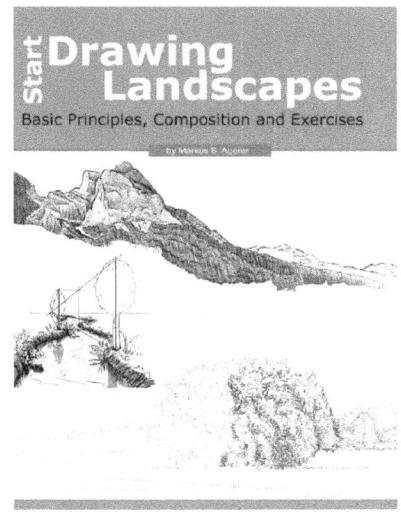

## Drawing Perspective & Space
Basic Principles of Drawing in Perspective

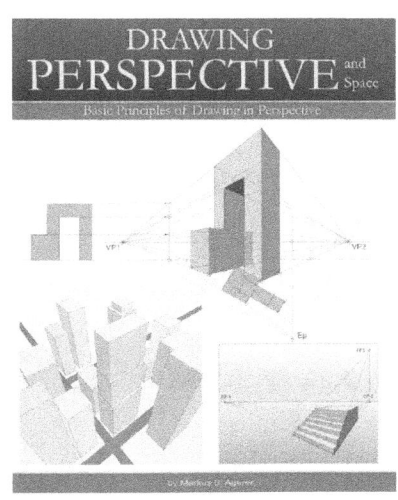

# Source

**Books:**

*"Underweysung der Messung mit dem Zirckel und Richtscheyt"*
Albrecht Dürer der Jüngere; Nürnberg 1525

„Leonardo da Vinci. Sämtliche Gemälde und Zeichnungen"
Autor: von Johannes Nathan (Autor), Frank Zöllner (Autor);
Verlag: TASCHEN Deutschland GmbH

„Der fotografische Blick - Bildkomposition und Gestaltung"
Autor: Michael Freeman;
Verlag: Markt+Technik Verlag; Auflage: 1 (1. Juli 2007)

„Meisterwerke 41 – Caravaggio"
Autor: Gaspare de Fiore, Luisa Cogorno, Giovanna Bergamaschi, Gianni Robba
Verlag: Fabbri Verlag (1991)

„How to Draw: Drawing and Sketching Objects and Environments"
Autor: Scott Robertson
Verlag: Design Studio Press


**Internet:**

www.art-class.net

zeichnen-lernen.markus-agerer.de

www.wikipedia.org

**Kunstgeschichte - 20. Vorlesung - DIE MALEREI IN HOLLAND UND FLANDERN IM 17. JAHRHUNDERT**
https://www.youtube.com/watch?v=hy-_259eRYs

**How Dutch Painters Invented Atmosphere – YouTube  Yale – University Art Gallery**
https://www.youtube.com/watch?v=MZyr4cLgS5E

www.ingramcontent.com/pod-product-compliance
Lightning Source LLC
Chambersburg PA
CBHW080457220526
45465CB00006B/2295